The Revolutionary Guide to Turbo Pascal

Yuri Borodich

Aleksandr Valvachov

Dr. Vitaly V. Leonenko

WROXPRESS®

The Revolutionary Guide to Turbo Pascal

Published by Wrox Press Ltd. 1334 Warwick Road,
Birmingham, United Kingdom.

Printed in the UK by Unwin Brothers Limited.

ISBN 1 - 874416 - 11 - 7

About the Authors

Yuri Borodich is a top programmer working at "Algorithm", a leading science and research centre in Belorus. He has written a number of books in Russian about programming in Pascal and his programs are used by over 450,000 PC experts throughout the C.I.S. In his spare time Yuri enjoys fishing and bodybuilding.

Aleksandr Valvachov is a visiting lecturer at several institutes and colleges in Belorus. He has written six books about programming and artificial intelligence, with more than 300,000 copies in print. He lives in Minsk with his wife and son, and in their free time he and his family enjoy mountain walking.

Dr. Vitaly V. Leonenko teaches Microelectronics at the Minsk Radio Engineering Institute in Belorus, where he previously studied as an undergraduate. He lives in Minsk with his wife and son and his interests include fishing, horticulture and walking his Airedale Terrier.

Technical Editors Andy Peppiatt and David Bates

Language Editor Victoria McCluskey

Translation Oleg Staravoitov

Book Design Nina Barnsley and Greg Powell

Cover Design Greg Powell and Paul Hougham

*Будем же учиться хорошо мыслить -
вот основной принцип морали.*

Б. Паскаль

Acknowledgements

Thanks to Ross Alderson for the cover image.

*Thanks also to Nan and Karen at Borland
for their help and support throughout.*

Trademark Acknowledgements

*Turbo Pascal and Borland are registered trademarks
of Borland International.*
Smalltalk is a trademark of Digitalk.
*MS-DOS is a registered trademark and Windows
is a trademark of Microsoft Corporation.*
*IBM is a registered trademark of International
Business Machines Corporation.*

CONTENTS

INTRODUCTION

About the Book

The Pascal programming language has been used for many years as the starting point for people learning about structured programming. It takes its name from the great French philosopher, mathematician and scientist Blaise Pascal who designed the first "computing machine". With the advent of Turbo Pascal from Borland International Pascal has developed into a powerful professional tool.

This book is aimed at both the beginner who is new to programming and to the professional programmer who is either learning or brushing up on the latest version of Turbo Pascal. The text begins with basic items of program structure and moves on to Object Oriented Programming and Turbo Vision, the new way of producing windowed programs.

The book contains a great number of practical examples that you will be able to use for every day work. Moreover, the authors give simple methods (i.e. without Turbo Vision) with worked examples that allow users who are new to the language to create useful programs. The examples in the book follow a theme that develops into a useful application for monitoring domestic finances. All of the Turbo Pascal code given in the book is stored on the diskette provided with the book. The text is reproduced in an interactive tutorial program which is also provided on the diskette. Using the book and diskettes together presents a very powerful way of learning Turbo Pascal.

Installing the Disk

The disk accompanying this book has three parts:

1. The source code for the programs in the book (if a program is shaded in the book it means it is included on the disk).

2. The HomeFinances program, which is described in the book and explored in full in Appendix A and Appendix B.

The tutorial program, which gives a visual representation of the information in the book.

Each part can be installed separately and will install into a special directory. The source code is copied to a directory named **SOURCE**, the HomeFinances program is copied to a directory called **HOMEFNCS** and the tutorial program is copied to a directory called **TPTUTOR**.

The files are compressed so you need to decompress them onto your hard disk. To install the tutorial program onto your C: drive, type **A:TUTOR** at the C:\> prompt. To install the HomeFinances program onto your D: drive, type **A:HOMEFNCS** at the D:\> prompt. To install the source code onto your C: drive, type **A:SOURCE** at the C:\> prompt.

Installing all three files onto your C: drive can be summarised as follows:

        C:\>**A:SOURCE**
        C:\>**A:TUTOR**
        C:\>**A:HOMEFNCS**

The Tutorial Program

To run the tutorial program you first need to install your mouse, if you have one. Then you need to go into the TPTUTOR directory. Simply type **CD \TPTUTOR** at the C:\> prompt (if you have installed onto your C: drive, at the D:\>prompt if you have installed onto your D: drive). Then type **TUTOR** and the program will start.

Use your mouse to choose a subject area. If you don't have a mouse then press the letter of the topic you are interested in. Use the arrow keys to highlight a subject and press **ENTER** to select. All the options (Selecting a topic, Exit, Help and Go to start of topic) are situated at the bottom of the screen. If in doubt, press **F3** (**Help**) and the option positions will be indicated on screen. To choose an item all you need to do is click on your selection with the mouse or press **ENTER** when the item is highlighted. To exit the program press **ESC**.

Starting the program can be summarised as follows:

        C:\>**CD \TPTUTOR**
        C:\TPTUTOR>**TUTOR**

Installing Turbo Pascal

If you have bought Turbo Pascal 6.0 you will want to get on and use it. Before installing this package on your computer though, it is advisable to make copies of the original Turbo Pascal disks. The DOS command **DISKCOPY** will let you do this.   If your computer has two floppy drives, type:

> **DISKCOPY A: B:**

if it has only one floppy drive, type:

> **DISKCOPY A: A:**

and press **ENTER**. DOS will prompt you what to do next. Having copied the Turbo Pascal disks, store the originals in a safe place and only use your copies.

Installation of Turbo Pascal is quite easy. Take the copy of the "INSTALL/COMPILER" disk and insert it in drive A:, then type

> **A:INSTALL**

and press **ENTER**. The installation of Turbo Pascal then starts working.

Your next move is to press **ENTER** and a window will appear asking you to enter the drive for the installation diskettes. If you want to use drive A: you can just press **ENTER** straightaway. Otherwise, select another option from the menu. When the next menu appears, use the arrow keys and **ENTER** to choose the type of disk you are going to install Turbo Pascal on (either a floppy disk or a hard disk).

The next stage is the main menu of the INSTALL program. You will be asked to pick the drive and subdirectory where you are going to allocate each component of Turbo Pascal. This is easy to do as the default paths are printed opposite every menu line. The names of the paths reflect the meaning of each part of Turbo Pascal. You can change any of the paths that do not suit you. Choose the **start installation** command from the menu and press **ENTER**. During the installation procedure the program will ask you to insert the following Turbo Pascal disks: "Turbo Vision/Tour, "Online Help" and "BGI/Utilities"

Changing DOS Configuration

Having finished the installation procedure you need to check the **CONFIG.SYS** file in the root directory. Turbo Pascal standard practice requires the following **FILES** command:

> FILES = 20

To check this, type the following at the DOS prompt:

> TYPE C:\CONFIG.SYS

If you need to alter the file you can either use a text editor or the DOS editor. Please note that before you edit any files it is advisable to take a copy first in case there are any problems with the alterations. You can also make your work with Turbo Pascal more convenient by changing the path command in the **AUTOEXEC.BAT** file in the root directory. This will enable you to start Turbo Pascal from anywhere on your PC. For example, assuming that the compiler is on drive D: in subdirectory \TP, the path command could look like this:

> PATH = C:\DOS; D:\TP

You can alter the **AUTOEXEC.BAT** file in the same way as the **CONFIG.SYS** file by using a suitable editor. After you have read this chapter, you can use the editor in Turbo Pascal to make alterations to the **AUTOEXEC.BAT** and **CONFIG.SYS** files. If you have followed all of our instructions, restart your PC and type the magic command **TURBO**.

CHAPTER 1

AN INTRODUCTION TO TURBO PASCAL

The Main Window

You are now dealing with the Turbo Pascal compiler. In contrast to previous versions it has a powerful integrated development environment (IDE). The IDE has interactive tools such as overlapping windows, scroll bars, dialogs, function keys and mouse support. The main menu of the IDE will appear once you have started the compiler. At the top of the screen you will see the menu bar. It is your primary access to all the main menu commands: ≡ (System menu), **File**, **Edit**, **Search**, **Run**, **Compile**, **Debug**, **Options**, **Window** and **Help**.

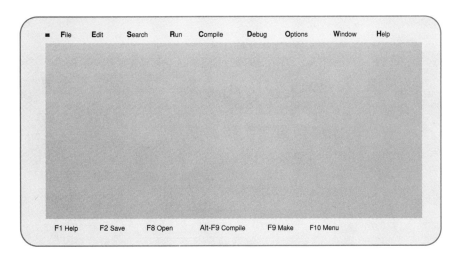

Figure 1-1
The Main Window

The line at the bottom of the screen is the status line which gives you information about the keys: **F1** - Help, **F2** - Save, **F3** - Open, **ALT-F9** - Compile, **F9** - Make, **F10** - Menu. The remaining part of the screen is called the desktop and will be used during the dialog as a work area.

There are 3 ways of calling an option from the main menu:

1. Press **F10**, then highlight the option with the left and right arrow keys and press **ENTER**.

2. Click on the option with the mouse (to click means to move the mouse cursor to the option on the screen and press the left mouse button).

3. Press **ALT** with the highlighted letter of the desired option: for example, press **ALT-C** to choose the **Compile** option. The only exception to this is that in order to call the System menu you have to press **ALT-SPACEBAR**.

The status line shows you basic keystrokes that invoke certain actions. To activate a function press the corresponding key or a quicker way is to click the shortcut with the mouse. For example, function key **F10** will return you to the main menu whenever you need to be there. Notice that you can only invoke active options from the status line - they are printed on a light background.

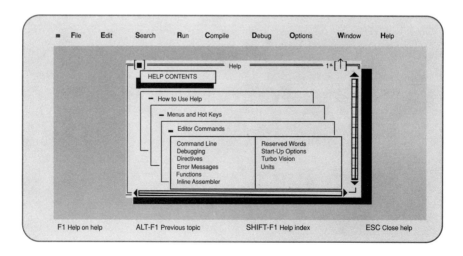

Figure 1-2
The Help Screen

Managing Windows

The windowing system is one of the most attractive features of the IDE. Windows are used for information exchange. You can open, move, resize, zoom, overlap and close each of them.

Figure 1-2 shows a **Help** window, opened by pressing the **F1** key. We'll start with some basic things that most of the IDE windows have in common. The first line consists of the **title bar** (Help) naming the window, a **window number** (1), a **zoom box** ([↑]) and a **close box** [■]. The right column and the bottom line may be used as vertical and horizontal **scroll bars**. The **resize box** is in the lower right corner of the window.

To close the window either click the close box with the mouse or press the hotkey **ALT-F3**. Every click on the icon of the zoom box can either **zoom** the window onto the whole screen or return it to the initial state (**unzoomed**) and the sign [↑] is substituted for [↕] and vice versa. The same effect is gained by double-clicking on the title bar or pressing **F5**. You can drag the resize box to make the window larger or smaller. You can also drag the title bar or double-line the border to move the window around. The same effect is achieved by pressing **CTRL-F3** and operating with the arrow keys. Once you have tried this you will be impressed by how convenient windows are.

The scroll bar is controlled in a similar way. You can use both the arrow keys and the mouse to move the text through the window. Practice with your mouse for a while; holding down the button move the mouse on the shadow area of the scroll bars. The text will move inside the window.

You may open as many windows as you want, you are only limited by the amount of memory available. To remove a window from the screen, you should close it first, to prevent overlapping by other windows. This is a specific feature of the new window system. Naturally, only one window should be active at any time. This is highlighted with a double line border. Each displayed window can be made active. To do this, press **ALT** with a window number and a new active window will be displayed above the others (of course you can only do this with the first nine windows because you've only got nine numeric keys on the keyboard). You are not faced with this problem when using the mouse. Even if there is only a small fragment of the window present on the screen, it is enough to click anywhere in it to make the window active. The **ALT-0** key also lets you see a list of the title bars. You can make your choice in the list as easily as in an ordinary menu.

Window operations are very important in the new version of the compiler, so a new option **Window** has been introduced in the main menu (see Figure 1-3).

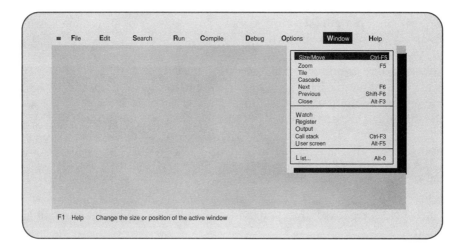

Figure 1-3
The Window Menu

Available commands will be highlighted with a corresponding color because most of them are determined by the existence of at least one open window on the screen.

Dialog Boxes

The **dialog box** is a type of Turbo Pascal window. It is responsible for controlling various commands of the IDE. You can define the initial values for some commands using a dialog box. Dialog boxes follow all menu items ending with ... (see Figure 1-4).

Unlike ordinary windows, the dialog box is always active on the screen. To continue work you must close the dialog box using the

ESC key. The dialog box can contain up to 5 different types of control elements: **action buttons**, **check boxes**, **radio buttons**, **input boxes** and **list boxes**. On the screen they form a control group with certain titles. For example, Figure 1-4 shows the following groups: **Text to find**, **New text**, **Options**, **Scope** and others. The active group has a highlighted title. You may switch over from one group to another either by using the mouse, or by pressing **TAB** or **SHIFT-TAB**. We will now look at all of the control elements we have mentioned taking the dialog box replace as an example.

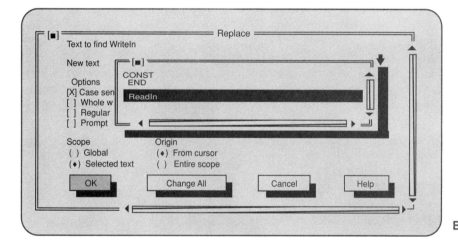

Figure 1-4
The Dialog Box "Replace"

Action Buttons

Figure 1-4 shows 4 **action buttons** or boxes: **OK**, **Change All**, **Cancel** and **Help**. Each of them performs certain actions. For instance, **OK** enters all input changes and starts command processing. The **Cancel** button is responsible for finishing and ignoring all changes. The **Help** box opens a help window for the current dialog box.

The action buttons listed above perform these standard actions for all dialog boxes in Turbo Pascal. We will not consider the **Change All** box at the moment because of its specific application in the **Replace** dialog box (see the section Search and Replace Commands)

The enter key allows you to leave the dialog box and to save all changes. It is initially equal to the **OK** button choice.

Check Boxes and Radio Buttons

Figure 1-4 shows a group of 4 **check boxes** called **Options**. As a rule, dialog boxes can have any number of check boxes. Their number is determined by how many are required to perform the command, and whether they can fit on the screen. Check boxes can have one of two settings: on or off. When a check box is selected, the sign [**X**] appears indicating that it is on. For example, in the dialog box **Replace**, the condition **Case sensitive** is on. When a group of check boxes is active on the screen, you can move between them using a mouse or the arrow keys. To change the setting of a check box you can either use the **SPACEBAR** or select the highlighted letter.

Radio buttons are different from check boxes in that only one button can be set at a given moment. They are intended for setting conditions that do not have a fixed number of options for each condition. In Figure 1-4 you can see two groups of radio buttons **Scope** and **Origin**. Note that only one condition is set in each group, marked by (•). To set a condition, make the group of radio buttons active and make your choice using either the mouse or arrow keys, or by selecting the highlighted letter.

Input Boxes and History Lists

In certain cases you might need to input some text to set a command condition. This is done using a special control element called **the input box**. For example, Figure 1-4 shows the input box **Text to find** with the string Writeln. This string should be found inside the program text. You can actually type any string you wish to find. The input box is made active in the usual way but this time notice that the cursor is in the entry field. You may use all of the alpha-numeric keys as well as **HOME**, **END**, **BACKSPACE**, **DEL** and **INS**. Pressing **ENTER** will close the dialog box and start the search. If you have not yet finished your work and you want to set up some check boxes or radio buttons, end the input of the string by pressing **TAB**.

If a special icon (↓) is given on the right of the entry field it means that the input box has a **history list**. The history list remembers all of the strings that have ever been entered in this input box and it can be used anytime. It saves the trouble of retyping similar strings. Both input boxes on Figure 1-4 have history lists. The history list of the **New text** box is active and is displayed on the screen. You may choose any line using either the mouse or the arrow keys and **ENTER**. The history box will be closed and the chosen line will appear in the input box. To open the history list press ↓ in the input box or click the (↓) icon.

List Box

The last control element of the dialog box is the **list box**. It looks very similar to the history list box but, unlike the latter, the contents can not extend beyond the limits of the screen. The list box contains a list of options for a certain command. The condition itself is defined by the title. If the list box is not active, its current value is displayed with a particular color. To make it active, either click anywhere in the box or use the **TAB** key. A cursor will appear on the line with the current value. Now you can choose any value using the mouse or the arrow keys. If the list of options does not fit in the screen you can easily rearrange its display.

Help

If you have any problems whilst using Turbo Pascal, there's always a friend at hand - online context-sensitive help. Press **F1** to call it up. A **Help** window will appear giving you information about the current part of Turbo Pascal that you are working on (see Figure 1-2). The **Help** window is manipulated like all of the other windows but there are some additional possibilities, for example, you can close the window just by pressing **ESC**.

All reference information in **HELP** is structured in separate interconnected **topics** and **help keywords**. They are displayed on the screen with a corresponding color. The big cursor can move along them as with ordinary menus. The cursor is controlled with the arrow keys, **TAB** key or the mouse. Move the cursor to the relevant keyword and press **ENTER** or double-click it with the mouse to get the information you need.

Help control commands are presented in a special menu (see Figure 1-5). You can switch over to it by pressing **ALT-H.**

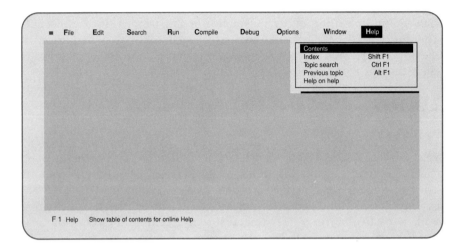

Figure 1-5
The Help Menu

Notice that here, as in many other menus, you can use a shortcut key combination. The shortcut combination is to some extent an addition to the status line. The **Contents** command from the Help window displays the table of contents (see Figure 1-2). There is an **Index** command to present a sorted list of keywords of the Help file. A fast search can be made by entering an initial letter. For example, if you press **R** the cursor will jump to the first help keyword beginning with **R**. Then if you press **E** the cursor will stop on the first keyword beginning with letters **RE**. For example, this would quickly get you information about the Readln procedure.

There is yet another way to get help on a subject, the **Topic search**. To use this command while editing, point to the relevant item with the cursor and press **CTRL-F1** (or point to it with the mouse and press the right button). **Topic search** will make Turbo Pascal easier to use, especially in the beginning.

You can use **Previous topic** or press **ALT-F1** to return to the last 20 help screens. When the Help window is active, the current status line (see Figure 1-2) contains all the keystrokes for the Help window shown. This means that you can try out any actions by clicking on the shortcut keys with the mouse. If you still find it somewhat difficult to use the Help system, use the **Help on Help** command or press **F1-F1**.

Using the Turbo Editor

The way in which you work with the source text in program design is very important, and can be very time-consuming, so the new version of the Turbo integrated editor will come as a relief. You can work with several files at once with files ranging up to 1 Mb in size. You can also move text between various windows and insert examples from the Help window.

To enter the editor choose the command **New** from the **File** menu. You will see an empty window named **NONAME00.PAS** (see Figure 1-6). The cursor will be in the upper left corner.

You can enter the editor just by pressing **ALT-F-N** (**ALT-F** calls the **File** menu, **N** calls the **New** command). You are now ready to enter some text. Before we get down to the editor commands, we will define some of the key concepts which are involved with the editor. These include **character**, **word**, **string**, **page**, **block** and **file**.

The meanings of character, string and file are fairly obvious but the others need some explanation. A word is a group of characters, delimited by blanks or special characters. Page consists of some text lines and its size is determined by the height of the editor window. A specially marked text area of variable size is called a block.

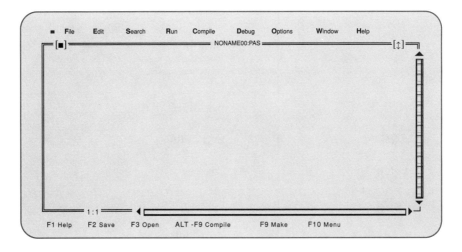

Figure 1-6
The Edit Screen

Editor Control Commands

All editor control commands can be divided into 5 groups:

1. **Cursor Movement**

2. **Inserting and Deleting**

3. **Blocking**

4. **Searching and Replacing**

5. **Miscellaneous**

Cursor Movement Commands

Most of these commands are similar to those used in other packages. Table 1-1 shows the list of cursor movement commands.

Key	Movement
←	Character left
→	Character right
↑	Line up
↓	Line down
HOME	Beginning of line
END	End of line
PgUp	Page up
PgDn	Page down
CTRL - ←	Word left

Table 1-1
Cursor Movement Commands

CTRL - →	Word right
CTRL-HOME	Top of window
CTRL-End	Bottom of window
CTRL-PgUp	Top of file
CTRL-PgDn	Bottom of file
CTRL-Q-B	Beginning of block
CTRL-Q-K	End of block

Table 1-1
Cursor Movement Commands (continued)

Insert and Delete Commands

There are two modes for entering text into the editor: **Insert** or **Overwrite**. When you enter a character in the Insert mode, the rest of the string to the right of the cursor is moved to the right. In the Overwrite mode, each new character replaces a character in its current position. You can switch modes by pressing the **INS** key. The form of the cursor changes so that you can easily distinguish between each mode.

Key	*Movement*
INS	Insert mode on/off
DEL	Delete character at cursor
BACKSPACE	Delete character left of cursor
CTRL-Y	Delete line
CTRL-Q-Y	Delete to end of line
CTRL-N	Insert line

Table 1-2
Insert and Delete Commands

Block Commands

You may find that you need to use a piece of text that has occurred before. Retyping is a nuisance and can be very time-consuming. Block commands will save both your time and your fingers.

First you have to define the block. Move the cursor to the beginning of the selected text and press **CTRL-K-B**. Then move the cursor to the end of the selected area and press **CTRL-K-K**. The selected block is now displayed with a different color. You can highlight a block by pressing **SHIFT-→**, or by using the mouse (with the button held down). To work with the block use the following commands:

Key	*Movement*
CTRL-K-C, SHIFT-INS	Copy block
CTRL-K-Y, CTRL-DEL	Delete block
CTRL-K-V, SHIFT-DEL	Move block
CTRL-K-H	Hide/display block
CTRL-K-P	Print block
CTRL-K-R	Read block from disk
CTRL-K-W	Write block to disk

Table 1-3
Block
Commands

These commands only affect blocks in the current editor window.

Block Commands in Multiwindow Editing

The latest version of the Turbo Editor can edit several files simultaneously and has a wider range of block commands. These commands use a special memory area called the **Clipboard**. Blocks being exchanged between various windows pass through this area.

For example, you decide to copy a text block from window 1 to window 2. First define the block in window 1 and copy it out to the Clipboard. Then switch over to window 2 by pressing **ALT-2**. Finally, press **SHIFT-INS** to copy the block from the Clipboard to the current window to complete the operation. You can also call these block commands from the main menu using the **Edit** option (see Figure 1-7).

In this example we used the hotkeys of the standard **Copy** and **Paste** commands. The Clipboard should now contain the block from the first window. To check that it really does, use the **Show clipboard** command. You can use the **Paste** command with a block all the time that it is selected in the clipboard window. The Clipboard window can be edited in the normal way. You can use the Clipboard as a rough draft for trying out different things without affecting your other files. In addition, a special **Copy example** command in the Edit menu is designed to copy examples from the Help window. You don't even have to mark these examples: just enter the editor window and press **SHIFT-INS**. The text will be copied from the Clipboard to the active window.

The **Cut** command is similar to **Copy**, but unlike the latter it deletes the copied block from the source file. You can restore the block to the current window by pressing the **SHIFT-INS**.

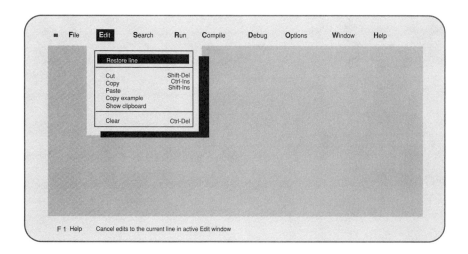

Figure 1-7
Edit Menu

Search and Replace Commands

These commands allow you to search for a line and replace it or to jump to a line according to its number. In all cases however you have to enter some additional information to set the necessary conditions. The sign ... in the menu is used to determine the initial command options. Choose the **Find** command or press **CTRL-Q-F** and you will see the **Find** dialog box.

Enter the string you have to find and set the necessary options. For example, in Figure 1-9 we are trying to find Writeln with case sensitive. The search starts from the current cursor position and finishes at the end of the file. Press **ENTER** or click the mouse on the **OK** box to start the command. If Writeln is found in the text it will be highlighted and the cursor will be set after the last character. You can continue to search by choosing the **Search again** command or by pressing **CTRL-L** until you get a window with the error message that the string is not found. In contrast to Find, the replace command finds the relevant string and substitutes the string with another one. If you have the prompt on replace operation confirmed, the **Change** box will automatically repeat the search as many times as the relevant line is found in the text.

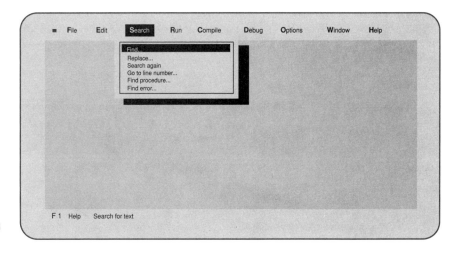

Figure 1-8
Search Menu

The **Go to line number** command requires you to enter the number of the line in which you want to set the cursor. Enter this number and the cursor will move to the first character of the line in the edited file.

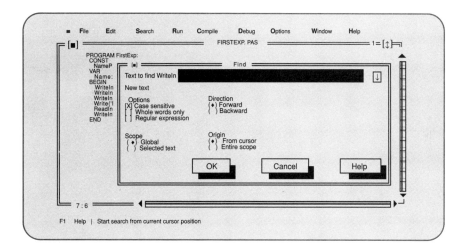

Figure 1-9
Dialog Box
"Find"

Miscellaneous Commands

These are certain specific commands which are not included in any of the above groups. One of the most useful is the **Restore line** command from the **Edit** menu (see Figure 1-7). It will restore the last edited line to its initial form, which is very convenient if you have made a mistake. To call this command press **CTRL-Q-L**. Remember that this command only works with the current line.

The **ESC** key will return you to the Editor window from the main window. **ALT-X** keys will complete work with the IDE and return you to DOS.

TASK-ALGORITHM-PROGRAM

PCs are tools that help you to solve many different types of problems. Contrary to popular belief, PCs can only do exactly as they are told. For a PC to perform a **Task** for you there are several things you need to establish:

1. The AIM
2. What data you need (INPUT)
3. The RESULT you expect
4. The means by which you achieve the result (ALGORITHM)
5. Any LIMITS

An **Algorithm** is a set of instructions that describes how to execute a task - similar to a cooking recipe.

Suppose you want to estimate your ideal weight. As a quick estimate you can say that it is equal to your height in centimetres - 100. This becomes:

AIM:	To estimate your ideal weight
INPUT:	Height
RESULT:	Ideal weight
ALGORITHM:	Ideal weight = height -100
LIMITS:	Metric system (Height is in centimetres, weight is in kilograms)

A good way to show the algorithm is by drawing a diagram which helps to show the logic involved (see Figure 2-1).

Some tasks are so complicated that it is almost impossible to understand them without a diagram. Diagrams are especially useful if you are using Turbo Pascal for the first time because they help to give a general outline to solve a particular task. Don't start to solve a task without drawing a diagram, you will be wasting your time!

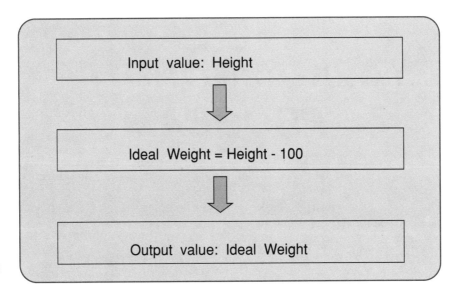

Figure 2-1
**Task Solving
Diagram**

Having completed the task specification and algorithm diagram you can get on with writing the program. A **Program** is a sequence of commands that perform an algorithm. The basis of any program is **Data**. Each piece of data should have a meaningful name associated with it. In the above example height and weight are items of data so we can assign the names "Height" and "Weight" to them. There are three basic components in every algorithmic programming language:

1. Input commands

2. Processing commands

3. Output commands

In Turbo Pascal the input and output commands can be fairly simple:

```
Read(Height);
Write(IdealWeight);
```

The processing commands are the widest set of instructions and are used for everything from arithmetic to menu design.

A First Look at a Pascal Program

A Turbo Pascal program consists of a title and a body. The command **PROGRAM** defines the title:

PROGRAM   IdealWeight;

The body contains a data specification section and an operator section. The data specification section must come first and defines all the data to be used in the program: it starts with the word **VAR**. The operator section contains commands which read data, execute actions and output results: it starts with   **BEGIN** and finishes with **END**. The entire program finishes with a full stop.

Turbo Pascal defines data in terms of integers, reals, strings and others (integers are whole numbers, reals are numbers with fractions, strings are a series of characters). In our example we will declare Height and Weight as integers:

```
PROGRAM IdealWeight;
VAR
  Height, Weight : integer;              { Data specifications }
BEGIN
  Write('Enter your height, please:');   { Input prompt }
  Read(Height);                          { Height value input }
  Weight := Height - 100;                { Ideal weight calculation }
  Write('Your ideal weight is ',Weight); { Output the result }
END.
```

Notice that we have added comments to the program - they can be used anywhere as long as they are enclosed in braces {}.

The most widely used Turbo Pascal programs look very similar to the above but their algorithms are usually more complicated and so a more complex set of instructions are used.

As you can see, the program text resembles ordinary English. Unfortunately however, your PC does not understand English, so you need to translate the Program into a language that it can understand before you can execute the program. A special program called a compiler is used to do the translation; it reads your **Source Code** and converts it into a form suitable for execution (a .EXE file). When you **Compile** your program you will often find that you have some errors in it. These are frequently caused by inaccurate typing. For example if you type

      PRGRM IdealWeight;

instead of

      PROGRAM IdealWeight;

the compiler will not be able understand the word PRGRM and will issue an error message. You will have to correct the error and compile the program again. This process is called debugging and it continues until there are no errors left. A .EXE file is then output and can be executed just like any other PC command.

Let us review the program design process:

1. Problem definition

2. Algorithm design

3. Input

4. Compiling

5. Debugging

6. Execution

The first two steps are carried out before you touch your PC, the last four are done with the aid of Turbo Pascal.

Your First Program

There is only one way to become a programmer, that is to do the routine work yourself. Now you can start your first Turbo Pascal program.

Creating

If you can't see the editor window after starting the compiler, start the **New** command or press **ALT-F-N**. Type the program below into the editor window (see Figure 1-6) exactly as it is shown, (including some possible errors). This should not be too hard as long as you know the Turbo Editor commands.

```
PROGRAM FirstExp;
CONST
   NamePro = 'HOME FINANCES ANALYSIS';
VAR
   Name : string;
BEGIN
   Writeln;
   Writeln(NamePro)
   Writeln;
   Write('Input your name: ');
   Readln(Name);
   Writeln(Name,'! Welcome to ', NamePro);
END.
```

Saving

Since you have probably spent quite some time entering the text, it would be a shame to lose your first program. To avoid unexpected problems, save your program in a file on the disk. To do this, use the Save command from the File menu. When you press **F2** (the hotkey of the Save command), a window will appear. You can now enter the name of the file to be saved. You may choose any name you like for example, **FIRSTEXP.PAS**. Press **ENTER** or click on the **OK** box after you have entered the name. A new file will be created in the current subdirectory and the title bar of the editor window will also change. If you don't enter any name, the file will automatically be called **NONAME00.PAS**

You can save your file in other subdirectories. All you have to do is to type a complete file specification, including the subdirectory and drive names. Another way to do this is to choose the relevant directory with the aid of the **TAB** key or the mouse, come back to enter the file's name and then press **ENTER** or click on the **OK** box.

Compiling

Once you have saved the program you can start compiling. The syntax of the statements is checked during this process. If there are no errors, the compiler creates an executable program.

To compile the example program, press **Alt-F9** or click on the **Compile** command in the Compile main menu. You will see the Compile window which presents some information about the compiling process. It will be replaced immediately by the editor window and the first string will carry a rather unpleasant error message and a possible reason for it (see Figure 2-2). The cursor is automatically fixed on either the error line or the line which follows.

You don't have to worry about this error as we deliberately included it in the program to demonstrate various functions. The comment on the error says

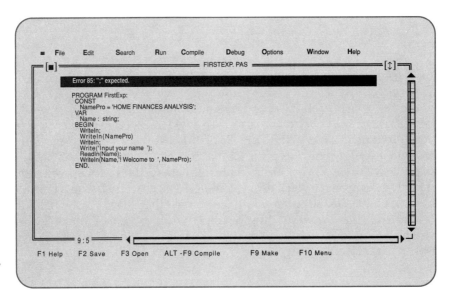

Figure 2-2
FIRSTEXP.PAS
Program Error
Message

that character **;** is expected. The cursor is pointing to line number 9. Consequently, you should look for a possible error either in this line or the adjacent ones. Even if the Turbo Pascal language is new to you, you should notice that the 8th line differs from others: it has no **;** character at the end:

```
Writeln(NamePro)
```

To correct the mistake you have to insert this character and perform the **Compile** command once again. If you have been careful and haven't made your own mistakes, the screen will display a compiling window very similar to the figure below:

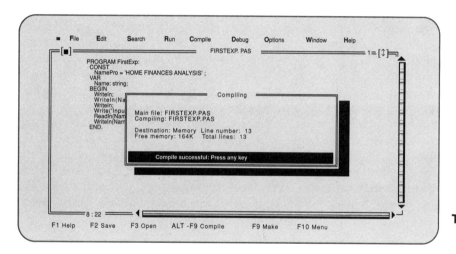

Figure 2-3
The Compiling Window

The bottom line of the window should inform you that the compilation has been a success. Let's save some new text by pressing **F2** and proceed to the most interesting step: running the program.

Running

To run the program press **CTRL-F9** or click on the **Run** main menu and then the **Run** command. Before using the **Run** program, make sure that the program has been compiled, otherwise you will get errors. Run-time errors affect how the program actually works. Turbo Pascal brings the relevant message onto the screen and automatically positions the cursor on the part of the program that has caused the error. After making the necessary changes run the program again.

Whilst running the program you can see that DOS replaces the IDE. DOS contains the information that you start with before calling the Turbo Compiler. This can make you think that you are working in the operating system.

Let's see how your first program works. You will be asked to enter your name, you will be welcomed by Turbo Pascal, and you will then return to the IDE shell. If you did not manage to read the message, you can see it again using the IDE.

Viewing the Result

There are two ways of viewing the text generated by your program. One way is to use the **Output** command from the **Window** menu. You will see a window with DOS screen copy. It may contain not only the output information but previous DOS commands too. Usually this window is placed at the bottom of the screen which enables you to compare the text program with its result. You may fling the output window onto the whole screen to get more information by clicking on the room box. Alternatively, you can use the **User screen** command from the **Window** menu. This will give you a complete DOS screen, unlike the **Output** command which presents the text in an ordinary Turbo Pascal window. Press any key or click the mouse to return to the IDE. Note that you can only view the results in graphics with the aid of the **User Screen** command, the screen must pause before you can switch over to it before the program continues.

Reloading the Program

If you have followed our instructions you have now successfully completed your first working program. You have seen its results on the screen and the program has been saved in a file on disk. If you find the results encouraging, you can try to run the program again or make some changes to it. To do this, reload the text from the file into the editor. Press **F3** or use the **Open** command from the **File** menu. A list of files for you to choose from will appear on the screen. In addition, the IDE has a list of all edited files that can be automatically loaded into the memory.

Other Menu Options

We'll now move on to some of the more interesting features of the IDE which can be very helpful. We won't consider all of the functions of the IDE as this would be very time-consuming.

Printing

It is quite probable that you will want to print the program text to work with it, or to keep it as a hard copy. For this reason there is a **Print** command in the **File** menu. To print the text, switch on your printer, insert some paper and select the command **Print**.

You also can print a portion of the text. To do so, outline it as a block and press **CTRL-K-P**.

Change Directory

You will have already noticed that the compiler always uses the current directory and drive to save files. If you want to save the file elsewhere, you have to perform some additional actions. To avoid this rather clumsy routine you can make the relevant drive or directory current using the **Change Directory** command from the **File** menu. It displays a window where you can make your choice (see Figure 2-4).

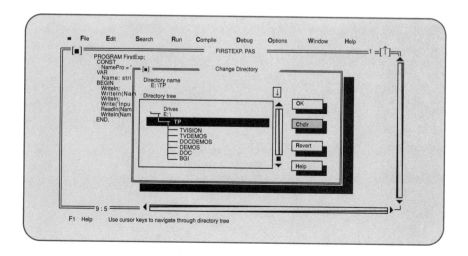

Figure 2-4
**Window
"Change
Directory"**

You can always enter a new directory from the keyboard, but it is often better to travel along the directory tree. This is quite easy: press **ENTER** on the highlighted tree item or double-click on it. A new drive or directory will appear at the top of the dialog box.

To enter a new drive, move to the **OK** box using the **TAB** key and press **ENTER**, or click on it. Clicking the **Revert** box will help you to restore the previous state of the directory tree as if no choice had been made before.

DOS Shell

Suppose you need to delete a certain file, for example, **FIRSTEXP.EXE** from the current directory. Unfortunately, the IDE has no way of doing this. Do you have any idea how to overcome this problem? The most obvious decision is to exit to DOS (by pressing **ALT-X**), delete the file and re-engage the compiler. This, however, is not the quickest way to delete a file. A more effective way is to use the **DOS shell** command from the **File** menu. This command allows you to temporarily enter DOS and perform any program or command. To return to the IDE type **EXIT**. For example, to delete the **FIRSTEXP.EXE** file you have to press **ALT-F-D**. You are now in DOS shell and you have to type:

        DEL FIRSTEXP.EXE

then type:

        EXIT

to return to the IDE.

CHAPTER 3

THE TURBO PASCAL BASICS

Identifiers

Turbo Pascal programs are made up of letters (A...Z, a...z), digits (0...9) and special characters (=, :, ;, etc.). All of these are represented on the keyboard and appear on the screen when you press the corresponding key. Groups of letters are called words and, as with most computer languages, words are divided into 3 groups: reserved words, standard identifiers and user's identifiers.

Reserved words are a special set of predefined words, and form the basis of Turbo Pascal. Some examples are: **PROGRAM**, **BEGIN**, **END**, **CONST**, **VAR**.

Standard identifiers are predefined procedures, constants and data types. For example, **Readln** and **Writeln** are standard identifiers which specify data input/output procedures; **String** defines a data type for strings. User's identifiers are, as their name implies, defined by a user. They can be used to identify any variable, procedure, or function. The words **NamePro** and **Name** in program 3-1 are examples of user's identifiers.

When creating an identifier, stick to the following rules:

1. Identifiers are made up of letters, digits, and underscore characters (_). No distinction is made between upper-case and lower-case letters.

2. The first character of an identifier must be either a letter or an underscore character.

3. Blanks can not be used in an identifier.

⚠ 4   Identifiers are delimited by blanks.

⚠ 5   An identifier may be of any length, so long as it does not extend beyond the end of the line. However, try not to use more than 10-15 characters in an identifier.

Here are some examples of right and wrong identifiers:

Right	*Wrong*	*Why it is wrong*
Document	1_Document	Starts with a digit
GoodName	Bad Name	A blank between Bad and Name
Unheard_of	Unheard-of	"-" is a wrong identifier character
Sum	5432	Starts with a digit

Table 3-1
Right and Wrong Identifiers

When using complex identifiers, there are two ways you can distinguish between the different parts. You can either separate the parts using the underscore character:

    PROGRAM My_Ideal_Weight;

or simply by using upper-case letters:

    PROGRAM MyIdealWeight;

In our experience the second way is easier to type in. So, all identifiers in this book will follow the second example.

The Concept of Data Types

All computer programs process data in some way. There are various types of data: integer, floating point, string, etc. In Turbo Pascal, a data type refers to a set of values and the ways in which they can be manipulated. For example, the data type Byte consists of all integer values between 0 and 255. The elements of Byte can be used in addition, subtraction, multiplication and division.

Each standard type definition uses a relevant identifier:

integer - for integers, real - for fractionals, etc.

If necessary, you can create your own data types. For example, if you are interested in zoology, you can specify a data type of Animals composed of animals' names. You declare a user's data type using the reserved word **TYPE**, followed by the type name and an admissible range of values:

```
TYPE
     Animals  =  (Cat,  Dog,  Horse,  Cow);
```

Standard (or predefined) and user-defined types are discussed below.

Constants and Variables

All the data in a Turbo Pascal program is classified as either constant or variable (see Figures 3-1 and 3-2). If the value is to remain unchanged, it is defined as a constant.

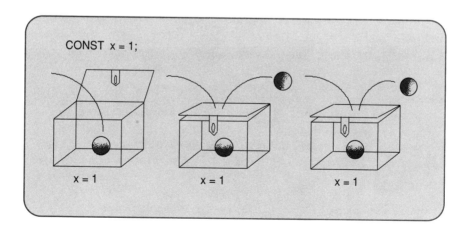

Figure 3-1
**Data
Classified
as a
Constant**

Figure 3-1 shows how a constant is similar to a closed box that has a name. The contents of the box are unchangeable.

A constant is usually either a number or a string; it is defined after the reserved word **CONST**. For example:

```
CONST
    MyHeight  =  184;
    MyName    =  'Donald';
```

Unlike constants variables can change their values if necessary.

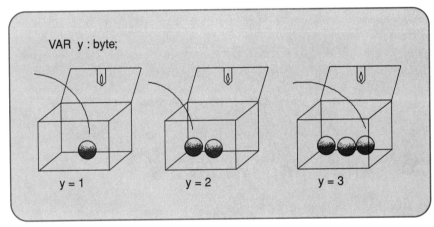

Figure 3-2
Data Classified as Variable

Figure 3-2. Shows how a variable is similar to an open box with a name. The box contents can be changed any time. The reserved word **VAR** is used to define them and is followed by identifiers of variables and indications of their type. A colon is placed between the identifiers and the words indicating the type. Each group of variables ends with a semicolon:

```
VAR
  MyWeight : integer;  { variable of standard data type
                                             Integer}
  MyAge : byte;{ variable of standard data type Byte }
  Animal : Animals;    { variable of a user's data type
                                             Animals }

  ...
  MyWeight := 100;     { 100 kg - too much for Donald }
                       { jogging every day ... }
  MyWeight := 80;      { Donald: I'm all right! }
```

Remember that in Turbo Pascal you have to describe all the data elements to be used in the **CONST** and **VAR** sections.

Numbers

There are two main numbering systems used in Turbo Pascal: decimal and hexadecimal. Decimal is used for arithmetic functions, hexadecimal is used mainly for accessing memory.

Decimal

Turbo Pascal number notation is similar to that of ordinary mathematics. There are integers and real numbers. Both integers and real numbers can be negative, zero or positive. Integers consist of digits and, sometimes, a positive or negative sign. If the sign is omitted and the number is not zero then it is considered positive:

```
      1      {  positive  }
    702      {  positive  }
   - 67      {  negative  }
```

Real numbers represent decimal fractions or integer values in fractional notation. For example, 0 is an integer number, but 0.0 is a real number. The integer and fractional parts of real numbers are separated by a decimal point. There are two notation forms for numbers: **fixed-point** and **floating-point** notation. The first one is used in an ordinary way:

```
5.18
0.01
3.14
```

Floating-point notation is used in mathematical calculations to allow for a greater range but can be less accurate:

```
5.18E+02        {5.18 multiplied by, 10 raised to
                the power  02}

10E-03          {10 multiplied by, 10 raised to the
                power  -03}

3.14E00         {3.14 multiplied by, 10 raised to
                the power  0}
```

We will only deal with fixed-point notation to simplify our explanations.

Hexadecimal

As you know, the computer's memory is made up of bits, which can have one of two possible values, 0 or 1. The computer "thinks" in a language made up of 1's and zeros. A bit is addressed and its contents specified using a special binary system. However, people naturally don't think in the same way as a computer - the binary number system is too laborious. You'll agree that the number 0001 0001 0001 0001 0011 0111 1000, for example, is hard to understand for someone who is used to the decimal numbering system - even for an experienced programmer. It is because of this that the hexadecimal number system was developed.

Each hexadecimal number corresponds to 4 bits, which means that a number stored in hexadecimal notation is 4 times shorter than a number stored in binary notation. It is very convenient for addressing the memory. Each digit in a hexadecimal number has a value within a range from 0 to 15. Each position has a power of 16. Hexadecimal values from 10 to 15 are written using the letters A to F respectively. Table 3-2 shows the corresponding binary, decimal and hexadecimal notation of numbers.

Decimal	Binary	Hexadecimal
0	0000	0
1	0001	1
2	0010	2
3	0011	3
4	0100	4
5	0101	5
6	0110	6
7	0111	7
8	1000	8
9	1001	9
10	1010	A
11	1011	B
12	1100	C
13	1101	D

Table 3-2
Number
Systems

14	1110	E
15	1111	F
16	10000	10
...	...	...
26	11010	1A
31	11111	1F
255	11111111	FF
256	100000000	100

Table 3-2
Number Systems (continued)

For example, the hexadecimal number 1F2 can be calculated as decimal 498. The $ symbol must appear before every hexadecimal number in a program. For example:

```
$4000      { hexadecimal value }
1234       { decimal value }
```

When addressing the memory we will usually use the hexadecimal system, giving the segment and offset.

Compiler Directives

The first set of advanced compiler features comes in the form of compiler directives. A compiler directive tells the compiler how to process your program. They are made up of various groups which perform different functions. For example, there's a group for debugging your program, another which makes it easier to create large programs, and so on.

In our programs we will often use compiler directives, such as {$R+}, {$I+}, etc. A compiler directive starts with an opening comment symbol and a dollar sign. Directives are placed at the top of a program, before any statement, and instruct the compiler to turn certain features on or off. For example,

```
{$I-}  -  off
{$I+}  -  on
```

disables or enables input/output checking.

Scalar Predefined Data Types

There are five scalar data types in Turbo Pascal: **integer**, **real**, **character**, **string** and **boolean**. From these simple types, you can build up complex types, such as arrays, records and sets.

Integer is the most basic of the Pascal data types. It represents whole numbers. More memory is required for storing large whole numbers than for storing small whole numbers: handling billions differs from handling dozens. Therefore Pascal offers you five integer data types.

Type	*Range of values*	*Size in bytes*
byte	0..255	1
word	0..65535	2
integer	-32768..32767	2
shortint	-128..127	1
longint	-2147483648..2147483647	4

Table 3-3
The Turbo Pascal Integer Types

We'll create some variables for month and year values as an example.

```
VAR
    Year    :  integer;
    Month   :  byte;
...
    Year    := 1991;
    Month   := 300;  { ERROR!  300  -  is  not  in
                             the  byte  range  }
    Year    := 10.0 + 2;  { ERROR!  10.0  -  is
                      not  an  integer  type  }
```

Real data types are used to store numeric data that requires a fractional part, thus maintaining a high degree of accuracy. Turbo Pascal offers five different data types for representing real numbers (see Table 3-4).

Type	Range of values	Size in bytes	Significant digits
real	2.9E-39..1.7E38	6	11-12
single	1.5E-45..3.4E38	4	7-8
double	5.0E-324..1.7E308	8	15-16
extended	3.4E-4932..1.1E4932	10	19-20
comp	-9.2E18..9.2E18	8	19-20

Table 3-4
The Turbo Pascal Real Number Types

The following examples illustrate real number variables:

```
VAR
  Income,            { monthly income }
  Food, Home,        { food and accommodation expenses }
  Clothing, Education : real;
                     { clothing and education expenses }
  ...
  Income := 1000.95+100;
  Food    := 210.00;
```

Turbo Pascal supports both fixed-point and floating-point notations. You should note that the use of **single**, **double**, and **extended** types is only effective if your computer has a maths co-processor chip. If this is not the case, you can emulate it by setting compiler directive {$N-}.

The **char** data type allows you to deal with ASCII characters. The IBM PC has a set of 256 ASCII symbols letters, digits, punctuation and control characters. A full list of ASCII characters can be found in Appendix C. Char type variables and constants allow operations with any character in the ASCII-table (see table 3-5).

Type	Range of values	Size in bytes
char	ASCII table	1

Table 3-5
Character Type

Character values in a program must be enclosed by two single quotation marks (' '), for example:

```
CONST
   First = 'A';
   Last  = 'Z';
VAR
  Symbol := char;
...
  Symbol := '+';
  Symbol := '<>'; { ERROR! Two characters for the Letter }
```

A string is a sequence of ASCII characters enclosed within single quotes. Strings are an integral part of Turbo Pascal programming, and you will find that you need to use them in practically every program. The following examples show how strings are made up:

```
'BASE.DTA'
'Our family Budget'
'Bob Simpson
      - error! Closing single quote is missing
```

To declare a string you use the reserved word **STRING**, followed by the length of the longest string you want to use. You should note that a string cannot be more than 255 characters long.

```
VAR
  Name : string[30];
  Address : string[60];
```

If you don't specify a maximum length:

```
VAR
  Job : string;
```

then the string length will automatically be 255 characters. You can define string variables by either defining the string type or by directly declaring a string variable. You can also use string constants:

```
CONST
  NamePro = 'WROX HOME FINANCES';
  FileName = 'BASE.DTA';
```

You cannot use a string variable as a selector value in a statement.

The **boolean** data type (after George Boole, who was one of the originators of formal logic) is provided by Turbo Pascal for handling True/False values. Figure 3-3 shows how it is used.

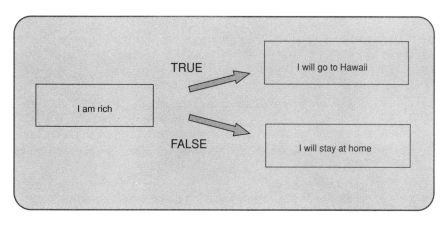

Figure 3-3
Use of the Boolean Variable

Boolean variables are not very useful by themselves. However, they are widely used in control statements, logical statements and mathematical expressions. In Turbo Pascal boolean variables are declared with the reserved word **boolean**   (see Table 3-6).

Type	*Range of values*	*Size in bytes*
boolean	True, False	1

Table 3-6
Boolean Type

For example:

```
VAR
  Flag : boolean;
  ...
  Flag := False;
```

User-Defined Data Types

One of Turbo Pascal's main advantages over other programming languages is its capacity to create user-defined data types. We will consider two scalar types: **enumerated data type** and **subranges**. Because they have a length of one byte, each of the enumerated data type's identifiers are assigned a value between 0 and 255. Whilst using the enumerated data type you have a problem with input/output. Standard input/output procedures do not apply, so you have to create your own method (see Chapter 6).

An Enumerated type is defined by simple specification of all of its elements:

```
TYPE
  Hobby = (StampCollecting, Cinema, Sport,
                            LoungingAround);
VAR
  MyHobby : Hobby;
...
  MyHobby := Sport;
  MyHobby := Pub; { ERROR! Pub is not
                        in Hobby type }
  Writeln(MyHobby); {ERROR! MyHobby is not
                     used with writeln}
```

The **Subrange** data type is defined by setting high and low limit values. The compiler uses special testing procedures to check whether the variable is in the defined range. Both of the constant limits must belong to the same scalar predefined type:

```
CONST
  Min = 1;
  Max = 41;
TYPE
  Temperature = Min .. Max;
VAR
  T : Temperature;
...
 T := 25;
 T := 120;   { An error occurs: the
              variable is out of range! }
```

Checking can be turned on or off using the {$R-} compiler directive.

Expressions

Constants and variables are used in expressions. An expression controls the order of data processing operations. It consists of operands, parentheses and operators. Constants, variables and function calls can all be operands. Operators define the processing operations of operands. For example:

```
(X  +  Y  -  10)
```

X, Y, and 10 are operands, +, and - are arithmetic operators. Parentheses are used to override precedence rules as in ordinary arithmetic expressions. The resulting type of an expression is the same type as its components.

Turbo Pascal operations are divided into several operational types, for example **arithmetic**, **relational**, **logical**, and **string** operations. Consequently, expressions are termed arithmetic, relational, logical and strings respectively. The first three groups are discussed later in this chapter, the remainder are considered with their corresponding data types.

Arithmetic expressions deal with integer and real operands:

Operator	*Operation*	*Operand type*	*Result type*
+	addition	integer	integer
		real	real
-	subtraction	integer	integer
		real	real
*	multiplication	integer	integer
		real	real
/	division	integer	real
		real	real
DIV	integer division	integer	integer
MOD	remainder	integer	integer

Table 3-7
Arithmetic Operators

Addition, subtraction and multiplication work just as you might expect:

Expression	Result
12 + 5	17
7 * 8	56
12.6 - 12	0.6
-(5 + 2)	-7
+(5 - 7)	-2

Division has three forms: **/, DIV and MOD**. To divide two real numbers, use a slash (**/**):

125.77 / 54.91 = 2.2905

The result is a real number.

To divide two integer values, use **DIV or MOD**. The **DIV** operator returns the quotient of the division of operands:

30 DIV 25 = 1   *then 30-25 = 5 to get remainder and store divisor*

The **MOD** operator returns the remainder of the division of operands:

30 MOD 25 = 5

The result of **MOD**- and **DIV** division is an integer. The following examples will help you understand the differences:

Expression	Result
4.0 / 2.0	2.0
5.0 / 2.0	2.5
11.0 / 4.0	2.75
5.0 / 10.0	0.5

Expression	Result
-10 DIV 7	-1 *gives divisor*
5 DIV 2	2
11 DIV 4	2
5 DIV 10	0

Expression	Result
-20 MOD 7	-6
5 MOD 2	1
11 MOD 4	3
5 MOD 10	5

gives remainder

Turbo Pascal relational expressions compare two operands, and return one of two boolean values: True or False. Operands may be of any scalar or enumerated type (see Table 3-8).

Operator	Operation	Expression	Result type
=	equal	A = B	True, if A is equal to B
<>	not equal	A <> B	True, if A is not equal to B
>	greater than	A > B	True, if A is greater than B
<	less than	A < B	True, if A is less than B
>=	greater than or equal to	A >= B	True, if A is greater than or equal to B
<=	less than or equal to	A <= B	True, if A is less than or equal to B

Table 3-8
Relational Operators

For example:

Expression	Result
45 = 50	False
45 <> 50	True
60 > 60	False
60 >= 60	True

Logical (or boolean) expressions operate only with the boolean operands (see Table 3-9).

Operator	Operation	Expression	A	B	Result type
NOT	Logical negation	NOT A	True False		False True
AND	Logical AND	A AND B	True True True False False True False False		True False False False
OR	Logical OR	A OR B	True True True False False True False False		True True True False
XOR	Logical EXCLUSIVE	A XOR B	True True True False False True False False		False True True False

Table 3-9
Boolean
Operators

For example:

Expression	Result
NOT (45 = 50)	True
(4 < 5) AND (10 > 7)	True
True OR False	True
False XOR True	True

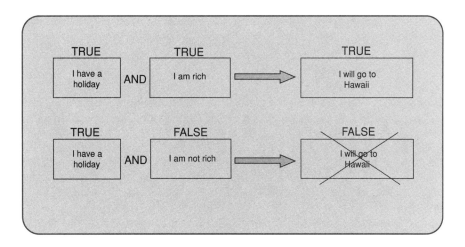

Figure 3-3
**The Use of
the AND
Operator**

Operator Precedence

Turbo Pascal uses a set of rules called operator precedence to evaluate expressions with more than one operator type. Turbo Pascal assigns a precedence level to each of its operators (see Table 3-10).

Operation	Level	Operation type
-, NOT, @	First (highest)	Unary minus, logical negation and @
*, /, DIV, MOD, AND, SHL, SHR	Second	Multiplying operators
+, -, OR, XOR	Third	Adding operators
=, <>, <, >, <=, >=, in	Fourth (lowest)	Relational operators

Table 3-10
*Precedence
Level*

For example, the expression 10 + 5 * 7 would be evaluated as follows:

```
7 * 5 = 35
10 + 35 = 45
```

The operator with the highest precedence is evaluated first, the sub-expression that contains operators with the next highest precedence is evaluated second, and so on.

Defining Precedence

There are 4 rules when defining precedence:

1. If the operand stands between two operators, it is connected first to the operator with the highest precedence. For example, in the expression X+Y/ C-K, first of all the operator / is calculated then + and - .

2. If the operand stands between two operators with the same precedence it is connected first to the left one. For example, in the expression X*Y*K, first of all X multiplied by Y is calculated and then this result is multiplied by K.

3. Surrounding a sub-expression with parentheses tells the compiler to evaluate the sub-expression first. For example, in the expression (X+Y)/C-K, the sub-expression (X+Y) is calculated first.

4. Sub-expressions with operators of equal precedence are evaluated strictly from left to right. For example, in the expression (X+Y)*(Z-T)/3.14 the sub-expression (X+Y) is calculated first, the result is then multiplied by (Z-T) then this result is divided by 3.14.

CHAPTER 4

STATEMENTS

Now that we've looked at data types, it is time to start processing. Data processing is done in the program's main body, the **statement section**. A Turbo Pascal **program** statement is a collection of identifiers, keywords, operators and constants that perform a specific action. A Turbo Pascal statement ends with a semicolon (;). There are two kinds of statements - simple and structured.

Simple Statements

A simple statement contains just one statement. For example, assignments, unconditional jumps and procedure calls.

As its name implies, the **assignment statement** assigns the result of an expression to a variable. The variable and the expression must be of the same type:

```
FuncKey := False;
Ch := 'G';
Sum := X+Y;
```

Sometimes program execution must branch to a different part of a program unconditionally. This unconditional jump is performed by the **GOTO** statement. **GOTO** requires that a **LABEL** declaration comes before any program **CONST** or **VAR** declaration. A Turbo Pascal label can be any series of digits in the range from 0 to 9999 or it can be an identifier:

```
GOTO 999;
GOTO EndBlock;
```

When using the **GOTO** statement, it is important to remember that any label is visible only inside the block where it was defined (see Chapter 5, Figure 5-2). An unconditional jump to another block is forbidden. If possible, try to avoid using **GOTO** statements. Debugging and maintaining programs full of **GOTO**'s is quite tricky.

The **procedure call statement** activates a standard or user-defined procedure:

```
ClrScr;
InitWork(True);
```

We will consider procedure calls in more detail later on.

Structured Statements

Structured statements are built from others, according to certain rules. There are 3 groups of structured statements: compound, conditional and repeat-statements.

Compound Statements

Compound statements are comprised of a group of statements, separated from one another by a semicolon. This group of statements is enclosed within **BEGIN...END**.

```
BEGIN
    <statement>;
    ...
    <statement>
END;
```

Although the idea of grouping several statements is straightforward, it is nevertheless one of the most useful features of Turbo Pascal. A compound statement is considered to be an entire unit, and can be used in any part of the program where the syntax of the language permits a statement.

Conditional Statements

There are two conditional statements in Turbo Pascal: IF and CASE. The IF statement is the common condition statement. It has two forms:

```
IF <condition> THEN <statement1>
            ELSE <statement2>;
```
and

```
IF <condition> THEN <statement>;
```

Any relational or boolean expressions can be used as a <condition>. In the first case if the condition is True, then the <statement1> is executed or else the <statement2> is executed (see Figure 4-1).

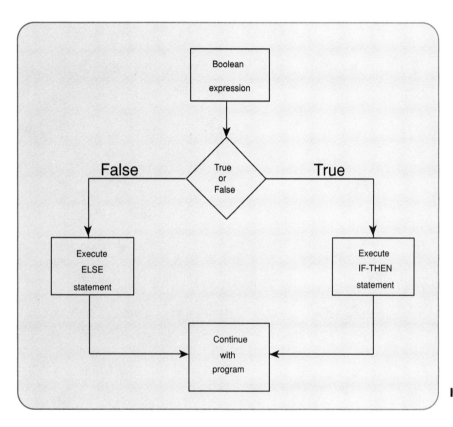

Figure 4-1
Flowchart of
IF-THEN-ELSE
Statement

For example:

```
IF Temperature > 37 THEN Write ('flu is possible')
                     ELSE Write ('OK!');
```

In the second case if a condition is True, then the statement following the **THEN** keyword is executed, otherwise the next statement after the **IF** is executed.

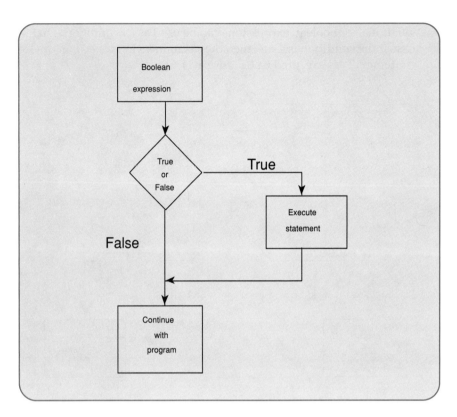

Figure 4-2
Flowchart of IF-THEN Statement

For example:

```
IF Reply <> Yes THEN Exit;
```

IF statements can be nested:

```
IF X > Y THEN
   IF X > 34 THEN
      IF Y <> 100 THEN <statement>;
```

You should avoid over-using nesting because it makes a program hard to understand.

Situations will arise in a program that require a variety of actions to be performed which are dependent on the value of the ordinal expression. For this reason, Turbo Pascal has the **CASE** statement. **CASE** provides a clear structure for multiple branching. It consists of an expression called a **selector** and a **list of case constants** and **corresponding statements**.

The **CASE** statement has two forms:

```
CASE <expression-selector> OF
  <list of case constants 1> : <statement 1>;
  <list of case constants 2> : <statement 2>;
  ...
  <list of case constants N> : <statement N>
  ELSE <statement>
END;
```

or

```
CASE <expression-selector> OF
  <list of case constants 1> : <statement 1>;
  <list of case constants 2> : <statement 2>;
  ...
  <list of case constants N> : <statement N>
END;
```

The selector can be of any scalar type except real or string.

The constant type must be compatible with the selector type. **CASE** is a widely used statement. Here are a few examples of possible applications:

CASE with integer type:

```
CASE I OF
  1,3,5 : Writeln('Odd number');
  2,4,6 : Writeln('Even number')
END;
```

CASE with user-defined enumerated type:

```
VAR Temperature: -20..40;
CASE Temperature OF
  -20..5  : Writeln('It is cold today');
  6..18   : Writeln('It is cool today');
  19..25  : Writeln('It is a beautiful day!');
  26..40  : Writeln('It is hot today')
END;
```

CASE with user-defined subrange type:

```
CASE MyHobby OF
  StampCollecting, Cinema : Writeln('Good hobby');
  Sport                 : Writeln('Excellent hobby');
  LoungingAround          : Writeln('Bad hobby')
END;
```

CASE with char type:

```
CASE Ch OF
  'a'..'z': Write('Lower-case letter');
  'A'..'Z': Write('Upper-case letter');
  '0'..'9': Write('Digit')
  ELSE      Write('Special symbol')
END;
```

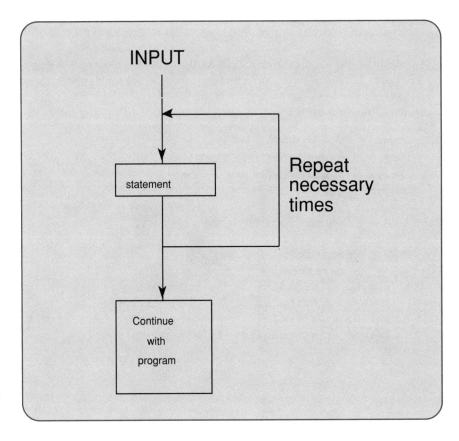

Figure 4-3
Flowchart of Loop

Repeat-Statements

FOR, **WHILE** and **REPEAT** statements are used for setting up various loops. The basic idea of all loops is shown in Fgure 4-3. The statement that is actually repeated is called the **loop body**. The keyword **FOR** is used to tell the program to execute a statement for a set number of times. In a **FOR** loop you must specify a starting and ending point, and use an integer variable as a counter. There are two formats of **FOR**:

```
FOR <loop variable>:=<S1> TO <S2> DO <statement>;
```

or

```
FOR <loop variable>:=<S1> DOWNTO <S2> DO <statement>;
```

S1 and **S2** define the start and the end of the <loop variable> values,

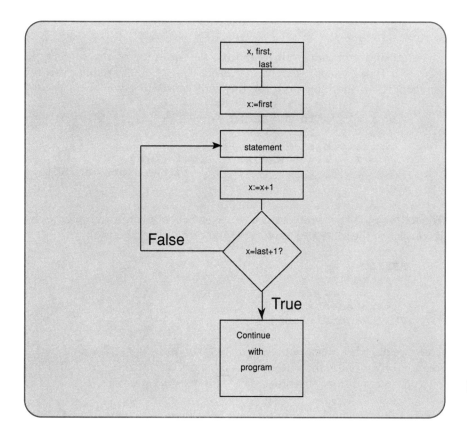

Figure 4-4
**Flowchart of
FOR-TO-DO
Statement**

<statement> is a loop body. If the **TO** keyword is used, program execution continues by checking to see if the variable's value is less than or equal to S2.

If the value is less than or equal to **S2** the statement after **DO** is executed. The loop variable is then incremented and its contents are once again checked. If the **DOWNTO** key is used, the variable is decremented and is checked to see if its value is greater than or equal to **S2**. If **S1 = S2** then the **FOR..DO** loop is executed only once, if **S2 > S1** then it is not executed at all.

We'll perform the calculation **FOR** Sum=1+2+3+...+10

```
VAR
  I, Sum : integer;
BEGIN
  Sum:=0;          { variable will store sum value }
  FOR I:=1 TO 10 DO Sum:=Sum+I;
  Writeln('Sum = ',Sum);
END.
```

The start and end values of loop variables must be of the same type. All scalar types, except real, can be used. The <Loop variable> can not be changed in the loop body as this will cause an error:

```
FOR I:=1 TO 10 DO BEGIN
  Sum:= I * 2;
  Write(Sum);
  I:= I + 2;  { ERROR! illegal change
                       of the <loop variable>}
END;
```

The **REPEAT** loop does not require you to specify a set number of iterations. It consists of the **REPEAT** keyword, loop body and end condition:

```
REPEAT
  <statement>;
  ..........
  <statement>
UNTIL <condition>;
```

The <loop body> does not need a **BEGIN..END** block. As long as the <condition> is False, the statement will be executed (see Figure 4-5). Thus, once the <condition> becomes True, the execution ceases.

The condition is checked after the loop body execution. Note that a **REPEAT** loop is always executed at least once, because <condition> is checked

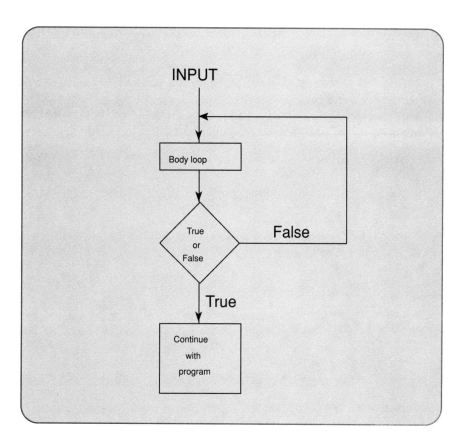

INPUT

Body loop

True
or
False

False

True

Continue
with
program

Figure 4-5
**Flowchart of
REPEAT Loop**

after the statement is performed. Don't forget to include a statement in the **REPEAT** body that influences the <condition>, otherwise the loop will be endless. The following example shows how the operator **REPEAT** is used to calculate 1+2+3+...+10:

```
PROGRAM DemoRepeat;
VAR
  I, Sum: integer;
BEGIN
  I := 1;
  Sum := 0;
  REPEAT
    Sum:= Sum + I;
    I:= I + 1           { influence <condition> variable }
  UNTIL I = 11;
  Writeln('Sum 1+2+...+10 = ',Sum);
END.
```

REPEAT loops can cause a lot of errors if you're using them for the first time, so be very careful with them!

The Turbo Pascal **WHILE** loop is similar to the **REPEAT** loop. There are two differences, the first is that the **WHILE** loop checks for a condition before it executes the loop body. The second difference is that the **WHILE** statement executes the loop body while <condition> is True.

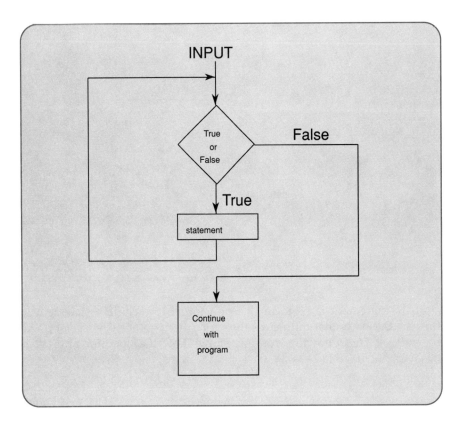

Figure 4-6
Flowchart of
WHILE Loop

Format:

```
WHILE <condition> DO
   <loop body>;
```

<loop body> - simple or compound statement.

As with the **REPEAT** statement, don't forget to include a statement in the loop body that influences <condition> to avoid an endless loop. In the example below we have added a **WHILE** loop to a task we considered earlier:

```
I := 1; Sum := 0;
WHILE I <> 11 DO BEGIN
  Sum := Sum +I;
  I := I +1      { influence <condition> variable }
END;
Writeln(Sum);
```

If <condition> = False at the very beginning, the **WHILE** body will not be executed at all:

```
Flag := False;
WHILE Flag DO BEGIN
  Writeln('Not run');
END;
```

WHILE is often used for creating special endless loops. Such loops can be used, for example, to input an unknown amount of data. The algorithm for this would be as follows:

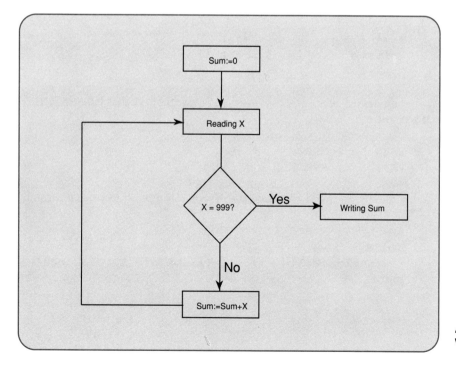

Figure 4-7
**Algorithm of
WHILE Loop**

```
PROGRAM DemoWhile;
VAR
  X, Sum : integer;
BEGIN
  Sum := 0;
  WHILE True DO BEGIN
    Readln(X);
    IF X = 999 THEN BEGIN { 999 - user's indication of end of data }
      Writeln('Sum= ',Sum);
      Exit                 { exits the program }
    END;
    Sum := Sum +X
  END;
END.
```

People using Turbo Pascal for the first time usually prefer **WHILE** loops to **REPEAT** loops, because they are clearer and cause less errors.

Syntax Rules

While writing statements you must adhere to the following syntax rules:

The semicolon delimits statements and its absence causes compiler errors:

```
X:=A + B;;;;      { legal ! }
Write(X)          { ERROR !}
X:=X+1;
```

A semicolon is not used after the reserved words **UNIT, USES, LABEL, TYPE, CONST, VAR:**

```
USES;    { ERROR }
VAR;     { ERROR }
```

A semicolon is not used after **BEGIN**. A semicolon before **END** is optional:

```
BEGIN;   { ERROR }
BEGIN
  Writeln('Hello!');   { (;) before END is legal }
END;
```

A semicolon is not used after **WHILE, REPEAT** and **DO**. A semicolon before **UNTIL** is optional:

```
WHILE True DO;        { ERROR! }
X:=1;
REPEAT
  X:=X+1;
  Writeln(X*X);       { (;) - legal }
UNTIL X<>11;
```

A semicolon is not used after **THEN** or before **ELSE**:

```
IF X <> 5 THEN Y:=Y+X;    { ERROR! (;) before ELSE }
ELSE Y:=Y-X;
```

CHAPTER

5

PROGRAM STRUCTURE

Sections of a Program

More often than not, a program has 7 sections (see Figure 5-1):

1. Included library units
2. Label definitions
3. Constant definitions
4. Type definitions
5. Variable declarations
6. Procedure and function definitions
7. Statements

Apart from the statement section, all these sections are optional. The defining sections (except **USES** - see below) can be placed anywhere within the program as many times as necessary. The only rule is that you must define the object of a program before you use it. For example constants, variables, functions, etc.

```
Program name ─────────┐
Compiler directives   ├──→ Program Heading
Unit names ───────────┘

Label declarations ───────┐
Constant declarations     ├──→ Data Declarations
Type declarations         │
Variable declarations ────┘

Procedures ───────┐
Functions         ├──→ Code Section
Program block ────┘
```

Figure 5-1
**The Structure
of a Typical
Program**

Program Heading

A Turbo Pascal program begins with the keyword **PROGRAM**, which allows you to name the program using a particular identifier. Note that assigning a program name is not absolutely necessary. This keyword is followed by a list of **global compiler directives**. The **USES** section begins with the reserved word **USES** and is followed by a list of included library units - this gives access to the standard Turbo Pascal routines:

```
USES Crt, Dos, { Crt, Dos are standard libraries }
     Service;  { Service is user-defined library }
```

We'll come back to units later in Chapter 8.

Data Declarations

Label Defining Section

By using a label, you can make a direct jump to any statement in a program. A label consists of an identifier (or simply a digit) followed by a colon. It should not have more than 127 characters. Don't forget that you must define a label before you use it. The label defining section begins with the reserved word **LABEL** followed by the list of label names, for example:

```
LABEL  999;
```

Note that the section ends with a semicolon. Now you can use the labels you have defined in your program:

```
PROGRAM DemoLabel;
LABEL 999;
VAR X : char;
BEGIN
  Writeln('Password, please:');
  Read(X);
  IF X <> 's' THEN GOTO 999;
  <statement>;
  ...
  <statement>;
  999:
END.
```

Constant Defining Section

The reserved word **CONST** is used for defining constants. It is followed by statements which assign constant values to certain identifiers. Each assignment ends with a semicolon:

```
CONST
  FileName = 'BASE.DTA';
  NamePro = 'WROX HOME FINANCES';
  CopyRight = 'Copyright (C) WROX 1992';
  Months : array[1..12] of String[9] =
            ('January','February','March','April',
          'May','June','July','August','September',
                  'October','November','December');
```

If you try to use names that actually mean something it will make your program text easier to understand.

Type Defining Section

This section is used for defining your own data types. It begins with the reserved word **TYPE**, which is followed by a type identifier and type specification:

```
TYPE
   Animals = (Cat, Dog, Cow);
```

You cannot use types directly in your programs. You should declare variables as particular types.

Variable Declaring Section

This section begins with the reserved word **VAR** followed by the list of variable names with a type specification:

```
VAR
  X,Y   : integer;   {variables of predefined types}
  Sum   : real;
  Animal: Animals; {variables of user-defined types}
  X     : 1..5;
```

Code Section

Procedure and Function Defining Section

The code section consists of a program block and often contains procedures and functions which are defined with the reserved words **PROCEDURE** and **FUNCTION**. The format for procedure definition is:

```
PROCEDURE <name> {(parameters)};
BEGIN
    <statement>;
    ...
    <statement>
END;
```

The format of function:

```
FUNCTION <name> {(parameters)} : <result type>;
BEGIN
    <statement>;
    ...
    <statement>
END;
```

You only have to define user-defined procedures and functions. Procedures and functions will be looked at more closely in Chapter 7.

Statement Section

This is the most important section of a Turbo Pascal program because it performs all the actions with variables, constants, and functions to give the result you want, which is of course, the main purpose of program design.

The statement section begins with the reserved word **BEGIN**. This is followed by the program statements, which are delimited by semicolons. The section ends with the reserved word **END** followed by a full stop:

```
BEGIN
    ...
END.
```

The words **BEGIN** and **END** are very similar to parentheses in standard arithmetic expressions. For more information about statement and syntax rules see Chapter 7.

Comments

Comments are simply used to provide extra information about the program. They do not perform any action.

They can be allocated in any place where a blank is legal. Comments are enclosed with the { } or (* *) characters and can contain any characters. For example:

```
PROGRAM WroxHomeFinances;
{*************************************************}
{ The analysis of a monthly/yearly family budget. }
{                                                 }
{            Copyright (C) WROX 1992              }
{*************************************************}
 BEGIN
 END.
```

If you use (*   *) delimiters any characters between '(' and '*' or '*' and ')' are illegal.

Neither can you use nested comments:

```
{  { comment }  }     - error
{ (* comment *) }     - correct
(* { comment } *)     - correct
```

Comments are ignored by the compiler and do not affect the program processing. They can be of any length and are used to specify the programmer's aim, clear up the use of an identifier, describe logically independent algorithm elements or explain complex actions. Good comments will help you to find mistakes and generally simplify your work with a program.

Scope

You will have already noticed that except for the heading, the kinds of items contained in programs, procedures and functions are the same: constant, type, variable definitions, definitions of procedures and functions and the body of statements. Part of a subroutine, or a program, other than the heading, is called a **block**. The main program body (the statements between **BEGIN** and **END**), together with the program defining sections, form a **global block**. Every procedure or function body with corresponding defining sections forms a **local block**. Each local block can contain several nested local blocks (Figure 5-2).

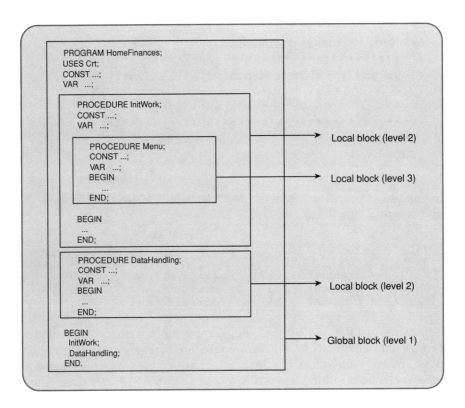

<figure>
```
PROGRAM HomeFinances;
USES Crt;
CONST ...;
VAR  ...;

  PROCEDURE InitWork;
  CONST ...;
  VAR  ...;                                        →  Local block (level 2)

    PROCEDURE Menu;
    CONST ...;
    VAR  ...;
    BEGIN                                          →  Local block (level 3)
      ...
    END;

  BEGIN
    ...
  END;

  PROCEDURE DataHandling;
  CONST ...;
  VAR  ...;
  BEGIN                                            →  Local block (level 2)
    ...
  END;

BEGIN
  InitWork;                                        →  Global block (level 1)
  DataHandling;
END.
```
</figure>

Figure 5-2
Local and Global Blocks

The **GOTO** statement operation area is limited to the local block in which it is declared.

The scope of an identifier is defined as the part of the program in which it has a particular meaning. The basic rule is that the scope of an identifier is the entire block in which it is declared, including nested blocks that do not contain a new declaration of this identifier.

Program Format

In this section we'll look at the various ways of tackling program layout.

A program consists of lines, and the maximum length for each line is 127 characters. Any further characters in the line are ignored by the compiler.

While typing a program text you can lay it out on the screen in any way you like. The main principle is that your program should be easy to read. The examples below demonstrate possible forms of program lay-out:

```
program sum;uses crt;var x,y:byte;begin
read(x);read(y);write(x+y) end.
```

```
PROGRAM SUM;
USES CRT; VAR X,Y:BYTE;
BEGIN READ(X);READ(Y);WRITE(X+Y) END.
```

```
PROGRAM Sum;
USES Crt;
VAR
 X,Y : byte;
BEGIN
 Read(X);
 Read(Y);
 Write(X+Y)
END.
```

In our opinion, the third option is probably the easiest to read, but of course you can create your own style.

CHAPTER

6

INPUT/OUTPUT

It is fairly obvious that the purpose of most programs is to gather data for processing and to output the result. In Turbo Pascal the **Read/Readln** and **Write/Writeln** procedures are used to perform these actions.

Data Input

The **Read** and **Readln** procedures are used for data input (see Figure 6-1).

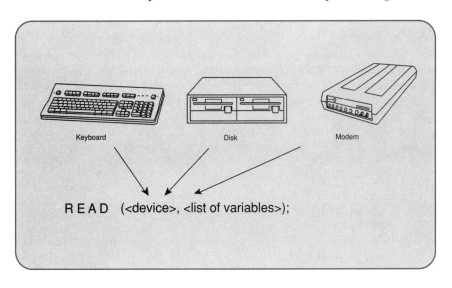

Keyboard   Disk   Modem

R E A D   (<device>, <list of variables>);

Figure 6-1
**Structure of
the Read
Procedure**

A <device> is a source of input data such as a keyboard, a display unit, a modem, etc. (more details about <devices> are given in Chapter 11). A keyboard is a predefined device for these procedures and does not need to be specified.

```
Read(X1,X2,...Xn);
```

where **X1,X2,...,Xn** are variable identifiers. In this chapter we'll look at data input from the keyboard.

The `X1,X2,...,Xn` values are typed on the keyboard and delimited by one blank. When characters are typed, they are displayed on the screen. The variable values must be input in exactly the same order as the variable type definition. For example, if you define `X1` as integer and then type a character value, an input/output error occurs. As an example we'll input 3 values:

```
VAR
  I : real;
  J : integer;
  K : char;
BEGIN
  Read(I,J,K);
```

First input:	Second input:
235.98 100 G	G 235.98 100

The first input is correct, because the input values 235.98, 100 and 'G' correspond to variable types `I`, `J`, `K`. The second input will cause an error because a character value has been assigned to the real variable `I`. The `Read` procedure reads the input only until its data arguments have been fulfilled. Any remaining data is used by the next **read** procedure.

```
VAR
  A, B, Sum1 : integer;
  C, D, Sum2 : real;
BEGIN
  Read(A, B);
  Sum1 := A + B;
  Read(C, D);
  Sum2 := C + D
END.
```

Press **ENTER** after typing each pair of values.

The `Read` and `Readln` procedures differ slightly in the way they function. Unlike `Read`, the `Readln` procedure keeps reading data until a new line is encountered. If any data remains after the `Readln` procedure's data arguments have been filled, the remaining data is ignored.

To avoid errors, you should separate the **Read** or **Readln** procedures for each input variable. For example:

```
     Bad:                              Good:

VAR                               VAR
  X,Y,Z : integer;                  X,Y,Z : integer;
BEGIN                             BEGIN
  Readln(X,Y,Z);                    Readln(X);
END;                                Readln(Y);
                                    Readln(Z);
                                  END;
```

Data Output

The **Write** and **Writeln** procedures are used to perform data output. They work with numbers, characters and boolean values (see Figure 6-2).

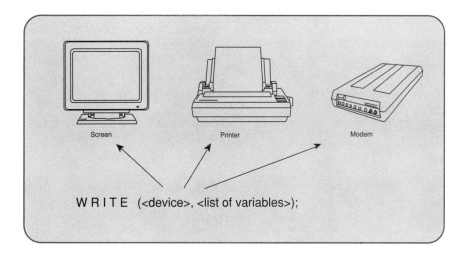

Figure 6-2
Structure of the Write Procedure

The <device> specifies the output device for data such as a screen, a printer, a modem, a disk, etc. The screen is a predefined device, so you don't need to worry about screen specification with the **Write** statement:

```
Write(Y1,Y2,...,Yn);
```

where **Y1,Y2,...,Yn** are constants, variables, or the result of an expression. The only real difference between the two procedures is that the **Write** procedure does nothing after it has sent data to the screen, while the **Writeln** procedure sends a new line (Carriage Return/Line Feed) to the screen. For example:

```
PROGRAM DemoWrite;
VAR
  X, Y : integer;
BEGIN
  Write('Input X: ');
  Readln(X);
  Writeln('Input Y: ');
  Readln(Y);
  Writeln('Sum X + Y = ', X+Y);
END.
```

Your screen display will look like this:

```
Input X: 5
Input Y:
6
Sum X + Y = 11
```

Figure 6-3
**A Run
of the
DemoOutput
Program**

Printer Output

In order to output data to a printer, you must specify the printer name LST in the **Write/Writeln** procedure and include the standard **Printer** module in the USES section:

```
PROGRAM DemoPrinting;
USES Printer;
BEGIN
  Writeln(LST, 'Output to printer');
  Writeln('Output to screen')
END.
```

Formatted Output

The **Write/Writeln** procedures can also display data in a formatted mode. You should define the width specification immediately after the data item name. For example:

Operator	Format of results
X := 74385;	
Writeln(X:9);	74385
Writeln(X:4);	74385
Writeln(X:14);	74385

Figure 6-4
Formatting Integer Output

The real values can be output in both fixed-point and floating-point formats. For floating-point you only have to specify the width:

    Writeln(X:n);

With fixed-point you also have the option of specifying decimal places:

    Writeln(X:n:m);

See the examples in Figure 6-5.

Operator	Format of results
Y := 74385.129;	
Writeln(Y:9:3);	74385.129
Writeln(Y:4:2);	74385.13
Writeln(Y:14:2);	74385.13
Writeln(Y:14:3);	74385.129
Writeln(Y);	7.4385129000E+04
Writeln(Y:5);	7.4E+04

Figure 6-5
**Formatting
Real Output**

With the operator **Writeln**(Y:4:2) the number of characters specified, that is 4, is not enough. In this case, the system automatically expands the output field to 8 characters.

User Type Output

If you are using Turbo Pascal for the first time you might have problems with the output of user-defined data types. A way round this problem is to define a corresponding string variable to each user defined element and output it. As an example we'll list a few types of hobbies and output one of them:

```
PROGRAM DemoUserTypeOutput;
TYPE
Hobby = (Music, StampCollecting, Sport, LoungingAround);
VAR
MyHobby : Hobby;
BEGIN
MyHobby := Sport;
CASE MyHobby OF
  Music              : Writeln('''Music'' is a good hobby');
  StampCollecting    : Writeln('''StampCollecting'' is a good hobby');
  Sport              : Writeln('''Sport'' is a good hobby');
  LoungingAround     : Writeln('''LoungingAround'' is a bad hobby')
END;
Readln
END.
```

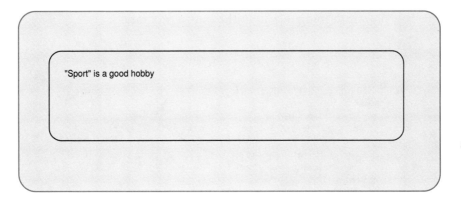

Figure 6-6
**A Run of the
DemoUser
TypeOutput
Program**

Dialog Programming

Most programs work in the dialog (interactive) mode. Your PC must tell you when and what data should be input. You can use the **Writeln** procedure to get this prompt, and then read the data using the **Readln** procedure. Example 6-7 shows a typical algorithm for you and your ATM (Automatic Teller Machine):

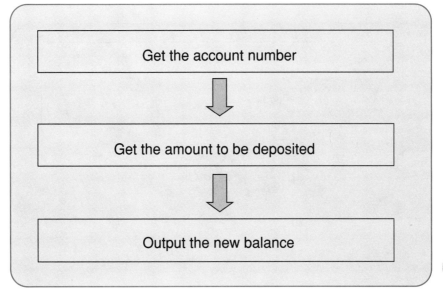

Figure 6-7
**Flowchart of
DemoDialogue
Program**

One way of transforming this algorithm into a program is:

```pascal
PROGRAM DemoDialogue;
VAR
   Number, Balance, Deposit: real;
BEGIN
   Writeln('Good morning.');
   Write('Please Enter your account number: ');
   Readln(Number);
   Balance:=1000.00; {in practice this value is read from a disk}
   Writeln('Your current Balance = ', Balance:8:2);
   Write('Please enter your deposit amount: ');
   Readln(Deposit);
   Writeln('Your account total has increased by ',Deposit:8:2,
                                          'Dollars');
   Writeln('Your balance is now ',Balance + Deposit:10:2);
   Writeln('Good bye.');
   Readln;
END.  { DemoDialogue }
```

Figure 6-8 shows the output results of Figure 6-7. These principles can be used as a base for any dialog you want to create.

```
Good morning.
Please enter your account number: 1242446
Your current Balance = 1000.00
Please enter your deposit amount: 1050.00
Your account total has increased by  1050.00 dollars
Your balance is now    2050.00
Good bye.
```

Figure 6-8
A Run of the DemoDialogue Program

PROCEDURES AND FUNCTIONS

Background

While programming, you will probably find that you need to repeat a particular group of statements more than once. Fortunately, Turbo Pascal has certain procedures and functions which mean that you can avoid rewriting frequently-used routines.

A **procedure** is a part of a program that has its own name, and performs certain actions. Procedures are like "programs within programs". You only need to write a procedure once, and you can then call it from any point in a program. When the procedure has completed all its actions, program execution continues from the next statement which follows the procedure call.

You cannot use procedure calls as operands in expressions.

Functions are similar to procedures. The only differences are that the function returns a value to the call point, and you can use the function's name as an operand in expressions.

There are **built-in (standard)** and **user-defined** procedures and functions.

Built-in procedures and functions are part of the Turbo Pascal language and you can use them without any preliminary definition. In this chapter we will look at some of the more basic standard procedures and functions. The others will be dealt with later on.

You build user-defined procedures and functions yourself. You must describe every procedure and every function before you use it.

Standard Library Units

Turbo Pascal 6.0 has a module structure. Version 3.0 has an entire library for all standard subroutines. Versions 4.0 to 6.0 contain separate groups of standard procedures and functions. These are located in different libraries which are called units. There are two types of units: standard and user-defined. In this chapter we will only look at standard units. User-defined units will be covered in the next chapter.

Name	*File*
Crt	TURBO.TPL
Dos	TURBO.TPL
Graph	GRAPH.TPU
Graph3	GRAPH3.TPU
Overlay	TURBO.TPL
Printer	TURBO.TPL
System	TURBO.TPL
Turbo3	TURBO3.TPU

Table 7-1
*Standard
Units*

Each unit consists of logically related procedures and functions.

Turbo Pascal 6.0 has 8 standard units: **Crt, Dos, Graph, Graph3, Overlay, Printer, System, Turbo3** and a special **Turbo Vision library**.

Before using a unit in a program, you must specify it in the USES statement. For example we will include the Crt, Dos and Printer units:

```
PROGRAM  MyProgram;
USES  Crt,  Dos,  Printer;
```

All standard units use the System unit. It is included automatically, and there is no need to specify it in the USES statement.

Turbo3 and **Graph3** units require you to specify the **Crt** module:

```
USES  Crt,  Turbo3,  Graph3;
```

Let's look at the units in turn:

System   is the "heart" of Turbo Pascal. Its subroutines provide the base for the work of all other units.

Crt   is used for display and keyboard control, such as graphics mode control, keyboard input, keystroke processing, window control and sound control.

Dos   allows you to implement various functions of DOS. It supports the processing of interrupts, disk and file operations, and environment and process control.

Graph3   supports the standard graphics procedures of Turbo Pascal 3.0.

Overlay   handles the overlay programs.

Printer   provides fast access to the printer. To use this unit you must specify LST in the output procedure:

```
Write  (Lst,'Printer  output');
```

Turbo3   provides maximum compatibility with Turbo Pascal 3.0.

Graph   provides effective work with the following adapters: CGA, EGA, VGA, HERC, IBM 3270, MCGA and AT&T 6300.

Specific standard subroutines will be explained in the relevant chapters. For the time being, we will look at the basic System unit subroutines.

System Unit Subroutines

Arithmetic Functions and Procedures

Arithmetic functions and procedures perform the most widely used mathematical operations. They fall into 3 groups: logarithmic, trigonometric and miscellaneous.

Logarithmic Functions

Exp(X)   Returns "e" ("e"=2.718282) raised to the power of X (real or integer). The result is real.

Ln(X)   Returns logarithm of X (real or integer) in base "e". X must be greater that 0. The result is real.

Examples:

Operator	Result
``Write(Exp(3.0));``	``4.4816894945E+00``
``Write(Ln(0.12*10));``	``1.8232155678E-01``

Trigonometric Functions

Arctan(X)   Returns arc tangent of X (real or integer). The result is real.

Cos(X)   Returns cosine of X (real or integer). The result is real.

Sin(X)   Returns sine of X (real or integer). The result is real.

All trigonometric functions require that X be in units of **radians**. The relationship of radians to degrees is:

```
Degrees := Radians * (180/Pi);
```

If you have degrees, but need radians, you can convert them using this formula:

```
Radians := Degrees * (Pi/180);
```

Examples:

Operator	Result
`Write(ArcTan(1)*180/Pi);`	`4.5000000000E+01`
`Write(Cos(60*Pi/180));`	`5.0000000000E-01`
`Write(Sin(60*Pi/180);`	`8.6602540378E-01`

Miscellaneous Functions

Abs(X)   Returns the absolute value of X (real or integer). The type of result coincides with the type of parameter.

Int(X)   Returns the integer part of X (real or integer). The result is real.

Frac(X)   Returns the fractional part of X (real or integer). Integer X always returns 0. The result is real.

Pi   Returns **Pi** value (3.1415926536E+00).

Random   Returns a random real value greater than or equal to 0 and less than 1.

Random(X) Returns a random integer greater than or equal to 0 and less than X.

Sqr(X)   Calculates the square of the X (real or integer) value. The result is real.

Sqrt(X)   Returns the square root of X (real or integer). The result is real.

Examples:

Operator	Result
`Write(Abs(4-6):2);`	`2`
`Write(Int(422.117):6:2);`	`422.00`
`Write(Frac(23.75):4:2);`	`0.75`
`Write(Sqr(-5));`	`25`
`Write('Pi =',Pi);`	`Pi=3.1415926536E+00`
`Write(Random(6));`	`4`
`Write(Sqrt(25));`	`5`

Transfer Functions

This group of functions allows you to convert one type to another type.

Ord(X)   Returns the ordinal number of an ordinal-type value, including type **Char**. The result is integer.

Round(X) Returns the rounded integer value of X (real) to the nearest whole number. The result is integer.

Trunc(X) Returns the truncated integer value of X (real). The result is integer.

Chr(X)   Returns a character of a specified ordinal number.

For example:

```
TYPE
   Animals = (Dog,Cat,Fox);
```

Operator	Result
`Write(Ord('A'));`	65
`Write(Ord(Cat));`	1
`Write(Round(5.5));`	6
`Write(Round(5.4));`	5
`Write(Trunc(5.7));`	5
`Write(Trunc(5.4));`	5
`Write(Chr(65));`	A

Chr(X) accepts an integer X and returns its equivalent ASCII value. For example, the following simple program displays the whole ASCII table:

```
PROGRAM DemoASCII;
VAR
   I : byte;
BEGIN
   FOR I:= 0 TO 255 DO
      Write(I:3, Chr(I), ' ')
END.
```

Scalar Procedures and Functions

Scalar procedures and functions work with all scalar types.

Inc(X {,N}) Increments X by N or by 1 when N is absent.

Dec(X {,N}) Decrements X by N or by 1 when N is absent.

Pred(S)   Returns the predecessor of the item expressed by **S**. The result type matches with the **S** type. If there is no predecessor the program is interrupted.

Succ(S)   Returns the successor of the item expressed by **S**. The result type matches the **S** type. If there is no successor the program is interrupted.

Odd(I)   Returns **True** if I reduces to an odd integer; otherwise it returns **False**.

For example:

Operator	Result
`Write(Inc(10,3));`	`13`
`Write(Pred(90));`	`89`
`Write(Succ(90));`	`91`
`Write(Odd(3));`	`True`

Program Control Procedures

These procedures control program processing, for example: running delays, exiting a program or routine, stopping program execution.

Delay(I)   Makes I millisecond delay in a program's execution.

Exit   Makes an immediate exit from the current block to the external one. If the main block exits, the program ends.

Halt(N)   Automatically ends the program and returns to the IDE or to DOS if you run EXE-file from the operating system.

For example:

```
Delay(3000);                    { 3 sec delay }
IF Count = 9999  THEN Exit;
IF Reply = 'Not' THEN Halt(1);
```

User-Defined Procedures And Functions

Procedures and functions are powerful tools for structured programming. You should be able to carefully divide a program into several logical parts and design them separately. Turbo Pascal procedures and functions allow you to do just this.

User-Defined Procedures

A procedure definition begins with the reserved word **PROCEDURE** followed by the name you want to give it. Procedure headings can also contain a list of formal parameters with type specification (see Figure 7-1).

Figure 7-1
**The
Structure
of a Turbo
Pascal
Procedure**

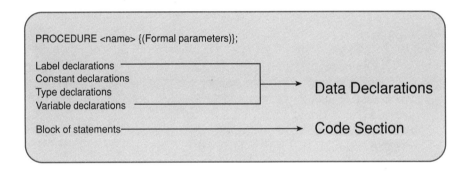

The main body of a procedure is called a **local block** and is similar to the body of a program. The parameters are used by the procedure to input or output data. All constants, types and variables declared within a procedure are called local and "are visible" (i.e. they can be used) only in the body of the procedure. You can use global constants and variables in any procedure.

As an example, we will write a procedure that will display the aim of the program and the author's intention on your screen (we will call this bit of information a title page).

```
PROGRAM DemoProcedure;

PROCEDURE TitlePage;
BEGIN
  Writeln('The calculation of the total,',
          ' the difference and the average');
  Writeln('                    of two numbers');
  Writeln('Author: Donald');
  Writeln('System: Turbo Pascal')
END;

BEGIN
  TitlePage;
  ...
END.
```

Such a simple display might strike you as being a little bit amateurish, but don't worry, in Chapters 15 and 18 you will learn how to create more advanced title pages.

User-Defined Functions

A function definition is similar to that of a procedure, in as much as it contains a heading, declarations and a body. The heading consists of the reserved word **FUNCTION**, the name you want to give it, an optional list of formal arguments and a result type (see Figure 7-2).

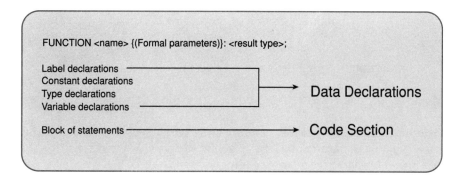

Figure 7-2
The Structure of a Turbo Pascal Function

The function body is called a **local block**. It is similar to the program body. Each function body must have an assignment to the name of the function as if the latter were a variable. This value is returned to the call point. To call the function you should place its name and a list of the actual parameters which correspond to the formal ones in the program. The following example shows a small function for raising to a certain power:

```
PROGRAM DemoPower;
VAR
  Z : real;

FUNCTION Power (X,Y : real): real;
BEGIN
  Power := Exp(Y * Ln(X))
END;
BEGIN
  Z := 5.31;
  Writeln(Power(Z, 4.0));   {raising Z to the 4-th power}
END.
```

If necessary, Turbo Pascal allows you to add user-defined subroutines to a user's library. We will explain how in Chapter 8.

Parameters

There are two ways in which you can pass parameters to either a procedure or a function. Usually a parameter is passed by a value. In this case the parameter's value is passed to the procedure after the call:

PROCEDURE DataIN (X, Y: real);

X and **Y** are passed to the procedure after the call.

Another method of passing parameters is passing by reference. In this case, you pass parameters by placing the **VAR** keyword before the parameter declaration in the heading:

PROCEDURE DataOUT (VAR A, B, C: integer);

The A, B, and C variables will be passed to the call point after the procedure execution.   Note that unlike the first method, actual parameters will be modified within the procedure.

You can use both the first and second methods:

PROCEDURE DataInOUT (X,Y: real; VAR A, B, C: integer);

Here **X,Y** values are passed to the procedure and **A,B,C** values are returned by it. As an example of how parameters pass values we will look at a procedure which takes the value of two numbers, calculates their total, difference and average, and returns the results:

```
PROGRAM DemoParameters;
VAR
   Tot, Dif, Av: real;

PROCEDURE Handling (X,Y:integer; VAR Total, Differ, Average: real);
BEGIN
   Total  :=X + Y;
   Differ :=X - Y;
   Average:=(X + Y)/2;
END;

BEGIN
   Handling(20, 10, Tot, Dif, Av);
   Writeln('Total = ', Tot:6:3);
   Writeln('Difference = ', Dif:6:3);
   Writeln('Average = ', Av:6:3);
   Readln
END.
```

See Appendix A for more examples of user-defined procedures and functions.

Scope

To ensure that you correctly define the scope of an identifier's application when using procedures and functions in your program, stick to the following rules:

1. Each identifier must be declared before use.

2. Identifiers are only visible within the block they are declared in.

▲③ All identifiers names within the block must be unique.

▲④ You can operate with the same names for different identifiers in different blocks.

▲⑤ You can define subroutines using the names of standard ones. In this case the standard subroutine will be invisible within the block where you have defined your subroutine.

Recursion

Recursion allows a Turbo Pascal subroutine to call itself, this can simplify the writing of some important routines, such as quick sort, binary search, etc. To ensure that the recursive procedure does not run endlessly, you have to set up conditions whereby the program can exit the call.

To demonstrate how recursion works, we'll calculate the factorial of a positive whole number: N!= N*(N-1)*...*2*1:

```
PROGRAM Recursion;
VAR   N: LongInt;

FUNCTION Factorial(N: LongInt): LongInt;
BEGIN
  IF N=1 THEN Factorial:= 1 {allows for exiting the recursion call}
  ELSE  Factorial:= N*Factorial(N-1)  { recursion call }
END;  { Factorial }

BEGIN { Recursion }
  Write('Enter number for factorial: ');   Readln(N);
  Write('Result = ', Factorial(N));
  Readln;
END.  { Recursion }
```

The recursion call will end only when parameter N equals 1. Figure 7-3 shows how a recursion program works where the value of parameter N is 3.

When the **factorial** function is first addressed, parameter N equals 3 (this is shown in box 1 of Figure 7-3). As this value is not equal to one the ELSE option of the IF operator is selected, and the **Factorial** function is addressed again (see box 2 of Figure 7-3). The **factorial** parameter N = 2 is now specified in the function and the **ELSE** option is selected again. This continues until the N parameter becomes equal to 1. The sequence of the Factorial function is completed and it returns the value 1. After this, values are calculated for the function where N = 2 and 3 (see Figure 7-3).

```
Factorial(2) = 2*Factorial(1) = 2*1 = 2

Factorial(3) = 3*Factorial(2) = 3*2 = 6
```

It follows that the result of the **Factorial** function where N = 3 will be 6.

Recursive calculations are performed by a function repeatedly calling itself. Every time the function is addressed the variables are stored in the memory, which means that every function can be considered independently of the previous call. If you use recursion calls carefully, you will be able to write compact code, especially when dealing with complex data such as linked lists, trees and dynamic arrays.

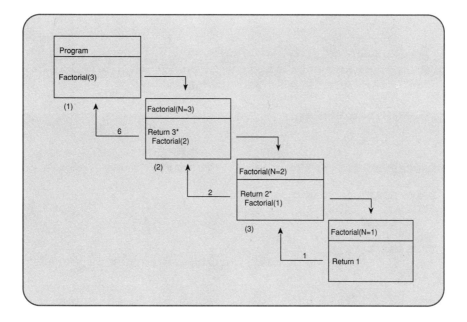

Figure 7-3
**Recursion
Call for the
Factorial
Function**

Forward Declaration

You must make sure that you have defined a procedure before you call it. Try out the following program:

```pascal
PROGRAM DemoForward;
VAR
  A : integer;

PROCEDURE P1 (VAR T : real);
BEGIN
  P2        { P2 has been not defined yet }
END;

PROCEDURE P2 (VAR V : real);
BEGIN
  ...
END;

BEGIN
  P1
END.
```

Having compiled this, you will notice that there is a mistake: **P2** is used before it has been defined. Fortunately, there is a way to avoid this problem. It is known as forward declaration. You simply write the keyword **FORWARD** after the **procedure** or **function** declaration. Once you have done this, any other subroutine can call it before definition:

```pascal
PROGRAM DemoForward;
VAR
  A : integer;

PROCEDURE P2 (VAR V : real); FORWARD;

PROCEDURE P1 (VAR T : real);
BEGIN
  P2
END;
PROCEDURE P2;
        { List of formal parameters is not repeated }
BEGIN
  ...
END;

BEGIN
  P1
END.
```

CHAPTER 8

USER-DEFINED LIBRARY UNITS

What is a User-Defined Unit ?

While writing Turbo Pascal programs you will find yourself repeating the same procedures and functions. To save time you can create a special Turbo Pascal library of commonly-used procedures and functions called a **unit**. These units are then included in a program by the **USES** command, similar to standard built-in units. Once you have included a unit, you have access to all of its subroutines. Note that user-defined units cannot be larger than 64K.

A Unit's Structure

A unit is a separately compiled module and is structured in the following way:

1. Heading
2. Interface
3. Implementation
4. Initialization

A **unit heading** consists of the reserved word **UNIT** followed by the unit's name. You must use the same name for the heading as the one you specified on the disk filename of the source file. For example, if the filename is **STAT.PAS**, the unit heading will be:

```
UNIT  Stat;
```

In the **interface** section you must list all the parts that are to be accessible to any program using the unit, such as global constants, variables, types, procedures and functions. The **interface** section begins with the reserved word **INTERFACE**. After this you place all declarations just as you would for a program or subroutine. Note that you can also include another unit here with the aid of the **USES** command.

In the **implementation** section you must specify the details Turbo Pascal needs to execute programs using the unit, such as local constants, variables, and procedures and functions to which you have no access. It also contains bodies declared in the procedures and functions of the previous section.

The **initialization** section always comes last in the unit. In this section you assign variables or default values. You can also use it to include any other code that needs to be executed before the program that uses the unit. Initialization codes are enclosed within the **BEGIN...END** pair. If a unit does not need an initialization section, you can omit the word **BEGIN**.

You declare a unit like this:

```
UNIT <name>;

INTERFACE { Global portion of the Unit}

    {Place a USES declaration for the global block}
    {Place global CONST,TYPE and VAR declaration here.}
    {Place PROCEDURE and FUNCTION declarations with the
                               parameters list here.}

IMPLEMENTATION     {Local portion of the unit}

    {Place a USES declaration for the
                               local blocks here.}
    {Place private LABEL, CONST, TYPE
                        and VAR declarations here.}
    (Place PROCEDURE and FUNCTION bodies declarations
                        in the INTERFACE section.}

BEGIN

    { Statements to be executed at the start of }
    { the program. These are not usually needed.}

END.
```

Building a Unit

As an example we will create the user library **MATH**, using four very simple functions which will add, subtract, multiply and divide two numbers. To do this you need to follow these steps:

1 Select the File option from the main menu.

2 Load the **MATH.PAS** file using the Open sub-option. The **MATH.PAS** file contains source texts of procedures and functions that you will want to include in your library:

```
FUNCTION Total(X,Y : real) : real;
BEGIN
   Total:= X + Y
END;
FUNCTION Difference(X,Y : real) : real;
BEGIN
   Difference:= X - Y
END;
FUNCTION Multiply(X,Y : real) : real;
BEGIN
   Multiply:= X * Y
END;
FUNCTION Divide(X,Y : real) : real;
BEGIN
   Divide:= X / Y
END;
```

3 Design your source texts in the way explained above. (i.e. heading, interface, implementation, initialization sections):

```
UNIT Math;

INTERFACE

FUNCTION Total(X,Y : real) : real;
FUNCTION Difference(X,Y : real) : real;
FUNCTION Multiply(X,Y : real) : real;
FUNCTION Divide(X,Y : real) : real;

IMPLEMENTATION

FUNCTION Total;
BEGIN
  Total:= X + Y
END;
```

```
FUNCTION Difference;
BEGIN
   Difference:= X - Y
END;
FUNCTION Multiply;
BEGIN
   Multiply:= X * Y
END;
FUNCTION Divide;
BEGIN
   Divide:= X / Y
END;

END.
```

4. Select the Compile option from the main menu.

5. Set the Destination sub-option of the compile menu to Disk.

6. Compile your text.

When you get a unit with the extension **TPU**: **MATH.TPU**, your library is ready!

Using a Unit

The following example shows you how to use the library unit while working with the program SimpleMath. Initially, the file **MYPROG.PAS** only contains three lines of this program:

```
PROGRAM SimpleMath;
BEGIN
END.
```

Suppose you wanted to write the program SimpleMath using **MATH.TPU**. You would need to take the following steps:

1. Load the program SimpleMath from file **MYPROG.PAS**:

```
PROGRAM SimpleMath;
BEGIN
END.
```

▲2▲   Specify the Math unit in the **USES** section of the program:

```
PROGRAM SimpleMath;
USES Math;
BEGIN
END.
```

All functions of the Math unit are now available to the user.

▲3▲   Now we'll use all the functions in our library to perform
addition, subtraction, multiplication and division of two
numbers: 20 and 10.

```
PROGRAM SimpleMath;
USES Math;
BEGIN
  Writeln('Total = ', Total(20.0, 10.0));
  Writeln('Difference = ', Difference(20.0, 10.0));
  Writeln('Multiply = ', Multiply(20.0, 10.0));
  Writeln('Divide = ', Divide(20.0, 10.0):6:2)
END.
```

▲4▲   Next we will tell Turbo Pascal where to find the file containing
MATH.TPU. Select the Options option from the main menu.
Select the Directories choice from the sub-options menu. Set
the path to the Math unit. Return to the main menu.

▲5▲   Make sure that the program is correct by starting it using the
Run option.

▲6▲   Now we will create an executable file from the program. Select
the Compile option from the main menu. Set the Destination
option in the compile menu to Disk. Compile your program.

MYPROG.EXE file is formed on the disk. It is a complete program design.
(You will find another example of library creation in Chapter 15).

CHAPTER
9

ADDING STRUCTURE TO DATA

Arrays

Declaration

Very often, you will find that you need to operate a set of data items of the same type. You can join these items together by declaring an **array**. For example, suppose you needed to work with a monthly salary received during the period of one year, you could treat these 12 values as an array with 12 elements of type real. As a rule an array element can be any type you like.

An **array** declaration looks like this:

```
VAR
   <name> : array [index range] of <type>;
```

So your income amount array will be:

```
VAR
  Income : array[1..12] of real;
```

The number of array elements is defined by the **index range**. In this case you have 12 elements, which is a fixed value for this program. If only one index range is written the array is termed one-dimensional, if two, two-dimensional and so on (see Figure 9-1). The number of dimensions you can have in an array is only limited by the capacity of your computer's memory.

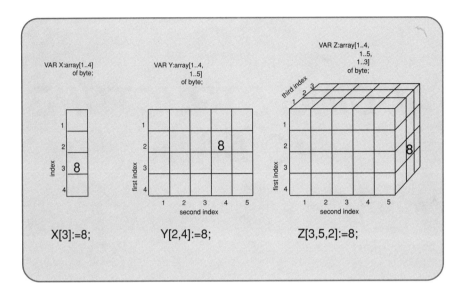

Figure 9-1
One-, Two-, and Three-Dimensional Arrays

Here Y is a two-dimensional array. It is analogous to a matrix with 4 rows and 5 columns in mathematics.

The elements are stored one by one, and a low element has a low memory address. When it comes to a multi-dimensional array, the elements are stored according to the following rule: the right index increases first. For example, if you had the following array:

```
VAR
    A : array[1..5,1..5] of integer;
```

it would be stored in the memory as:

```
A[1,1] A[1,2] ... A[1,5] A[2,1] A[2,2] ... A[5,5]
```

In Turbo Pascal, index range control is provided by the R compiler directive. Its default value is passive: { $R-}. If you set R to the active $R+ value, the compiler automatically organizes **index range control**. For example, if you declare the array

```
VAR
    W : array[1..10] OF real;
```

and set {$R+} directive, then the following assignment

```
W[20] := 0.0;
```

will result in exiting the program and will display an error message. If you set {$R-} then this illegal array index will not be noticed and you will get an unexpected error situation.

There are several ways you can declare an array. We have already looked at the following way:

```
VAR
   InData  : array[1..12] of real;
   OutData : array[1..12] of real;
```

Another way is to define the array as a new data type:

```
TYPE
   ArrR = array[1..12] of real;
VAR
   InData,OutData : ArrR;
```

You can also set the index range with constants which you have defined earlier:

```
CONST
   VertValue  = 639;
   HorizValue = 349;
VAR
   EGAScreen : array[0..HorizValue, 0..VertValue];
```

Operating With Arrays

To use an array as one item, you must write the array identifier without index specification. The whole array can be used in equal, not equal and assigning operations. In this case, each array must have the same structure (i.e. have the same element type and index range). As an example we'll declare the arrays A and B, then look at some operations:

```
VAR A,B : array[1..20] of real;
```

A = B   True, if each element of array A matches
               the corresponding element of array B.

A <> B   True, if at least one A element does not match the
               corresponding B element.

A := B   All B element values are assigned to corresponding
               A elements. B elements remain unchangeable.

The above operations are the only ones you can perform with a whole array, any other operation you try will cause an error.

Operating With Array Elements

To access an array element you must write the array identifier with the relevant index. For example, **Arr[2]** denotes the second element of the Arr array. If you are working with a two-dimensional array you have to write two indices, with an n-dimensional n indices. For example, to access the element in the 4-th row and 4-th column of array **X**, you would have to write **X[4,4]**.

You can use array elements in the same way as you would use simple variables. They can be operands, used in **FOR**, **WHILE** and **REPEAT** statements, which you input and output using the read and write commands.

To demonstrate the use of array elements we'll have a look at some typical operations. Start by declaring the following arrays:

```
VAR
    A, D : array[1..4] of real;
    B : array[1..10,1..15] of integer;
    I, J, K : integer;   S : real;
```

Then initialize the **A** and **B** arrays with zeroes:

```
A := 0;     { error! You cannot initialize }
B := 0;     { a whole array with zeros directly }
FOR I:=1 TO 4 DO A[I]:=0;  { correct }
FOR I:=1 TO 10 DO          { correct }
   FOR J:=1 TO 15 DO
      B[I,J]:=0;
```

A more effective way of initializing an array is to use the **FillChar** procedure and the **SizeOf** function. This function returns the size of memory needed to allocate certain variables or data types:

```
FillChar(A, SizeOf(A), 0);
FillChar(B, SizeOf(B), 0);
```

For a more detailed explanation of **FillChar** see Chapter 14. Turbo Pascal is not able to input and output an entire array. You have to do this element by element:

```
Readln(A);                              { error }
FOR I:=1 TO 4 DO BEGIN
  Write('Enter element A[', I, ']: ');
  Readln(A[I]);
END;
```

or for a two-dimensional array:

```
FOR I:=1 TO 10 DO
  FOR J:=1 TO 15 DO BEGIN
    Write('Enter element B[', I, ',', J, ']: ');
    Readln (B[I,J]);
  END;
```

Naturally, you can also input separate elements:

```
Readln(A[3]);
Readln(B[6,9]);
```

Both of these values are typed on the same line from the current cursor position. Sometimes you will find it useful to declare an array constant, which is done in the following way:

```
CONST
  Months:array[1..12] of string[9] =
  ('January','February','March','April','May','June',
   'July','August','September','October','November',
                                'December');
```

In this case, you don't need to organize data input, as it is already contained in the memory.

Output elements are similar to input ones, the difference being that you use the **Write** and **Writeln** statements:

```
FOR I:=1 TO 4 DO Writeln(A[I]); { output A array }
```

and for B array:

```
FOR I:=1 TO 10 DO
  FOR J:=1 TO 15 DO
    Writeln(B[I,J]);        { output B array }
```

Now copy D array to A:

```
FOR I:=1 TO 4 DO A[I]:=D[I];
```

D elements remain unchanged, **A** elements are now equal to **D** elements. It goes without saying that **A** and **D** arrays must have the same structure. You will also need to know how to conduct a search in an array. Suppose you wanted to find the number of zero elements in **A**, you would use the following operation:

```
K:=0;
FOR I:=1 TO 4 DO
  IF A[I]=0 THEN K:=K+1;
```

After finishing this loop, variable **K** will contain the number of zero elements in array **A**. The operation below will enable you to exchange the first and the fifth elements of **A** array:

```
Addit:= A[5];    { Addit is additional variable }
A[5] := A[1];
A[1] := Addit;
```

Sets

Type declaration

A **set** is a user-defined type that deals with a collection of objects of the same ordinal type or a subrange of an ordinal data type. You should declare sets of integers or characters, but not of real numbers or strings. A set cannot have more than 256 values.

The following examples show set declaration:

```
TYPE
  Letters = set of 'a'..'z';
  Digits = set of 0..9;
  Schoolboys = (Tom, Bob, Nick, Steve, Andy);
VAR
  Let : Letters;           { elements are letters }
  Dig : Digits;            { elements are digits }
  Sportsmen, ExcellentPupils, GoodMusicians,
            TroubleMakers : SET OF Schoolboys;
```

Here's another way you can declare a set variable;

```
VAR
  Let : set of 'a'..'z';
  Dig : set of 0..9;
  Sportsmen,
  ExcellentPupils,
  GoodMusicians,
  TroubleMakers : SET OF (Tom, Bobby, Nick, Steve,
                                      Tony, Andy);
```

Now that you have declared your set, you can start to work with it. The following example shows how a set of schoolboys can be divided into subsets of sportsmen, excellent pupils and good musicians.

```
BEGIN
  Sportsmen:= [Bobby, Andy];
  ExcellentPupils:= [Tom..Andy];
  GoodMusicians:= [Alex]; { error! Alex is not in
                                    Schoolboys set }
...
END.
```

A set may also be empty in which case it is a set which has no elements. An **empty set** is written as: []. For example:

```
TroubleMakers:=[];
```

Set Operations

You can use the following operators to work with sets: **=, <>, >=, <=, IN,** union, difference, intersection. The result of all these operations is True or False.

The **set equal to** operator (=) compares two set expressions to see if they are equal. The element order is ignored:

Expression	Result
[1,2,3,4] = [1,2,3,4]	True
['a','b','c'] = ['c','a']	False
['a'..'z'] = ['z'..'a']	True

The **set unequal to** operator (<>) compares two set expression to see if they are not equal in value or have an unequal number of elements:

Expression	Result
[1,2,3,] <> [3,1,2,4]	True
['a'..'z'] <> ['z'..'a']	False
['c'..'t'] <> ['c'..'t']	False

The **set greater than or equal to** operator (>=) compares two set expressions to see if all the elements of the second set are in the first one. If this is true, the operator returns the value **True**. Otherwise the operator returns the value **False**.

Expression	Result
[1,2,3,4] >= [2,3,4]	True
['a'..'z'] >= ['b'..'t']	True
[] >= ['c','x']	False

The **set less than or equal to** operator (<=) compares two set expressions to see if all the elements of the first set are in the second one. If it is true, the operator returns the value **False**:

Expression	Result
[1,2,3] <= [1,2,3,4]	True
['d'..'h'] <= ['z'..'a']	True
[1,2] <= []	False

The **set IN** operator tests whether the result of the ordinal expression is an element of two set expressions (see Figure 9-2).

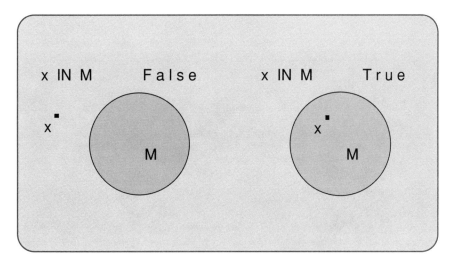

Figure 9-2
**Venn
Diagram
Showing the
Operation
of IN**

This operation is usually used in conditional statements:

A value	Expression	Result
2	IF A IN [1,2,3] THEN ...	True
'V'	IF A IN ['a'..'n'] THEN ...	False
X1	IF A IN [X0,X1,X2,X3] THEN ...	True

You can also use the **IN** operator to simplify your programs. For example you only need to write:

```
IF a IN [1..6] THEN ...
```

instead of

```
IF (a=1) OR (a=2) OR (a=3) OR (a=4)
        OR (a=5) OR (a=6) THEN ...
```

Beware of the following error which is often made:

```
X NOT IN M   - is a wrong expression
NOT (X IN M) - is a right expression.
```

The **set union** operator (+) returns the set that contains elements from both set expressions.

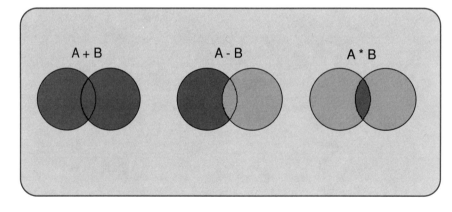

Figure 9-3
Venn diagrams showing the set operations (+), (-), (*)

Example:

Expression	Result
[1,2,3,] + [1,4,5]	[1,2,3,4,5]
['A'..'D'] + ['E'..'Z']	['A'..'Z']
[] + []	[]

The **set intersection** operator (*) returns the set that contains elements common to the two set expressions.

Expression	Result
[1,2,3] * [1,4,2,5]	[1,2]
['A'..'Z'] * ['B'..'R']	['B'..'R']
[] * []	[]

The **set difference** operator (-) returns the set of elements found in the first set that are not also found in the second set:

Expression	Result
[1,2,3,4] - [3,4,1]	[2]
['a'..'z'] - ['d'..'z']	['a'..'c']
[X1,X2,X3,X4] - [X4,X1]	[X2,X3]

Using data type sets has distinct advantages. By simplifying statements, programs become more understandable, they need less memory and are compiled faster. The only serious difficulty is with input and output. Turbo Pascal has no inbuilt procedure for dealing with these operations and you have to create them yourself.

Records

Type declaration

The **user-defined record type** allows you to work with items of different types. To declare a record type you begin with the reserved word **RECORD** followed by a list of field declarations. Field declarations consist of a **field identifier** and **field type**. You finish the **type** declaration with the reserved word **END**.

As an example we'll declare a record for operating with a family budget:

```
TYPE
   Base = RECORD
                Month   : byte;
                Year    : integer;
                Income  : real;
                Food,
                Accommodation,
                Clothing,
                Education,
                MedicalCare,
                Leisure,
                Other   : real
            END;
VAR
   wRec, NewRec : Base;
             { variables for access to record fields }
```

To refer to a field you must separate the variable identifier and the field identifier with a full stop (.). For example you would refer to the Base record fields like this:

```
wRec.Month, wRec.Year, wRec.Income, etc.
```

You can use these field references as simple variables:

```
wRec.Month   := 4;
wRec.Year    := 1991;
wRec.Income  := 577.00;
```

They are also easily input and output:

```
Read(wRec.Month);
Write(wRec.Year:4, wRec.Income:7);
```

And you can operate with the entire records:

```
NewRec := wRec;
```

This statement will assign fields of the **NewRec** record with the values from **wRec** fields. Such an assignment is legal if both records have the same type. The memory volume needed to store the record is defined by the length of all the fields.

You should note that a field identifier can't be used without a variable identifier. You have probably noticed that working with long field references is a bit clumsy, especially when field identifiers are more than 6 characters long. Fortunately Turbo Pascal has a statement which makes this easier:

```
WITH <variable identifier> DO <statement>
```

When typing a variable identifier, as well as using field identifiers such as:

```
WITH wRec DO BEGIN
  Month:= 4;
  Year := 1992;
  Income:= 577.0;
END;
```

Turbo Pascal also allows you to use **nested records** (i.e. a field may be a record too). The **WITH** statement can be nested too:

```
WITH RV1 DO
  WITH RV2 DO
    WITH RVn DO ...
```

is the same as:

```
WITH RV1, RV2,..., RVn DO ...
```

Records are usually used for work with dynamic structures and files. You can also use them for work with complex numbers:

```
TYPE
  Complex = RECORD
              Realp  : real;  { real part }
              Imagep : real;  { imaginary part }
            END;
VAR
  A : Complex;
BEGIN
  A.Realp := 6.3;
  A.Imagep := 1.9;
  ...
END.
```

Variant Records

In the previous section we looked at records with static structure. The record was made up of a list of static fields with identifiers and type for each field. This kind of list is called a **variant**. Variant records are also made up of variant parts, which are defined by the **CASE** operator and the **tag field**. Variant records are declared in the following way:

```
<record identifier> = RECORD
   field declaration;   { fixed fields }
   ...
   field declaration;
   CASE <case identifier> : <type specification> OF
    <case label1> : (field declaration);{ variant
                                          fields }
     ...
     <case labelN> : (field declaration);
END;
```

First of all place the valid static field declarations. The variant **CASE...END** structure must be separated by a semicolon. Use the tag identifier to define the variant of the field to be used according to the case labels specification:

```
TYPE
   DataType = (TInt, TString);
   GetRec = RECORD
              X, Y: byte;
              CASE Kind: DataType OF
                TInt: (VInt: integer);
                TString: (VString: string[20]);
   END;
VAR
   WorkRec: GetRec;
```

The **X** and **Y** fields are static and are not dependent upon the **Kind** tag identifier (see Figure 9-4). The **vInt** field can be used only if **Kind = TInt.** If **Kind = TString** then the **VString** field is accessible. The amount of memory available for the variant record depends on the size of the largest variant.

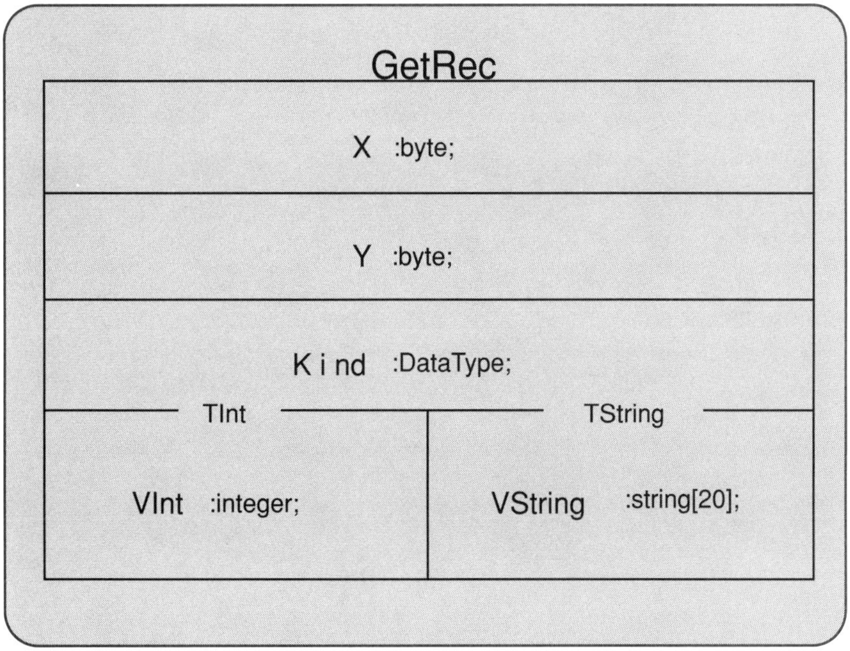

Figure 9-4
**Record for
the GetRec
Type**

This structure allows you to access all fields in all variants depending on the value of the tag field. The following example shows how variant records work in the **GetRec** type.

```pascal
PROGRAM DemoRec;
USES Crt;
TYPE
  DataType = (TInt, TString);
  GetRec = RECORD
           X, Y: byte;
           CASE Kind: DataType OF
           TInt: (VInt: integer);
           TString: (VString: string[20]);
  END;
VAR
  WorkRec: GetRec;
BEGIN
  ClrScr;
  WITH WorkRec DO BEGIN
     X:= 5;   Y:= 5;
     Kind:= TInt;             { variant with VInt }
     GotoXY(X, Y);   ClrEol;
     Write('Enter number: ');  Readln(VInt);
     Write('New data: ', VInt);
     Kind:= TString;       { variant with VString }
     GotoXY(X, Y);   ClrEol;
     Write('Enter string: ');  Readln(VString);
     Write('New data: ', VString);
  END;
END.
```

When the **WorkRec** record addresses the **Readln** procedure for the first time, it contains the **VInt** field values. After the second address, the same record will have its own variant values and instead of containing all the figures from the **VInt** field, it will contain a string entered in the **VString** field. This is made possible because the values of the flag have changed.

CHAPTER 10

WORKING WITH STRINGS

String Length

In order to estimate the size of memory needed to store a string, you have to add 1 to the **string length**. For example, if you have the following variables:

```
VAR
  Fstr : string[125];
  St1 : string[34];
  St2 : string[50];
```

126, 35 and 51 bytes respectively, are needed to store them. An additional byte with length specification is a zero byte of the string. For example, if you declare a name variable as a string and assign the value 'DONALD' to it:

```
VAR  Name : string[8];
  ...
  Name := 'DONALD';
```

then this string will be allocated in memory as follows:

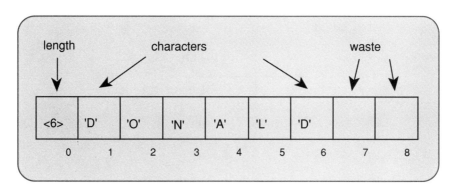

Figure 10-1
The Location of a String in Memory

String Expressions

String expressions refer to expressions with string operands. They are made up of string constants and variables, function calls and operators.

The **concatenation operator** (+) is used to combine characters and strings in to one string:

Expression	Result
'I' + 'B' + 'M' + ' PC' + ' AT'	'IBM PC AT'
'A' + 'B' + 'C' + 'D'	'ABCD'

The resulting string must not be more than 255 characters long.

The **relational operators** (=, <>, >, <, >=, <=) compare two string operands. They have less precedence than a concatenation operator and are consequently performed after concatenations in expressions. Strings are compared from left to right up to the first unmatched characters. In comparisons, the string containing a character that has a greater ASCII number is considered the **greater**. The result of relational operations is always boolean:

Expression	Result
'DOS4.0' < 'DOs4.O'	True
'chord' > 'CHORD'	True

If the strings being compared are of different lengths, the longer string is considered the **greater**. Strings of equal length and matched characters are considered **equal**:

Expression	Result
'Printer' > 'Printer'	False
'XXXXXX' > 'XXXX'	True
'Office' = 'Office'	True

The **assignment operator** (:=) assigns the result of a string expression to a string variable:

```
Str1 := 'Group of students';
Str2 := Str1 + 'and workers';
Family := 'Simpson D.G.';
```

If an assigning value is longer than a string variable, then the unnecessary characters on the right are omitted:

Declaration	Expression	Result A value
A : string[4];	A := 'Group';	'Grou'
A : string[5];	A := 'Group';	'Group'
A : string[2];	A := 'Group';	'Gr'

You can operate with both string and character operands in an expression. If you assign a character variable to a string value then this string must be one character long in order to avoid an error.

You can refer to the components of string variables by indexing. For example, **Str2[1+2]** denotes the third character of **Str2**, and **Str2[7]** denotes the 7-th one. The zero byte of each string contains length specification. For example you can find out the current length of the string **Name** using the function **Ord**:

```
Name := 'DONALD';
Writeln(Ord(Name[0]));
```

String Procedures

The procedure **Delete(S, Pos, N)** deletes **N** amount of characters from the **S** string, **Pos** indicates the position of the first character to be deleted. Of course the program will not work if Pos > 255 :

S value	Expression	Result
'abcdef'	Delete(S,4,2)	'abcf'
'BigBen'	Delete(S,4,4)	'Big'

Insert (S1, S2, Pos). Insert **S1** in **S2** from the **Pos** position. Example:

```
VAR  S1, S2, S3 : string[11];
...
S1 := 'IBM ';
S2 := 'PC AT';
S3 := Insert(S1,S2,1);
```

The result will be **S3** string: 'IBM PC AT'.

The **Str(X, St)** procedure converts the numeric value **X** to the **S** string. **X** may be followed by output format (see Chapter 3). If the format specification is not great enough to output a string, it is automatically extended:

X value	Expression	Result
1500	Str(X:6,S)	'_ _1500'
4.8E+03	Str(X:10,S)	'_ _ _ _ _ _4800'
76854	Str(-X:3,S)	'-76854'

The **Val(S, X, Code)** procedure converts the **S** string to an integer or real value **X**. You should note that you cannot use blanks at the beginning or at the end of the **S** string. **Code** is an integer. If the conversion is successful, then **Code = 0**. If an error occurs then **Code** contains an ordinal number of the error character (i.e. the first non-conversional character, a letter, for example). **S** in this case is undefined:

S value	Expression	Result	
'1450'	Val(S,IBR,Code)	1450	Code=0
'14.2E+02'	Val(S,IBR,Code)	1420	Code=0
'14.2A+02	Val(S,IBR,Code)	?	Code=5

String Functions

The function **Copy (S, Pos, N)** returns a substring **N** characters long and **Pos** is the first position which is copied. If **Pos > Length(S)**, then the result will be blank; if **Pos > 255** an error will occur. The **Length** function is explained in detail below.

S value	Expression	Result
'ABCDEFG'	Writeln(Copy(S,2,3))	'BCD'
'ABCDEFG'	Writeln(Copy(S,4,10))	'DEFG'

Concat (S1,S2,...,Sn) - concatenates **S1, S2, ..., Sn** strings from left to right:

Expression	Result
Writeln(Concat('My',' dog'))	'My dog'
Writeln(Concat('Index',' 220100'))	'Index 220100'

When two strings are combined the total string length must not be more than 255 characters. The function **Length(S)** returns the number of characters in the **S** string. The result will be an integer.

S value	Expression	Result
'123456789'	Writeln(Length(S))	9
'System 370'	Writeln(Length(S))	10

The **Pos(S1,S2)** function finds the first occurrence of the **S1** substring in **S2**.The result is an integer number. If **S1** is not found in **S2** the result is zero

S value	Expression	Result
'abcdef'	Writeln(Pos('de',S))	4
'abcdef'	Writeln(Pos('r',S))	0

You will often need to convert lower-case letters to upper-case ones. Fortunately, Turbo Pascal has a special function **Upcase(Ch)** which allows you to do this. **Ch** is a character of the 'a'..'z' range. As an example we'll convert the 'donald' string to 'DONALD':

```
PROGRAM DemoUpcase;

VAR
  S : string[10];
  I : byte;
BEGIN
  S := 'donald';
  FOR I:=1 TO Length(S) DO  S[I] := Upcase(S[I]);
  Writeln(S);
  Readln;
END.
```

Application

The following program will give you a practical example of working with strings. It demonstrates what is known as a "running line" algorithm:

```
PROGRAM DemoStringGo;
USES Crt;
TYPE
  Str160 = string[160];
VAR
  WorkStr: Str160;

PROCEDURE GoString(X, Y: byte; InSt: Str160);
{ X and Y are the coordinates of the "running line" }
VAR
  St1 : Str160;
  I : byte;
BEGIN
  St1 := '  ';
  ClrScr;
  St1 := St1+InSt;
  FOR I:= 1 TO Length(St1) DO BEGIN
    Delete(St1, 1, 1);
    GoToXY(X, Y);
    Write(St1);
    Delay(90); DelLine
  END
END;  { GoString }
```

```
BEGIN
  GoString(1, 10, 'Turn on your printer!!!');
  WorkStr := 'Set the paper !!!';
  GoString(1, 14, WorkStr);
  ...
END.
```

The **GoString** procedure is used for attracting the user's attention to the screen.

CHAPTER 11

FILES

File Handling Concepts

You will probably find that you use your programs more than once, which means that you are continually having to re-input the relevant data. Obviously this is very time consuming, so the best way to get round this problem is to store the data in a file on a floppy disk or hard disk, and to use this file any time you need the data. Each **file** has its own **name** (of not more than 8 characters) and **extension** (of not more than 3 characters). For example:

```
BASE.DAT
README.TXT
```

You access a file by using what's known as a **file pointer** (see Figure 11-1). A file component is pointed to by a file pointer and is accessible for reading and writing. When you read or write a particular component, the file pointer moves on to the next one. For example, Figure 11-2 shows a file with byte components. The file pointer is placed on the second component which means that this component is now accessible for processing.

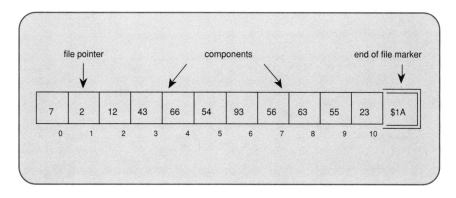

Figure 11-1
**Structure
of File for
Byte Type
Components**

Each reading or writing operation moves the file pointer to the next component. Components are numbered from zero: 0,1,2.... The last one is followed by the **end of the file marker** (^Z, ASCII code 26). The number of components is only limited by the size of the disk.

There are three types of files: **text files**, **typed files** and **untyped files**, which we will explain in turn.

Text Files

Declaring

We'll start with the simplest of the files. What exactly is a text file? It consists of a string containing characters, words and sentences. You can use your text files to store letters, documents, instructions, etc. Each string ends with a two character combination: **carriage return** (CR, ASCII code 10) and **line feed** (LF, ASCII code 13).

You can only move the file pointer from the beginning to the end, which means that you can only organize sequential access. Work with a file is usually divided into 3 stages:

1. File creation on the disk.

2. File extension adding new strings.

3. File output on the screen or a printer.

As we have already mentioned, you can only access the string using the file pointer:

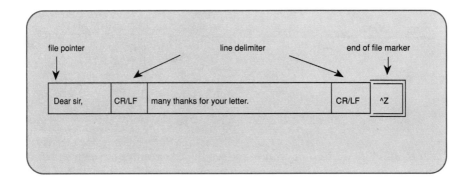

Figure 11-2
A Typical Text File Structure

You declare text files using the reserved word **TEXT**:

```
VAR
    FV  :  TEXT;
```

Handling procedures

Turbo Pascal provides a set of procedures and functions for handling text files.

`Assign(FV, N)`	assigns file name N to file FV.
`Rewrite(FV)`	creates new disk file for output.
`Reset(FV)`	opens a file that already exists on the disk.
`Append(FV)`	opens text file FV ready to accept new lines.
`Write(FV, S)`	sends value S to an output file. Does not write CR/LF.
`Writeln(FV, S)`	sends value S to an output file. Writes CR/LF.
`Read(FV,S)`	outputs one or more variables from the disk file.
`Readln(FV, S)`	outputs one or more variables only from text file.
`Flush(FV)`	writes buffered sectors from text file to disk.
`Eoln(FV)`	function returns True when reaching the CR/LF.
`SeekEoln(FV)`	function returns True when it finds CR/LF or ^Z.
`SeekEof(FV)`	function returns True when it finds ^Z.

Table 11-1
Text File Handling Procedures

These procedures will be explained in more detail later on.

Creating a Text File

As an example we'll create the file **Letter.001**. It will contain a business letter which you can print out. First you need to declare a file variable using the reserved word **TEXT**:

```
VAR
     Document  :  TEXT;
```

The next file variable, "**Document**", must be linked to a name that the file is to receive on the disk:

```
Assign(Document,'Letter.001');
```

As you can see, the file does not exist yet so you have to open the file using the **Rewrite** procedure:

```
Rewrite(Document);
```

You can also use the **Reset** or **Append** procedures. The reset procedure opens a file which already exists on the disk and sets the file pointer at the beginning of the file. The **Append** procedure sets the file pointer after the last file string and is used to add a new string to the file. Now the file is ready for writing. You can use two procedures, which you have already worked with, for writing. They are:

```
Write (Document,S);
Writeln (Document,S);
```

where the **Document** is a file variable declared above and S is the input string. The difference between **Write** and **Writeln** is the same as it is for displaying text on the screen. Of course, you have to declare S as a string variable and assign a value to it before writing. We'll now create the **Letter.001** file. Input the strings in the file from the keyboard until the **END** string is entered:

```
REPEAT
  Writeln('Input the string');
  Readln (S);
  IF S <> 'END' THEN Writeln (Document,S)
UNTIL S = 'END';
```

You have now created the **Letter.001** file. When you have finished working with this file you have to close it using the **Close** procedure:

```
Close (Document);
```

This procedure breaks the link between the file variable **Document** and the **Letter.001** file. So if you want to access this file you have to open it once again with the **Reset** or **Rewrite** procedures.

Reading from the Text File

Reading from the text file is also performed using standard procedures:

```
Read (Document,S);
Readln (Document,S);
```

After executing every **Readln** statement the file pointer is moved to the next string. You can now print the **Letter.001** file using the **WHILE loop** and **Eof** function:

```
Reset(Document);
WHILE NOT Eof(Document) DO BEGIN
  Readln(Document,S);
  Writeln(LST,S)
END;
```

The reading and printing of the string will continue until the file pointer reaches the end of the file. Don't forget to close the file:

```
Close (Document);
```

Expansion of the Text File

Sometimes you will want to add information to an existing file. When you want to add strings to the file, you open it with the **Append** procedure and then perform the input and close procedures as usual:

```
Append(Document);
REPEAT
  Writeln('Input the string: ');
  Readln(S);
  IF S <> 'END' THEN  Writeln(Document,S)
UNTIL S = 'END';
Close(Document);
```

Typed Files

Declaring

Typed files can contain any valid Turbo Pascal components. You define a typed file using the reserved words **FILE OF** followed by a component type specification:

```
VAR
  DataX : FILE OF real;
              { components of this file are real }
  DataY : FILE OF integer;
              { components of this file are integer }
```

The most frequently used are files of records which you declare in the following way:

```
TYPE
   <name> = RECORD
                <field:type>;
                ...
                <field:type>
            END;
VAR
   <FV> : FILE OF <name>;
   <RV> : <name>;
```

FV is used for file access, and RV is used for the record fields access (it does not deal with the file at all). The FV variable is used as a parameter in all file processing procedures.

Means of Processing Typed Files

Turbo Pascal procedures and functions provide you with a number of ways of processing typed files (processing refers to any action performed with a file). The abbreviations FV and RV have been used for file variables and record variables respectively.

`Assign(FV, N)`	assigns file name N to file FV.
`Rewrite(FV)`	creates a new disk file for output.
`Reset(FV)`	opens a file which already exists on the disk.
`Write(FV, RV)`	sends value RV to an output file FV.
`Read(FV, RV)`	outputs variable RV from disk file FV.
`Erase(FV)`	deletes file FV from the disk directory.
`Truncate(FV)`	deletes all components from the current pointer to the ^Z marker.
`Seek(FV,N)`	moves file pointer from the current position to record N.
`Close(FV)`	closes file FV.
`FilePos(FV)`	returns the current file pointer position.
`IOResult`	returns the input/output error code.
`Eof(FV)`	returns **True** if the file it reaches the ^Z.
`FilePos(FV)`	returns the number of the record, pointed at by the file pointer.
`FileSize(FV)`	returns the total number records in file FV.

Table 11-2
Typed File Handling Procedures

Access to the File Components

There are two ways you can access the relevant file record: **sequential access** and **random access**. The first way has already been mentioned in the explanation of text files. According to this method, data records are read one by one. The **WHILE** loop and **Eof** function are usually used for this. For example, if you wanted to find out the income for November 1990 using a file with components of the **Base** type:

Month	Year	Income		Other
01	1990	4500.00	...	50.00
02	1990	4100.00	...	96.00
	...			
10	1990	4850.00	...	10.00
11	1990	4900.00	...	47.00
12	1990	5000.00	...	32.00

Figure 11-3
File
BASE.DTA

you could do it by conducting a sequential search in the list of records until the record with the field Month = 11 is found. If you have a lot of records, the search process can be very time consuming so it's more convenient to organize direct access, which you can do if you know the record's number. This method is called random access and is carried out using the **Seek** procedure:

```
Seek(wFile, 11-1);
Write('Income sum = ', wRec.Income);
```

Note that the **Seek(wFile, 11-1)** statement has been used here instead of **Seek(wFile,11)** because the first record is record 0. Your choice of method will depend on the task you want to perform.

Creation of Typed Files

To create a typed file you have to perform the following actions:

1.   Assign a name to it.

2.   Open the file as you would open a new one.

3.   Input the data and write the components into the file:
         input the data for the first component;
         write the first component into the file;
         .....
         input the data for the nth component;
         write the nth component into the file;

4.   Close the file.

We'll now show you how to create the **BASE.DTA** file which will contain information about a family budget. First you must name and declare it:

```
CONST
  FileName ='BASE.DTA';     { name of file }
TYPE
  Base = RECORD
            Month: byte;
            Year : integer;
            Income : real;
            Food,
            Accommodation,
            Clothing,
            Education,
            MedicalCare,
            Leisure,
            Other : real
         END;
VAR
  wFile : FILE OF Base; { wFile - variable for
                                  file access }
  wRec  : Base;    { wRec - variable for record
                                  fields access }
  Flag  : boolean;
  N     : integer;
```

Now you can create your file. First you have to assign a name to it:

```
Assign (wFile,Filename);
```

Then you open the file using the **Rewrite** procedure:

```
Rewrite(wFile);
```

Finally, you can input data. We suggest that you input data from the keyboard and enter 99 to stop the process.

```
Flag := False;
WITH wRec DO
  REPEAT
    Write('Month: ');  Readln(Month);
    IF Month = 99 THEN    Flag := True
    ELSE BEGIN
       Write('Year: ');       Readln(Year);
       Write('Income: ');   Readln(Income);
       ...
       Write(wFile,wRec);    { writing to the file }
    END;
  UNTIL Flag;
Close(wFile);
```

You have now finished creating the file **BASE.DTA** and can start processing.

Processing

Processing usually consists of the following steps:

1.   Assign a name to a file.

2.   Open a file already existing on the disk.

3.   Read file components.

4.   Perform any actions with it.

5.   Close file.

As an example we'll output the income amount for the year 1990 from the **BASE.DTA** file. First you have to link the file variable and **BASE.DTA** file:

```
Assign (wFile,'BASE.DTA');
```

Then you open the existing file with the **Reset** procedure:

```
Reset(wRec);
```

Notice that we've used the **Reset** procedure here instead of **Rewrite** because the **Rewrite** procedure is used for opening new files. If you used the **Rewrite** procedure here, all the information in the file would be deleted and you would be left with a new "clean" file. The special compiler directive $I allows you to create a universal opening procedure:

```
Assign(wFile, FileName);
{$I-} Reset(wFile); {$I+}
                { this will cause an error if the
                file does not exist on the disk }
IF IOResult <> 0 THEN BEGIN
  Rewrite(wFile);
  Writeln('New file !')
END;
```

You can now print the data that you need. You should search for the data until you reach the end of the file:

```
WHILE NOT Eof(wFile) DO BEGIN
  Read(wFile, wRec);
  WITH wRec DO
    IF Year = 1990 THEN   Writeln(LST, Income);
END;
```

Now that you have performed all the necessary actions you can close the file:

```
Close(wFile);
```

Any file processing can be handled in the same way.

File Editing

Sometimes you'll need to rewrite the data in a file, to add records, to change certain record fields, etc.

Adding New Records to a File

To add new records to a file you have to move the file pointer using the **Seek** procedure. The process is similar to file creation, the only difference being that the new records are placed after the last file record. The algorithm for this would be:

1. Open the already existing file.

2. Position the pointer after the last record in the file.

3. Enter the new record(s) at this position.

4. Close the file.

We'll add new records to our **BASE.DTA** file to demonstrate this. This time, you should input records until 99 is typed instead of the monthly value:

```
Assign(wFile, FileName);
Reset(wFile);
Seek(wFile, FileSize(wFile));
Flag := False;
WITH wRec DO
  REPEAT
    Write('Month: ');  Readln(Month);
    IF Month = 99 THEN    Flag := True
    ELSE BEGIN
      Write('Year: ');    Readln(Year);
      Write('Income: '); Readln(Income);
      ...
      Write(wFile,wRec);    { writing to the file }
    END;
  UNTIL Flag;
Close(wFile);
```

Changing Fields of File Records

If you want to change certain record fields you should use random access. Suppose you needed to rewrite a particular monthly income amount, the algorithm would be as follows:

1. Open the already existing file.

2. Point to the relevant record using the Seek procedure.

3. Read the record (the file pointer will point to the next record, return the file pointer to the editing record using the Seek procedure and change the necessary fields of the record).

4. Write the changed record in the same place.

5. Close the file.

Here is part of a program that illustrates this algorithm:

```
Assign(wFile,FileName);
Reset(wFile);
Flag := False;
REPEAT
  Writeln ('Number of editing record: ');  Readln(N);
   IF N = 999 THEN    Flag := True
   ELSE BEGIN
     Seek(wFile,N-1);
     Read(wFile,wRec);
     Seek(wFile,N-1);
     Write('New Income amount: ');
     Read(wRec.Income);
     Write(wFile,wRec)
   END;
UNTIL Flag;
Close(wFile);
```

If you type 999 instead of the record number you will automatically exit the program. If you don't know the number of the record you want to edit, you should use sequential access.

Deleting File Records

You can delete any record by simply rewriting it. You can also use a flag (i.e. a special field) to indicate whether a record exists or not. If you want to delete it from the memory completely, you have to rewrite the file onto a new place.

This chapter shows only the main ideas and methods for operating with files.

Untyped Files

Reading and writing the components of a file on a disk takes up a lot of time. Fortunately, however, Turbo Pascal allows you to work with whole blocks of information rather than having to work with just single file components. These blocks of information are referred to as untyped files. Each file is made up of a set number of blocks of 128 bytes, which you can read or write.

You declare an untyped file in the following way:

```
VAR
   FV : FILE;
```

These files are opened and closed just like typed ones. The main difference is in the reading and writing, for which you use a special procedure which is detailed below (see Table 11-3).

Table 11-3
Binary Files Handling Procedures

`BlockRead(FV, Buf, Num)`	reads Num blocks from file FV to Buf.
`BlockRead(FV, Buf, Num, Res)`	reads Num blocks from file FV to Buf.
`BlockWrite(FV, Buf, Num)`	writes Num blocks from Buf to file FV.
`BlockWrite(FV, Buf, Num, Res)`	writes Num blocks from Buf to file FV.

In these procedures FV is an untyped file variable. **Buf** is a variable of any type (usually an array). **Num** is the number of blocks that you want to read or write. Each block is 128 bytes. **Res** specifies the number of blocks which is actually read/written. As an example we'll create and read the following untyped file.

```
PROGRAM DemoIOBlock;
CONST
  FileName = 'BINFILE.DAT';
VAR
  Buf : array[1..1280] of byte;
  FV : FILE;
  Res, I : integer;
BEGIN
  Assign(FV,FileName);
  Rewrite(FV);
  { fill array Buf with a number - in our example 9 }
  FOR I:=1 TO 1280 DO  Buf[I]:= 9;
  FOR I:= 1 TO 10 DO  Writeln(Buf[I]);           { checking output }
  BlockWrite(FV,Buf,10,Res);         { write 10x128 bytes to file }
  Writeln(Res);
  Close(FV);
  Readln;
  Reset(FV);
  BlockRead(FV,Buf,10,Res);     { read 10x128 bytes into memory }
  FOR I:= 1 TO 10 DO Writeln(Buf[I]);            { checking output }
  Close(FV);
  Readln;
END.
```

CHAPTER 12

POINTERS

Creating Pointers

So far we have only considered fixed data types, where you have all the information you want to process ready at the compilation stage. However, you will often find that you don't know the number of data elements to be processed before execution - when you're working with an array of arbitrary length, for example. So, you need to have variables that can be created and deleted during the execution process. Turbo Pascal provides a special data type for this purpose called a **pointer**.

Each memory byte has its own address which you can use to access the byte and read or write its value. When you declare a variable its identifier is linked with a specific memory cell. When assigning a value to the variable you store it in the corresponding memory cell. Unlike the variable, a pointer contains a memory address, that is, it only points to a particular memory cell. Each address stored in the pointer is 4 bytes long. The first word (first 2 bytes) is called a **segment** and the second word (second 2 bytes) an **offset**. By using a segment and an offset you can address up to 1M of memory. The whole memory is divided up into sections of 64K, known as segments. The precise address is determined by the offset. A memory address is usually written as follows:

```
<address> = <segment>:<offset>
```

Hexadecimal notation is the best system to use for address specification. Suppose you wanted to point to the first and the last addresses in the $4000 segment:

```
<first address> = $4000:$0000
<last  address> = $4000:$FFFF
```

The segment address is justified within a 16-byte boundary. It means that addresses $4000:$0000 and $4001:$0000 differ by 16 bytes.

Figure 12-1 shows some examples of addressing:

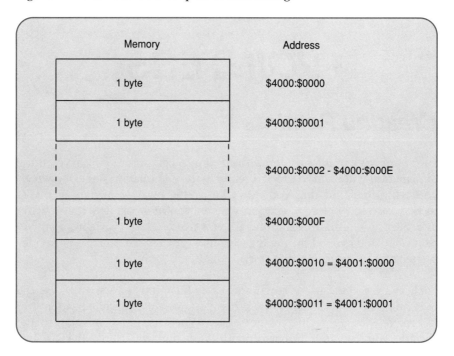

Figure 12-1
**The Memory
Address of
the $4000
Segment**

The pointer can point to any data type: integer, real, string, record, etc. **Pointer** declaration is very similar to **ordinary variable** declaration. The only difference is that you have to write the character ^ before the type specifier:

```
TYPE
  WindowPtr = ^WindowRec; { pointer type for the
                                  record WindowRec }
  WindowRec = RECORD
              X, Y : byte;
              H, W : byte;
              END;
VAR
  iPointer : ^integer;
  wPointer : WindowPtr;
  sPointer : ^string;
  AnyPointer : pointer;
```

The **iPointer** variable points to an integer value, the **sPointer** points to a string, the **wPointer** points to a record of the **WindowRec** type. The **Anypointer** variable can hold a pointer for any type. All declared pointers contain memory addresses, but each of them specifies different data types (see Figure 12-2).

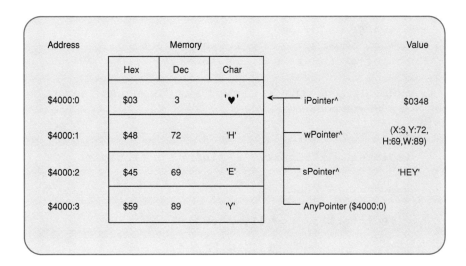

Figure 12-2
Pointers in the Memory Address $4000:$0000

If you want to define a pointer to a particular structured type (such as array, set, record, etc) you have to declare this type in the **TYPE** section.

Operations with Pointers

When you declare a pointer a place is reserved for it in the memory. This place is used for storing the variable's address and there is no initial value assigned to the pointer. So, you have to assign the address of a particular variable to the pointer before you use it. The standard procedure **New** will allocate memory for such a variable and assign its address to the specified pointer:

```
New(iPointer);
New(sPointer);
```

Dynamic variables are allocated to a special memory section called **Heap. Heap** contains all memory that is left over after allocating space for the operating system, run-time library, your program and variables declared within the program. The procedure **New** reserves the number of bytes according to the type specification. The address of this memory area is assigned to the pointer. Now you can gain access to these dynamic variables using pointers. To do this, put the character ^ after the pointer identifier:

```
iPointer^ := 58;
sPointer^ := 'Hello !';
Writeln('iPointer^ = ', iPointer^);
Writeln('sPointer^ = ', sPointer^);
```

You can use dynamic variables as static ones. For example, declare the following integer pointers:

```
VAR
   iPointer1, iPointer2, iPointer3 : ^integer;
```

and allocate memory to them:

```
new(iPointer1);  new(iPointer2);
```

Now you can use the following statements:

```
iPointer1^ := 58;   iPointer2^ := 97;
iPointer1^ := iPointer1^+iPointer2^;
                       { iPointer1^ equals 155 }
iPointer2^ := iPointer1^; { iPointer2^ equals 155 }
```

You can operate with the pointer values too:

```
iPointer3 := iPointer1;   { now iPointer3 and
           iPointer1 point to the same value: 155 }
AnyPointer := iPointer1;
```

After executing these statements three pointers (**iPointer1**, **iPointer3**, **AnyPointer**) now point to the same memory area. This means that **iPointer1^** and **iPointer3^** are equal. Note that you should initialize **iPointer3** without the **New** procedure. Using identical addresses for different pointers gives interesting results. For example, if you now perform the following statement:

```
iPointer3^ := 247;
```

and then print both iPointer1^ and iPointer3^:

```
Writeln('iPointer3^ = ', iPointer3^,
                ' iPointer1^ = ', iPointer1^);
```

You will see that iPointer1^ and iPointer3^ both have a value of 247.

Be careful while working with the dynamic variables. You should make sure that you differentiate between operations with the pointers and operations with the value of the pointer.

```
iPointer := iPointer2;        { pointers }
iPointer^ := iPointer2^;      { value of the
                                dynamic variables }
```

Absolute Variables and Pointers

We'll now show you how you can gain direct access to the memory. Turbo Pascal allows you to give variables a specified absolute address. The keyword **ABSOLUTE** sets this address:

```
VAR
   Work : integer Absolute $5000:$0100;
```

The variable work is now located at the address $5000:$0100. You can assign a value to it:

```
Work := 473;
```

You can also arrange direct access to a particular byte using the pointers. To do this, you should assign a concrete value to the pointer using the **Ptr** function:

```
iPointer := Ptr($5000, $0100);
                        { initializes the pointer }
```

The **Ptr** function calculates the absolute memory address. Now you can gain access to specified bytes:

```
iPointer^ := 473;
```

This type of pointer is known as an **absolute pointer**. Note that there is a significant difference between an absolute variable and an absolute pointer. An absolute variable doesn't need any additional memory - you link it with a specified memory cell and arrange access to this cell. An absolute pointer needs 4 bytes of memory to store a memory address. Its advantage is that you can change a pointer value and operate with different memory cells.

Comparing Pointers

You can use pointers in relational operators. The following example shows a comparison of the values of the pointers:

```
IF iPointer1^ >= iPointer2^ THEN
   iPointer1^ := iPointer1^ +1;
```

Both iPointer1 and iPointer2 are integer pointers. You can't use pointers of different types in relational operators.

It is more difficult to compare pointer values themselves. Computer experts can't seem to agree on how to compare memory addresses, such as: which address is greater. So, relational operators are limited to two definitions: equal or unequal:

```
IF iPointer1 = iPointer3 THEN              { equal }
   iPointer1^ := 0;
IF iPointer1 <> iPointer3 THEN             { unequal }
   iPointer3 := iPointer1;
```

Relational operators are usually used for cases when you need to find a boundary element. The special pointer **Nil** allows you to do this.

Nil Pointer

The Nil specifier indicates that the pointer has no special meaning (i.e. it is not linked with any memory cell):

```
iPointer := Nil;
```

You can initialize all pointers with the **Nil** value and then test them within the program to avoid meaningless operations:

```
IF iPointer = Nil THEN
   New(iPointer);
```

It is a good idea to use the **Nil** pointer in linked data types, such as lists, to indicate the boundary elements.

Memory Management

As we have already indicated, the **New** procedure locates pointers in a special section of the memory called **Heap**. If you don't specify its size before compilation, the heap area will occupy all accessible memory. The **Heap** size automatically decreases when you allocate pointers. You can see this by following this simple program:

```
PROGRAM TestNew;
TYPE
WindowPtr = ^WindowRec; { pointer type for the record WindowRec }
 WindowRec = RECORD
             X, Y : byte;
             H, W : byte;
           END;
VAR
 iPointer : ^integer;
 wPointer : WindowPtr;
 sPointer : ^string;
BEGIN
 Writeln('Start of the program. Heap: ', MemAvail);
 New(iPointer);
 Writeln('Heap after iPointer allocation: ', MemAvail);
 New(sPointer);
 Writeln('Heap after sPointer allocation: ', MemAvail);
 New(wPointer);
 Writeln('End program. Heap: ', MemAvail);
END.
```

The standard **MemAvail** function was used in this program. It returns the **Heap** size. Figure 12-3 shows memory allocation in **Heap**.

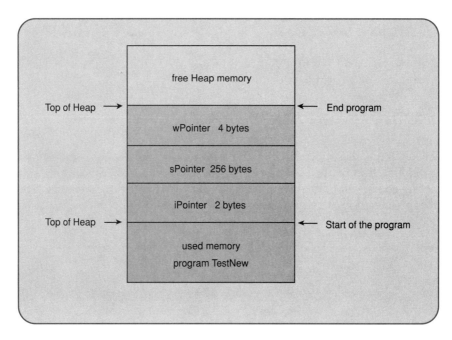

Figure 12-3
Allocation of Heap Memory

Pointers are allocated from the lower addresses up to the DOS memory. To operate with the Heap area it is quite enough to know its original, current, and end positions. You set these values using the following three pointers in the system unit: **HeapOrg**, **HeapPtr**, **HeapEnd**. In our example we have called the current position the top of the Heap. When the **HeapOrg** matches the **HeapPtr** the Heap area is clear. When **HeapEnd** matches the **HeapPtr** the Heap area is full. When you allocate memory the **HeapPtr** value increases.

The main advantage of dynamic variables is that you can reallocate them at any time and delete them from the memory. The **Dispose** procedure frees Heap memory occupied by the **New** procedure:

```
Dispose(sPointer);
Dispose(iPointer);
```

The new sPointer and iPointer are unlinked from the memory addresses in **Heap**. Don't assign new values to these pointers after the **Dispose** call while working with the pointers. Try to follow this order:

1. Allocate memory

2. Operations with the pointer

3. Reallocate memory

You have to follow each **New** procedure call with the **Dispose** call.

Reallocating Memory

Now we'll look at the problem of memory reallocation. Suppose you decided to free only the iPointer memory:

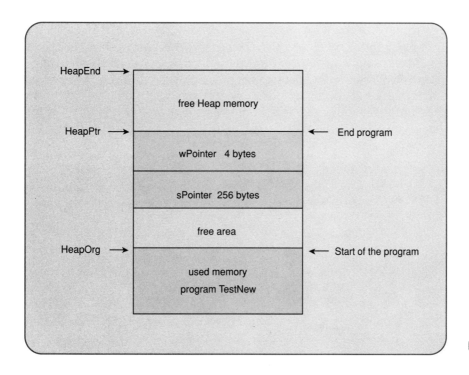

Figure 12-4
Free Area Caused by the iPointer Reallocation

You have reallocated the memory cell, but the **HeapPtr** points to the previous address after the **wPointer**. When operating with dynamic variables in large programs such free blocks can take up essential parts of the memory. Turbo Pascal allocates a new pointer in the following way:

1. It searches for a suitable free block and allocates the pointer to it.

2. If there is no suitable free block its allocates the pointer to a file section of the Heap memory.

These actions are performed automatically. You can find out the size of the maximum memory block available in Heap using the **MaxAvail** function:

```
IF SizeOf(string) <= MaxAvail THEN   New(sPointer)
ELSE   Writeln('Not enough memory in Heap');
```

Mark and Release Procedures

There is another way you can create dynamic variables. The **Mark** procedure assigns the current **HeapPtr** value to the specified pointer. Then you allocate any variables using the **New** procedure. Now, however, you can free all occupied memory by one operation: the **Release** procedure reallocates all variables that lie above the specified parameter, that is, the pointer. **HeapPtr** is assigned the pointer value. Figure 12-5 shows the memory allocation dynamics:

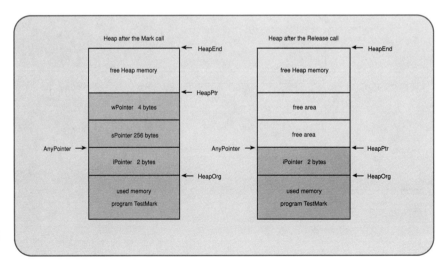

Figure 12-5
Memory Allocation in the TestMark Program

```
PROGRAM TestMark;
TYPE
  WindowPtr = ^WindowRec; {pointer type for the record WindowRec}
  WindowRec = RECORD
                 X,Y: byte;
                 H,W: byte;
              END;
VAR
  iPointer:^integer
  wPointer:WindowPtr;
  sPointer:^string;
  AnyPointer:pointer; {this pointer will contain the HeapPtr value}
BEGIN
  Writeln('Start of the program. Heap: ', MemAvail);
  New(iPointer);
  Writeln('Heap after iPointer allocation: ', MemAvail);
  Mark(AnyPointer);
  New(sPointer);
  Writeln('Heap after sPointer allocation: ', MemAvail);
  New(wPointer);
  Writeln('Heap after wPointer allocation: ', MemAvail);
  Release(AnyPointer);
  Writeln('End program. Heap: ', MemAvail);
END.
```

Getmem and Freemem Procedures

There is yet another method for creating dynamic variables. **GetMem** and **FreeMem**, like **New** and **Dispose**, allocate and reallocate only one dynamic variable. The **GetMem (VAR P: pointer; Size: word)** procedure creates P^ variable of **Size** size. The procedure **FreeMem (VAR P: pointer; Size: word)** reallocates P^ variable of length **Size**.

GetMem and **FreeMem** can completely duplicate the **New** and **Dispose** procedures:

```
    New(wPointer);
    Dispose(wPointer);
```

or

```
  GetMem(wPointer, SizeOf(WindowRec));  {the result
                                         here will be the}
  FreeMem(wPointer, SizeOf(WindowRec)); {same as
                                  for New and Dispose}
```

Unlike **New** and **Dispose**, the **GetMem** and **FreeMem** procedures can alter the size of allocated memory:

```
GetMem(AnyPointer, 40);    { allocates 40 bytes
                                  for AnyPointer }
...
FreeMem(AnyPointer, 40);
GetMem(AnyPointer, 2000); { allocates 2000 bytes
                                  for AnyPointer }
...
FreeMem(AnyPointer, 2000);
```

Linked Lists

These data structures can be realized in two ways: with the help of static arrays and with help of dynamic variables. Using arrays poses some serious problems. The most obvious one is that you have to declare a size to the compiler. If you choose the largest option it will often waste memory space. If you choose the smallest option, the program will not work for certain tasks. A good idea is to use dynamic variables. With their help you can create data structures of a particular size during the program's execution. Figure 12-6 shows a **linked list**:

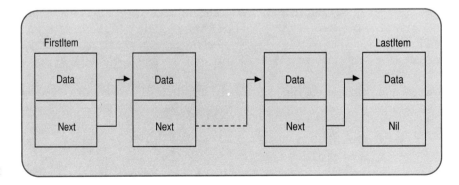

Figure 12-6
A Linked List

Each list item has two logical fields: **Data** and **Next**. The first contains data, the second, an ordinary pointer, which points to the next list item. Clearly, if you know the first item you can then gain access to any list item. The last item has a **Nil** value for the **Next** pointer. It indicates the end of the list.

Try this example which will create a list for a telephone directory. First you must define its item structure:

```
TYPE
   ItemPtr = ^ItemRec;
   ItemRec = RECORD
      Name : string[25];        { data fields }
      Company : string[30];
      Phone : string[15];
      Next : ItemPtr;
   END;
```

This is a recursive data structure because the Next field points to an item of the same type.

There is a set of basic operations that you use for lists. They are: **insert, delete, search, sort**. In order to work with linked lists you must know the **first record in the list**: the FirstItem, and **current record**: the CurrItem. This SimpleList program demonstrates the creation of a list for a telephone directory:

```
PROGRAM SimpleList;
USES Crt;
TYPE
  ItemPtr = ^ItemRec;
  ItemRec = RECORD
   Name  : string[25];      { data fields }
   Company : string[30];
   Phone : string[15];
   Next  : ItemPtr;
  END;
VAR
  FirstItem, CurrItem : ItemPtr;
  AnyPointer : pointer;
  Ch : char;

PROCEDURE InputItem(VAR Item : ItemPtr);
{ input item from the keyboard }
BEGIN
  WITH Item^ DO BEGIN
   Write('Input name: ');   Readln(Name);
   Write('Input company: ');   Readln(Company);
   Write('Input phone: ');   Readln(Phone);
  END;
END; { InputItem }
```

```
PROCEDURE AddItem;
{ adds new item in the list }
VAR  NewItem : ItemPtr;
BEGIN
  New(NewItem);                    { create a new item }
  InputItem(NewItem);              { input data for item }
  IF CurrItem <> Nil THEN
     CurrItem^.Next := NewItem;    { connection between the items }
  CurrItem := NewItem;             { the current item is a new item }
  CurrItem^.Next := Nil;           { the current item is the last item
                                                       of the list }

  IF FirstItem = Nil THEN          { is the list empty? }
     FirstItem := CurrItem;        { set the first item of the list }
END; { AddItem }


PROCEDURE OutputItems;
{ outputs all items on the screen }
VAR  WorkItem : ItemPtr;
BEGIN
  WorkItem := FirstItem;
  WHILE WorkItem <> Nil DO BEGIN
     WITH WorkItem^ DO
        Writeln(Name, ' ', Company, ' ', Phone);
     WorkItem := WorkItem^.Next;  { go to the next item }
  END;
  Ch := ReadKey;
END;   { OutputItems }


PROCEDURE SearchItem;
{ sequential search of the item }
VAR
  St : string[25];
  WorkItem : ItemPtr;
  SearchFlag : boolean;
BEGIN
  Write('Input name for search: ');
  Readln(St);
  SearchFlag := False;
  WorkItem := FirstItem;
  WHILE (WorkItem <> Nil) AND (NOT SearchFlag) DO BEGIN
     IF WorkItem^.Name = St THEN  SearchFlag := True
     ELSE  WorkItem := WorkItem^.Next;  { go to the next item }
  END;
  IF SearchFlag THEN BEGIN     { is the search successful? }
     WITH WorkItem^ DO
        Writeln(Name, ' ', Company, ' ', Phone);
     Writeln;  Writeln('Will you pass to edit ? (Y/N)');
```

```
      REPEAT;
          Ch := ReadKey;  { read control character from keyboard }
      UNTIL Ch IN ['Y','y','N','n'];
    IF Ch IN ['Y','y'] THEN   InputItem(WorkItem);
    END;
END; { SearchItem }

BEGIN { SimpleList }
  Clrscr;
  Mark(AnyPointer);
  FirstItem := Nil;   CurrItem := Nil;
  REPEAT
      GotoXY(1,25);
      Write('(A)dd, (O)utput, (S)earch, (E)xit');
      REPEAT;
          Ch := ReadKey;  { read control character from keyboard }
      UNTIL Ch IN ['A','a','O','o','S','s','E','e'];
      ClrScr;
      CASE Ch OF
          'A','a' : AddItem;
          'O','o' : OutputItems;
          'S','s' : SearchItem;
      END;
      ClrScr;
  UNTIL Ch IN ['E','e'];
  Release(AnyPointer);
  Clrscr;
END.   { SimpleList }
```

You can add to the set of procedures using the **DeleteItem**, **SortItem** or any other procedure. You should save this list in the file on your disk. The structure of the file record will be the same as the **ItemRec**, but without the field pointer:

```
TYPE
  FileRec = RECORD
    Name    : string[25];      { data fields }
    Company : string[30];
    Phone   : string[15];
  END;
VAR
  DataFile : file of FileRec;
```

First you form the list from the file records, then work with it, and finally save all the list items back in the file.

Double linked lists contain two pointers: a pointer to the next item and a pointer to the previous one (see Figure 12-7).

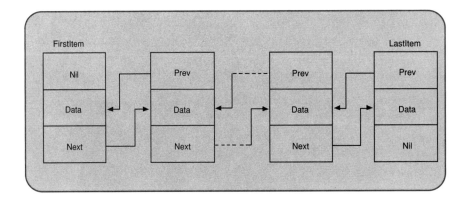

Figure 12-7
**Double
linked list**

The **ItemRec** definition is as follows:

```
TYPE
  ItemPtr = ^ItemRec;
  ItemRec = RECORD
    Name : string[20];
    Company : string[30];
    Phone : string[12];
    Prev : ItemPtr;
    Next : ItemPtr;
  END;
```

Now you can move in two directions within the list which significantly speeds up access and search processes.

DISPLAY CONTROL

So far you have only used the **Write** and **Writeln** procedures to output data onto the screen. However, with Turbo Pascal you can create attractive-looking output even on a black and write screen simply by understanding a few details about your display. All the procedures which control the screen display are situated in the CRT unit.

About Display

A display is similar to an ordinary television set. It can be black-and-white or color and works in both text and graphic modes. The main difference between the two modes is that in the text mode you output characters, and in the graphic mode you output pixels. In this chapter we will only look at text modes. Graphic modes will be discussed in Chapter 16.

You need to know the following basic details about the display screen:

- There are black-and-white (monochrome) and color screens.

- The cursor position is specified by X-Y coordinates.

- The top left hand corner always has the coordinates (1,1).

- The number of lines and columns depends on the display type and text mode.

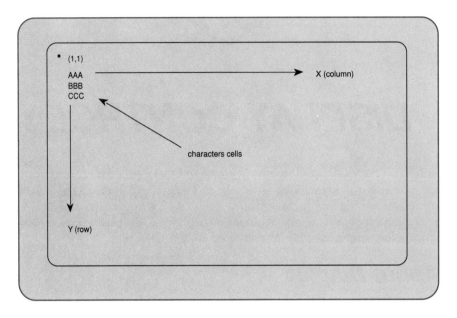

Figure 13-1
Coordinate Frames in the Text Mode

The text mode allows you to perform the following operations:

1. Change the brightness of the output characters.

2. Use 16 colors for characters and 8 for background.

3. Start blinking.

4. Move the cursor.

5. Make windows.

6. Manipulate lines on the screen.

Obviously, if you have a monochrome display you will get various shades of gray instead of colors.

Text Modes

There are 5 different text modes (see Table 13-1), each of which you set using the **TextMode(N)** procedure, where **N** specifies the required text mode:

```
TextMode(3);  is equivalent to   TextMode(CO80);
```

Mode	Value	Size	Description
BW40	(0)	25x40	monochrome
CO40	(1)	25x40	colour
BW80	(2)	25x80	monochrome
CO80	(3)	25x80	colour
Mono	(7)	25x80	monochrome

Table 13-1
Text modes

The majority of computers with color monitors use the CO80 mode. It provides 25 lines and 80 columns, i.e. 2000 characters, and is the default mode when you start Turbo Pascal. LAPTOP computers usually use the BW40 or CO80 mode.

Controlling the Brightness

The simplest way of varying your output picture is to change the brightness. You can do this using the procedures **HighVideo**, **LowVideo** and **NormVideo** which set high, low and normal brightness respectively. Suppose you wanted to output a prompt:

Find   Correct   Print

with highlighted initial letters, the simplest method would be:

```
GotoXY (20,24);  {  set  start  point  }
HighVideo;      Write('F');
NormVideo;      Write('ind    ');
HighVideo;      Write('C');
NormVideo;      Write('orrect    ');
HighVideo;      Write('P');
NormVideo;      Write('rint    ');
```

Note that changing the brightness is particularly effective if you have a monochrome display. **GoToXY** is explained later.

Text Color and Background

Dark Colors		Light Colors	
Value	*Const*	*Value*	*Const*
0	Black	8	DarkGray
1	Blue	9	LightBlue
2	Green	10	LightGreen
3	Cyan	11	LightCyan
4	Red	12	LightRed
5	Magenta	13	LightMagenta
6	Brown	14	Yellow
7	LightGray	15	White
		128	Blink

Table 13-2
Color
identifiers

Turbo Pascal provides **TextColor(C)** and **TextBackGround(C)** procedures for specifying character and background colors. **C** - is a specific color number. For the **TextColor** procedure **C** can have values in the range of 0...15, for **TextBackGround** - 0...7. You can specify any color using the number or color identifier (see Table 13-2).

```
TextBackGround(Blue);  is equivalent
                       to TextBackGround(1);
```

If you look at the bottom of the table you will see the **Blink** constant. You can set blinking by simply adding this constant to the color number:

```
TextColor(Green);
Writeln('Green color without blink');
TextColor(Red+Blink);
Writeln('Red color and Blink');
TextColor(Red);
Writeln('Red color without blink');
```

Cursor Control

If you want to place data on the screen in a particular order you must specify the cursor position, which you do using **GotoXY(X,Y)**. This procedure moves the cursor to the (X,Y) position. Suppose you wanted to output the message 'Press any key to continue' from position (25,24):

```
GotoXY(25,24);    { position cursor at X=25, Y=24 }
Write('Press any key to continue');
```

WhereX and **WhereY** functions return X and Y cursor coordinates respectively:

```
Write('Current cursor coordinates are ',
                        WhereX,' ',WhereY);
```

Clearing the Screen

Once you have finished working with one image on your screen you obviously need to clear it before you can begin work on another. To do this you use the **ClrScr** procedure. If you have previously specified a background color using **TextBackGround** then this color will automatically be returned after the **ClrScr** procedure. For example:

```
FOR I:= 1 TO 2000 DO Write('*');
                    { fills the screen with * }
TextBackGround(Green);
ClrScr;   { clears the screen then colors it green }
```

The same procedure applies to text windows, which is explained below.

Text Windows

Sometimes you will want to work with only part of the screen - a window. For example, you might need to input and output data in different places on the screen independently. This is what you use the **Window(X1,Y1,X2,Y2)** procedure for. **X1**, **Y1** are coordinates at the top left corner, **X2**, **Y2** are coordinates of the bottom right corner (see Figure 13-2).

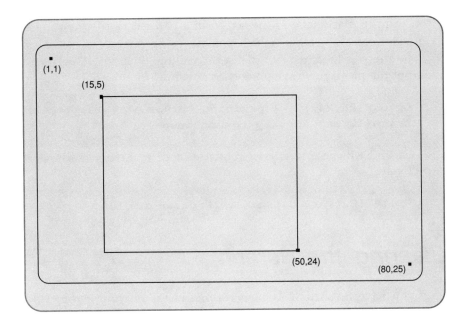

Figure 13-2
Window
(15,5,50,24)

Once this procedure has been called, Turbo Pascal acts as if the new window is the whole screen. The maximum screen size you can use is full screen, the minimum is one line and one column. The algorithm for working with windows is quite simple:

1. Open window.

2. Clear it using the **ClrScr** procedure.

3. Output into the window.

As an example we'll write a program that calculates the sum of 3 input values and outputs the result (see Figure 13-3).

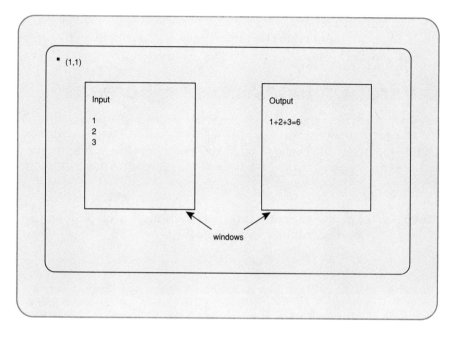

Figure 13-3
**Full Screen
and Two
Windows**

You can now input and output data in different windows:

```
PROGRAM DemoWindow;
USES Crt;
VAR  A, B, C, Sum : integer;
BEGIN
  TextBackGround(Black);
  ClrScr;                     { clear screen }
  Window(10,5,35,20);         { open input window }
  TextBackGround(blue);       { window background will be Blue }
  ClrScr;                     { clear first window }
  TextColor(LightGreen);      { output characters will be LightGreen }
  Writeln('Input');
  Writeln;
  Readln(A);
  Readln(B);
  Readln(C);
  Sum := A+B+C;
  Window(40,5,65,20);         { open output window }
  TextBackGround(Yellow);     { window background will be Yellow }
  ClrScr;                     { clear second window }
  TextColor(LightBlue);       { output characters will be LightBlue }
  Writeln('Output');
  Writeln;
  Write(A,'+',B,'+',C,' = ',Sum);   { output result }
  Readln;
END.
```

After studying this program you shouldn't have any problems using windows. There are more examples of windows in Chapter 15 and Appendices A and B.

Control of Lines on the Screen

The **ClrScr** procedure will clear the whole screen or window, whereas for this type of work you will often only want to clear a line or even part of a line. You can do this by following the procedures detailed below.

ClrEol   clear the current screen line from the cursor position to the right edge of the screen.

InsLine   insert a blank line onto the screen at the current cursor position. All lines below the new line are scrolled down.

DelLine   delete the line on which the cursor is located. Lines below the deleted line scroll up one line.

As an example try out the following program which will fill the screen with 24 lines comprised of the * symbol. You can then practice different ways of manipulating the screen image using the various procedures described above.

```
PROGRAM DemoScreenLine;
USES Crt;
VAR  I:integer;
BEGIN
  ClrScr;
  FOR I:= 1 to 24 DO
    Writeln(I:2,'*********************************');
  FOR I:=1 TO 24 DO BEGIN        { ClrEol demonstration }
    Delay(200);
    GoToXY(10,I);
    ClrEol;
  END;
  FOR I:=1 TO 24 DO BEGIN        { DelLine demonstration }
    Delay(200);
    GoToXY(1,1);
    DelLine
  END;
  Delay(1000);
  FOR I:= 1 to 24 DO
    Writeln(I:2,'*********************************');
  Delay(200);
  GoToXY(1,10);
  InsLine;                       { InsLine demonstration }
  Delay(2000)
END.
```

CHAPTER 14

ADDITIONAL POSSIBILITIES

Procedural Types

Using the procedural types, ordinary procedures and functions can be interpreted as kinds of variables. Procedural type declaration is quite simple:

```
TYPE
  MyProc = PROCEDURE(S : string; VAR V : byte);
  MyFunc = FUNCTION(X,Y : integer) : real;
```

As you can see, you simply use the reserved words **PROCEDURE** and **FUNCTION**, and follow them with parameter definition. Parameter identifiers are arbitrary, so you don't necessarily have to use them. You declare procedural variables in the same way as you declare ordinary variables:

```
VAR
    P  :  MyProc;
    F  :  MyFunc;
```

When you use these variables with parameters in the program, a particular procedure or function is called.

As procedural variables are very similar to pointers, they can be called procedural pointers. You have to assign an initial value to them before use, and they are compatible with the standard pointer type. In order to get the usual 4-byte (segment : offset) pointer you have to use the **FAR** keyword. In this case, the procedure or function call is **far**. If you don't do this, the procedural pointer is only 2 bytes long and the call is **near**.

```
PROGRAM TestFunc;
TYPE
  MyFunc = FUNCTION(X,Y : integer) : real;
VAR
  F : MyFunc;

FUNCTION Multiply(X,Y : integer) : real; FAR;   { far call }
BEGIN
  Multiply := X*Y;
END;   { Multiply }

FUNCTION Divide(X,Y : integer) : real; FAR;     { far call }
BEGIN
  IF Y <> 0 THEN   Divide := X/Y
  ELSE  Divide := 0;
END;   { Divide }

BEGIN  { TestFunc }
  F := Multiply;
  Writeln ('Multiply: 221 and 44 = ', F(221,44));
  F := Divide;
  Writeln ('Divide: 221 and 44 = ', F(221,44));
END.   { TestFunc }
```

Besides using them for direct initialization you can operate with procedural variables as with ordinary ones, by assigning the value of one to another.

Fillchar and Move Procedures

In addition to the **SizeOf** function (see Chapter 9), Turbo Pascal has two standard procedures which allow you to work effectively with the memory: **FillChar** and **Move**. Both procedures use the fast memory move instructions, which means that including them increases the speed at which your program works.

The procedure **FillChar (VAR V; Count: word; FillCh: char)** fills an area of the memory, specified by **Count**, with the character specified by **FillCh**. The address at which the area starts in the memory is determined by the variable **V**. As you'll agree, using the **FillChar** procedure is an ideal way of initializing complex data types (arrays, records, strings).

```
PROGRAM DemoFCH;
VAR
    A: array[1..10] of integer;
    St: string;
BEGIN
    { initialization of the elements of array A }
    FillChar(A, SizeOf(A), 0);
    { fills the string with 40 characters '_' }
    FillChar(St[1], 40, '_');
    St[0]:= Chr(40);          { sets the length of the string }
    Writeln('St = ', St);
END.
```

The procedure **Move (VAR Source, Dest; Count: word)** allows you to copy a given number of bytes, specified by **Count**, from the variable **Source** to the variable **Dest**.

```
PROGRAM DemoMove;
VAR
    A: array[1..10] of integer;
    B: array[1..5] of integer;
    I: byte;
BEGIN
    FOR I:= 1 TO 10 DO
        A[I]:= I;    { initialization of the elements of array A }
                { copies the last 5 elements from array A to array B }
    Move(A[6], B, SizeOf(B));
    FOR I:= 1 TO 5 DO   { outputs the elements of array B }
        Writeln('B[', I, '] = ', B[I]);
END.
```

Using Special Symbols

Turbo Pascal will let you output complex images on the screen and to a printer, such as histograms, frames, titles, etc. In the text modes there are special characters that you should use for this: horizontal and vertical sections of a line, shading characters and others. All these characters come in the 176..223 range of the ASCII table. There are 3 ways in which you can output special characters: using the **Chr** function, using the '**#**' character, or pressing the **ALT** combination.

Suppose you wanted to draw two lines using the ASCII character number 196 (that is '—'). The first two methods work as follows:

```
FOR I := 1 to 50 DO  Write(Chr(196));{ using Chr }
FOR I := 1 to 50 DO  Write(#196);    { using # }
```

If you want to actually see these characters in the text of your program you should use the **ALT** key. Type the ASCII character number while holding down the **ALT** key (you must use the numbers on the right hand side of keyboard). When you then release the **ALT** key the character which corresponds to the number you pressed will appear on the screen.

Suppose you wanted to draw horizontal lines using the **Writeln** procedure:

```
Writeln(' ———————— ');
```

It is very easy to do:

1. Enter **Writeln('**

2. Press ALT and hold it down while you type 196

3. Release ALT, now you can see **Writeln('—** on the screen;

4. Repeat steps 2 and 3 four times to get **Writeln(' ————————**

5. End the statement with ': **Writeln(' ———————— ');**

You can now see the statement in the program that draws an uninterrupted line on the screen. The following statement will enable you to view the number and the symbol itself at any time:

```
FOR I:= 176 TO 223 DO  Writeln(I:4, Chr(I));
```

Formatting Output for a Printer

The printer will let you output text in various formats. For example, you can use double, underlined, draft or high quality fonts. There are certain control characters which you must use to make your choice of font. Of course, the characters themselves are not output on the paper. As an example, we'll set up a high quality print for an EPSON 1050 printer:

```
Writeln(Lst, #27, 'x', '1');
Writeln('High quality output!');
```

Each control character works until its opposite appears in the text. For example:

```
Writeln(Lst, #15, 'CONDENSED FONT', #18);
```

#15 - indicates the beginning of CONDENSED print, #18 - indicates a change. Different printer models use different symbols to indicate which type face is to be used. Specific information about a particular printer is always given in the printer manual.

Keyboard Control

Standard keyboards have three types of keys: character keys (digits and letters), control keys (cursor movement, **INSERT**, **DELETE**, etc), and special keys (**CTRL**, **ALT**, **NUMLOCK**, etc). The microprocessor's own keyboard generates unique codes for each key pressed. Turbo Pascal transforms these codes into what are known as scan codes (see Appendix D). Keyboard control in the program is based on the processing of key scan codes. Each of the three groups of keys mentioned above generates individually structured scan codes.

Character keys return one value only, which is known as a simple code.

Control keys on the other hand return two values. The first is zero (which indicates that it is a control key) and the second is the code for this key (this is usually called an extended code). Special keys do not have scan codes, however, they affect the scan codes of keys pressed simultaneously.

The **Readkey** and **KeyPressed** functions of the **Crt** unit are used for keyboard control in Turbo Pascal programs. The **ReadKey** function reads a key from the keyboard and returns the character value:

```
USES Crt;
VAR Ch : char;
...
Ch:= ReadKey;
IF Ch = #121 THEN     {#121 - is scan code
                                for 'y' key }
   Writeln(' y key is pressed');
```

If you press the 'y' key for example, the **ReadKey** function returns the letter 'y'. The character is not displayed on the screen which can be very useful, for example, when you are organizing menu systems. The **KeyPressed** function returns the boolean value **True** if any key is pressed or **False** in other cases. The **KeyPressed** function influences the **ReadKey** function: if **KeyPressed** returns **True**, **ReadKey** does not wait for next key to be pressed and reads the current key. Otherwise, the **ReadKey** waits until you press any key. Table 14-1 explains how the **KeyPressed** and **ReadKey** functions work.

Keys	Function	
	KeyPressed	ReadKey
Character	True	code
Control	True	#0 + code
Special	False	-

Table 14-1
The Structure of Keyboard Return Codes

The following example shows how scan codes are processed for the character and control keys:

```pascal
PROGRAM DemoScanCode;
USES Crt;
CONST
  Esc = #27;              { #27 is the ESC key code }
  F1 = #59; F10 = #68; { #59 and #68 codes for F1, F10 }
  InsKey = #82;          { #82 is code for INS key }
VAR
  ExtendKey : boolean;
  Ch : char;

FUNCTION GetKey : char;
{ function waits for a key to be pressed }
VAR  Ch : char;
BEGIN
  ExtendKey := False;
  Ch := ReadKey;         { reads the first byte of code }
  IF Ch = #0 then BEGIN   { function key is pressed }
    ExtendKey := True;
    Ch := ReadKey         { reads the second byte of code }
  END;
  GetKey := Ch
END;   { GetKey }

BEGIN { DemoScanCode }
  ClrScr;
  REPEAT
    Ch := GetKey;
    IF NOT ExtendKey THEN
      Writeln('Symbol key is pressed with the code ', Ord(Ch))
    ELSE
      CASE Ch OF
        F1..F10: Writeln('function key is pressed');
          InsKey: Writeln(' INS key is pressed')
            ELSE  Writeln('extended code #00+', byte(Ch));
    END { case }
  UNTIL (Ch <> Esc)
END.   { DemoScanCode }
```

Processing Input and Output Errors

Error processing is organized by compiler directives and the standard function **IOResult**. There are always three steps to any error processing:

1. Disable input/output error checking operations using the **{$I-}** directive.

2. Test the result of the **IOResult** function.

3. Process the error according to the error number.

We'll take the following program as an example. Suppose you were trying to calculate the sum of an unknown quantity of real numbers that you were inputting from the keyboard. We'll consider the input of a letter, instead of a digit, as an error. If this happens the program will print the current sum and exit.

```
PROGRAM DemoIOResult;
VAR
  X, Sum : real;
BEGIN
  Sum := 0;
  WHILE True DO BEGIN
    {$I-}              { disables input/output control }
    Write('Input the number ');
    Readln(X);
    {$I+}                { enables input/output control }
  IF IOResult > 0 THEN BEGIN { tests the return value IOResult }
      Writeln('Input character is not a digit');
      Writeln ('Current sum is ', Sum:8:3);
      Halt;
    END;
    Sum := Sum + X;   { calculates the sum }
  END
END. { DemoIOResult }
```

You cannot handle file operations without error processing. For example, a common mistake is loading the wrong file. Usually you have to reload the whole program, which takes a long time. So, when the wrong filename is entered it is a good idea to prompt for the correct filename again.

Below is an example of a program that positions the file marker at the top of the file. The program prompts for the filename until the right value is input:

```
VAR
  FV : file;
  FileName : string;
  IOres: integer;
...

REPEAT
  Write('Input filename: ');
  Readln(FileName);
  Assign(FV, FileName);
  {$I-}        { disables system control }
  Reset(FV);
  {$I+}        { enables system control }
  IOres:= IOResult;
  IF IORes <> 0 THEN
    Writeln('File is not found: repeat once again.')
UNTIL IORes = 0;
```

Sound Effects

A General Outline

The ASCII-symbol number 7 (^G), and the standard Crt procedures **Sound**, **NoSound**, and **Delay** are used for making sound effects. Using ^G is remarkably simple, it is entered as a parameter in the **Write** and **Writeln** procedures. The number of times a sound signal is produced depends on the number of times you specify the ^G character. The example below will result in 3 signals:

```
Write('End  of  handling!',^G,^G,^G);
```

For more sophisticated sound effects there is a special procedure, **Sound(X)** which produces a sound at X hertz frequency. The sound lasts until the **Nosound** procedure turns it off. The following example will produce a sound at a frequency of 500 hertz for 2 seconds:

```
Sound(500);
Delay(2000);
NoSound
```

You can use these procedures to imitate the sound of a siren, an alarm-clock, a telephone ringing, etc. This is achieved by setting sounds at various durations and frequencies which correspond to the notes of the octave (see Table 14-2).

Note	Big octave	Small octave	First octave	Second octave
Do	130.81	261.63	523.25	1046.50
Re	146.83	293.66	587.33	1174.07
Mi	164.81	329.63	659.26	1318.05
Fa	174.61	349.23	698.46	1396.09
So	196.00	392.00	784.99	1568.00
La	220.00	440.00	880.00	1760.00
Ti	246.94	493.88	987.77	1975.00

Table 14-2
Note
frequencies

N.B. when you're using a sound routine you have to round off these values. We'll now have a look at some practical examples that you might want to use in your work.

Creating Melodies

One way in which you can produce a melody is to set up sounds with frequencies that correspond to the notes. You should load the sound durations in one array and the sound frequencies in another. The example below demonstrates how you can play a scale with increasing note duration:

```
PROGRAM DemoScale;
USES Crt;
CONST
  M : array[1..7] of integer = (262,294,330,349,392,440,494);{note}
  T : array[1..7] of integer = (10,11,12,13,14,15,16);{duration}
VAR
  I : byte;
BEGIN
  WHILE NOT KeyPressed DO BEGIN
    FOR I := 1 TO 7 DO BEGIN
      Sound(M[I]);
      Delay(T[I]);
      NoSound
    END;
  END
END.  { DemoScale }
```

You can produce quite a good tune by changing the values of the **M** and **T** arrays.

An Accompaniment for Output Operations

You can also use sound effects in your programs to accompany the output process. It means that you can output prompts, various error messages and screen headers. As an example we'll prompt two lines in the middle of the screen, accompanying them with a sound signal.

```
PROGRAM DemoAccomplish;
USES Crt;

PROCEDURE Accomp(X,Y: integer; St: string);
{Outputs the St string accompanied by sound effects}
VAR
  I : byte;
BEGIN { Accomp }
  GoToXY(X,Y);  { start coordinates for outputting the string }
  FOR I := 1 TO Length(St) DO BEGIN
    Write(St[I]);  { outputs the I-th character of the string }
    Sound(12000);
    Delay(90);
    NoSound;
  END
END;   { Accomp }

BEGIN { DemoAccomplish }
  Accomp(23, 12, 'E X P E R T   S Y S T E M');
  Accomp(20, 15, 'Text output is followed by sound!');
END.   { DemoAccomplish }
```

Using Sounds to Accompany Error Situations

There are a lot of different errors that can occur during program execution: output errors, overflow errors and many more. Sound signals in these cases will help to attract the user's attention to critical situations. The signals can be single, continuous (interrupted by the user) or intermittent. The following example will simulate a ringing telephone:

```
PROGRAM DemoRinging;
USES Crt;
VAR  R,I: integer;
BEGIN
  REPEAT
    FOR R := 1 TO 2 DO BEGIN
    FOR I := 1 TO 8 DO BEGIN
        Sound(600);
        Delay(60);
        NoSound
      END;
    Delay(110)
  END;
  Delay (1000)
UNTIL KeyPressed;
END.
```

Similar signals can also be used to accompany prompts, to input new data, to insert another floppy disk, etc. Generally, sound signals are used when the PC operator's involvement is required.

The Electronic Composer

You can also use the sound procedures to create your own electronic composer. To do this you have to write an algorithm for random sound generation, and then you should be able to produce some relatively pleasant tunes!

```
PROGRAM  MakeMusic;
USES  Crt;
VAR
  I  :  integer;
BEGIN
  I  :=  1;
  REPEAT
```

```
        I := I + 1;
        Sound(Random(180) + 40 + I);
        Delay(170);
        NoSound;
        Delay(100)
    UNTIL KeyPressed
END.
```

Imitating a Musical Instrument

The sound procedures will also let you simulate musical instruments. The keys 1..8 (scan codes #49..#56) on your PC's keyboard can act as a piano keyboard. The zero key (scan code #48) exits the program. The following program shows how you can do this:

```
PROGRAM DemoInstrument;
USES Crt;
CONST
 M : ARRAY[1..8] OF integer=(262,294,330,349,392,440,494,523);
VAR
 I : integer;
 Ch: char;
BEGIN
  WHILE True DO BEGIN
   Ch := ReadKey;
   CASE Ch OF
      #49 : I := 1;
      #50 : I := 2;
      #51 : I := 3;
      #52 : I := 4;
      #53 : I := 5;
      #54 : I := 6;
      #55 : I := 7;
      #56 : I := 8;
      #48 : Halt  { exits when the key '0' is pressed }
    ELSE  Write('Key sound not specified. Repeat!')
   END;
   Sound(M[I]);
   Delay(100);
   NoSound;
  END
END.
```

This type of program is particularly useful for teaching children how to use the computer keyboard. However, we advise you not to overload your programs with musical and sound effects as it can become annoying. A good program will always let you turn off sound effects for people who don't like them.

Pascal + Assembler

Assembler Insertion

While writing programs you might find that Turbo Pascal doesn't give you enough scope for your ideas, for example it's difficult to organize good access rights protection without using an assembler. Fortunately, however, Turbo Pascal 6.0 allows you to insert assembler language into your Turbo Pascal program. A built-in assembler supports all the commands of 8086/87 80286/87 microprocessors and most Turbo Assembler statements.

If you are using assembler language you must place the assembler statements within **ASM ... END**:

```
ASM
    < assembler statements >
END.
```

If you put more than one statement in a line you must delimit each of them with a semicolon:

```
ASM
    Mov Ax,0; Mov Ds,Ax; Push Cx
END;
```

If each statement has a separate line you don't need the semicolon:

```
ASM
    Mov Ax,0
    Mov Ds,Ax
    Push Cx
END;
```

The following is an example of assembler insertion. The program tests the input value (which is a password of some kind) and if it is not 17 it reboots MS-DOS:

```
PROGRAM DemoAsm;
USES Crt;
VAR  PW : string;

PROCEDURE Defence;
BEGIN
  ASM   { MS-DOS reboots - if the password is wrong }
    cli
    mov  AX,0
    mov  DS,AX
    mov  CX, 1234H
    mov  [0472H], CX
    mov  CX, 0FFFFh
    push CX
    push AX
    retf
  END
END;  { Defence }

BEGIN  { DemoAsm }
  ClrScr;
  Write('Password: ');
  Readln(PW);
  IF PW <> '17' then Defence;
    ...        { password is correct, continue normal performance }
END.   { DemoAsm }
```

This unexpected reboot will act as a warning for anyone who tries to use this program without permission.

Machine Code Insertions

Turbo Pascal allows you to have sections in your program that are actually in machine code. The **Inline(Statements)** procedure is used to insert machine code, where Statements refers to the machine code. Machine codes must be delimited by /. The following example performs the same task as the assembler insertion, it reboots MS-DOS:

```
PROCEDURE  Defence;
BEGIN
    InLine($EA/$00/$00/$ff/$ff);
END;
```

You should note that the machine code insertion of only 5 bytes is more compact than the assembler one.

CHAPTER 15

YOUR UNIVERSAL LIBRARY

The Service Unit - A Great Time-Saver

By now you should feel at ease with Turbo Pascal. You have written your first programs and have seen the results. Of course, the work you've done will have a very modest design and a poor input/output interface compared with modern commercial products, but don't despair, such professional programs take hours of hard work on a computer. In this chapter we'll help you on your way to professional programming by explaining the **Service** unit library. It contains procedures and functions that make menus, draw frames, and control text output. While building a program you can use them as "ready-made bricks". This way you will save time, and money!

The list of **Service** unit subroutines is fairly universal. All of them deal with the general functions for designing a user's interface. It is hard to imagine, for example, a good input service without cursor movement and frame drawing. Also, it is practically impossible to create complex program systems without a menu. Every programmer should have programs like this in their repertoire. The reasons for arranging such a library in units are as follows:

- The functional independence of units.

- The ease with which you can include any unit in your program.

The **Service** unit contains several logical sections, and each of them consists of functions and procedures for the same application area. Every section is followed by standard Turbo Pascal comments. At the end of the chapter you will find a general structure which you can use to arrange a ready-to-use **Service** unit, but you can change the unit structure any time you like. The following descriptions give a detailed explanation of each separate section.

Text Output on the Screen

Output problems have already been considered in previous chapters and we will not waste time going over them again here. The **Write**, **GotoXY**, **TextColor**, and **TextBackGround** procedures, with which you are already familiar, are used for text and color operating.

You should think of each screen with output information, as a set of color logic elements: frames, titles, and text strings. To operate with the colors you need to set an attribute for each logic element. In the **Service** unit there are five color attributes:

```
VAR
   TxtColor, NormColor, HighColor,
   SelColor, FrameColor: byte;
```

The **TxtColor** variable lets you set the color of the menu lines, **SelColor** is used for highlighted menu lines, **NormColor** for standard screen output, **HighColor** for title lines, and **FrameColor** for frames. The first four bits of the attribute (which is the length of a byte) define the foreground character color **(TextColor)**, the last four bits define the background color **(TextBackGround)**. This strange representation is used because it matches the storage structure of the attribute in a video buffer. The **Service** unit contains several procedures for attribute processing.

The **SetCol** procedure sets the color for output strings. The **Color** parameter defines the attribute:

```
PROCEDURE SetCol(Color: byte);
BEGIN
   TextColor(Color MOD 16);   TextBackGround(Color DIV 16);
END;  { SetCol }
```

You can also set a specific color for frame output:

```
SetCol(FrameColor);
```

The **ColorByte** function forms an attribute from the foreground (C parameter) and background (Bg parameter) colors:

```
FUNCTION ColorByte(C, Bg: byte): byte;
BEGIN
  ColorByte := C + Bg *16;
END;    { ColorByte }
```

The **ColorByte** function, which we will use in the **MenuColors** procedure, is only accessible in this **Service** unit. For this reason, we have included it in the **IMPLEMENTATION** section (see Chapter 8).

We have already defined five global variables for attributes, so now we can add the **MenuColors** procedure which allows you to assign values to these variables. There are five foreground and five background colors you can choose from. If you decided to change the number of attributes you would also have to alter the **MenuColors** procedure:

```
PROCEDURE MenuColors(Tc,Tbg, Nc,Nbg, Hc,Hbg, Sc,
                                      Sbg, Fc,Fbg : byte);
BEGIN
 TxtColor := ColorByte(Tc, Tbg);
 NormColor := ColorByte(Nc, Nbg);
 HighColor := ColorByte(Hc, Hbg);
 SelColor := ColorByte(Sc, Sbg);
 FrameColor := ColorByte(Fc, Fbg);
END; { MenuColors }
```

In the **INITIALIZATION** section you assign the initial values:

```
MenuColors(Black, LightGray, LightGray, Blue,
            Yellow, Blue, Black, Green, White, Blue);
```

After this initialization, the **SelColor** variable will contain the attribute for a black foreground and a green background.

We can now move on to dealing with procedures that output strings on the screen. As you'll have already noticed, the **GotoXY** and **Write** procedures are often used together, so it's much more convenient to join them together to make one procedure: **WriteXY(S, X, Y)**, where S is the output string, and X, Y are coordinates of the initial output point:

```
PROCEDURE WriteXY(S : string; X,Y : byte);
BEGIN
  GotoXY(X,Y);  Write(S);
END;  { WriteXY }
```

You can add to the **WriteXY** procedure by including color specification. In such a way, the **WriteXYc** procedure outputs a string of a specific color:

```
PROCEDURE WriteXYc(S : string; X, Y, Color : byte);
BEGIN
 SetCol(Color);  WriteXY(S,X,Y)
END;  { WriteXYc }
```

You can use the **WrtCenter** procedure for outputting a string in the middle of the screen. The X coordinate is calculated automatically (according to string length and initial screen length - 80):

```
PROCEDURE WrtCenter(S : string; Y, Color : byte);
BEGIN
  SetCol(Color);  WriteXY(S,(80-Length(S)) DIV 2,Y)
END;  { WrtCenter }
```

For example, you could output the following string:

```
WrtCenter('WROX HOME FINANCES', 14, HighColor);
```

Frames

Frames are used in the majority of programs that involve work with windows. To create frames in the text mode you should use graphics characters, the relevant characters being located in the second part of the ASCII table. You can use them to draw single, double and mixed frames:

The **FrameChar** type is used to specify which characters you have chosen to create a frame:

```
TYPE
    FrameChar = array[1..8] of char;
```

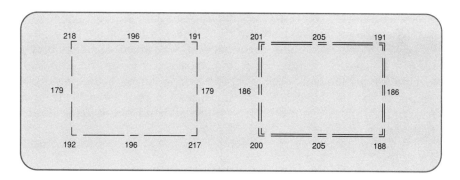

Figure 15-1
**The Use of
Graphics
Characters
to Create
Frames**

Now we will define two sets of characters (for single and double frames respectively) using a typed constant:

```
CONST
    MaxFrames = 2;
    Frames : array[1..MaxFrames]
        of FrameChar = ('┌─┐║│└_┘', '╔═╗║║╚═╝');
```

You use **MaxFrames** to define the number of sets you want. If you want a new type of frame you have to change these constants. Suppose you needed to draw all the frames in the same style (i.e. using the same type of lines in each case). You could define a special variable:

```
VAR    CurFrame  :  FrameChar;
```

The assigning of this variable determines what kind of drawing frame will be output. For ease of reference we will call this frame the current frame. The **SetFrame** procedure sets the current **CurFrame** value. The **Ind** parameter is the index in the **Frames** array and defines what kind of frame drawing you will have:

```
PROCEDURE SetFrame(Ind : byte);
BEGIN
    IF Ind <= MaxFrames THEN CurFrame := Frames[Ind];
END;  { SetFrame }
```

We have set the initial **CurFrame** value for drawing single-line frames in the **INITIALIZATION** section:

```
SetFrame(1);
```

The **Frame** procedure, as its name suggests, draws a frame. It has five parameters: the X1, Y1, X2, Y2 are similar to standard window parameters and define the top left and bottom right hand corners of the frame, and the **Name** parameter contains the frame title. We have used the following colors: **FrameColor** for the frame, **HighColor** for the title, and **NormColor** for the frame window. The title is output in the middle of the upper part of the frame, and for cases where it is too long, it is truncated. The frame is output from the top left hand corner to the bottom right hand corner:

```
PROCEDURE Frame(X1, Y1, X2, Y2 : byte; Name : string);
VAR  I, J : byte;
BEGIN
   Window(X1, Y1, X2, Y2);
   SetCol(NormColor);
   ClrScr;          { clears the window }
   Window(1, 1, 80, 25);
   SetCol(FrameColor);
   WriteXY(CurFrame[1],X1,Y1);
   FOR I := X1+1 TO X2-1 DO   Write(CurFrame[2]);
   Write(CurFrame[3]);
   I := Length(Name);   J := X2-X1-1;
   IF I > J THEN BEGIN
     I := J;   Name[0] := Chr(J);      { truncates the title }
   END;
   WriteXYc(Name, X1+1+(J-I) DIV 2, Y1, HighColor);  { title }
   SetCol(FrameColor);
   FOR I := Y1+1 TO Y2-1 DO BEGIN
     WriteXY(CurFrame[4],X1,I);
     WriteXY(CurFrame[5],X2,I);
   END;
   WriteXY(CurFrame[6],X1,Y2);
   FOR I := X1+1 TO X2-1 DO   Write(CurFrame[7]);
   Write(CurFrame[8]);  SetCol(NormColor);
END;  { Frame }
```

We'll practise drawing various frames:

```
SetFrame(1);
Frame(5, 5, 35, 15, 'Single');
SetFrame(2);
Frame(40, 5, 70, 15, 'Double');
```

Program Design

In your program you will probably want to remind the user about current hotkeys or generally give other information. You can do this in the last screen line using the **WrtHelp** procedure:

```
PROCEDURE WrtHelp(S : string);
BEGIN
  SetCol(NormColor);   GotoXY(1, 25);   ClrEol;
  WriteXY(S, 2, 25)
END;   { WrtHelp }
```

You can use help lines to accompany any action in a program.

Here are some constants, made up of commonly used keys, which you might want to use. They should simplify your work considerably:

```
CONST
    NULL = #0;      Enter = #13;    Esc = #27;
    HomeKey = #71;  EndKey = #79;   UpKey = #72;
    DownKey = #80;  LeftKey = #75;  RightKey = #77;
```

We'll now demonstrate the **WrtLabel** procedure that uses the **AnyKey** procedure. This routine will help you standardize your programs.

```
PROCEDURE AnyKey;
VAR CH : char;
BEGIN
  REPEAT UNTIL KeyPressed;      { wait for the key to be pressed }
  CH := Readkey;                { read scan-code of pressed key }
  IF (CH = NULL) THEN           { has the function key been pressed? }
    CH := ReadKey;              { read extended scan-code }
END; { AnyKey }
```

When placed at the beginning of a program, the **WrtLabel** call will clear the screen, output the program title and the author's copyright line:

```
PROCEDURE WrtLabel(Name, Copyright : string);
BEGIN
  SetCol(NormColor);   ClrScr;
  Frame(20, 12, 60, 16, '');
  WrtCenter(Name, 14, HighColor);      { output name and }
  WrtCenter(CopyRight, 17, NormColor); { author's copyright line }
  WrtCenter('Press any key to continue...', 25, NormColor);
  AnyKey;   ClrScr;
END; { WrtLabel }
```

For example, the beginning of your program might look like this (see Figure 15-2):

```
WrtLabel('WROX HOME FINANCES',
                        'Copyright (C) WROX 1992');
```

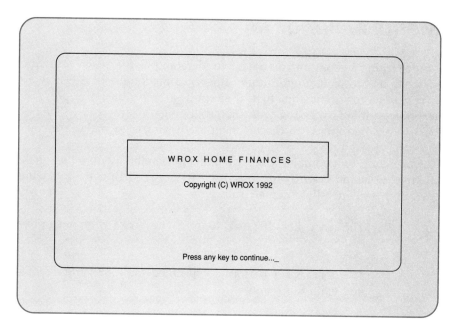

Figure 15-2
**Screen
Display After
the WrtLabel
Procedure**

At the end of the program you must return the screen to full size, restore the initial attribute and clear the screen. The **ExitProgram** which uses the **CopyAttr** constant will perform these functions:

```
CONST
  CopyAttr: byte = TextAttr;

PROCEDURE ExitProgram;
BEGIN
  TextAttr := CopyAttr; Window(1,1,80,25);  ClrScr;
END;  { ExitProgram }
```

The **Service** unit is included in the program and the program already contains the byte of the current color attribute. Of course, you can modify the initialization and exit procedures to suit your own needs.

Menu Making

While writing a program you have to understand its functional structure, so try to divide your program into different functional blocks. There are two reasons for doing this: first, it simplifies the writing of a program, secondly, it makes working with the program easier for a user. The best way to arrange access to these functional blocks is to make a menu.

The **Service** unit contains a vertical and a horizontal menu which make up the **Hmenu** and **Vmenu** functions respectively. We'll operate the menus according to generally-accepted rules:

1. The arrow keys are used to move the cursor from one option to another.

2. The **ENTER** key performs a specified command and the **ESC** key exits the menu.

The **Getkey** function reads data from the keyboard and identifies the menu command. It waits for any key to be pressed, identifies it and returns the menu command that corresponds to that key. This approach allows you to change the menu control simply by rewriting the **Getkey** function. For example, you can arrange the mouse support by including input from the relevant port.

In the **Service** unit we have defined a number of constants that correspond to the menu control commands:

```
CONST
    mcExit = 0;      mcSelect = 1;  mcLeft = 2;
    mcRight = 3;     mcHome = 4;    mcEnd = 5;
    mcNoComand = 6;
```

Now you can write the **Getkey** function:

```
FUNCTION Getkey : byte;
VAR
  Ret : byte;
  Ch : char;
BEGIN
  Ret := mcNoComand;
  REPEAT
    Ch := Readkey;
    IF (Ch = NULL) AND KeyPressed THEN BEGIN  { control keys }
      Ch := ReadKey;
      CASE Ch OF
  DownKey, RightKey : Ret := mcRight;
    UpKey, LeftKey : Ret := mcLeft;
      HomeKey : Ret := mcHome;
        EndKey : Ret := mcEnd;
      END;
    END
    ELSE
      CASE Ch OF { alphanumeric keys }
  Enter : Ret := mcSelect;
    Esc : Ret := mcExit;
      END;
  UNTIL (Ret < mcNoComand);
  GetKey := Ret;
END; { Getkey }
```

As the **Getkey** function is only accessible in the **Service** unit we have included it in the **IMPLEMENTATION** section.

Horizontal Menu

This menu consists of a line with a list of options, one of which (usually the first) is highlighted by a different color. The line number that will be used for the menu line is set by the **Y** parameter. The menu keywords are stored in the **MenuStr** strings array and this array is passed using the untyped parameter **ArrSt**. The maximum size of the array is the **ItemsMenu**. If you want, you can reduce the array length by setting the **Size** parameter:

```
TYPE  MenuStr = string[20];
CONST ItemsMenu = 20;
```

Keywords are output using the **TxtColor** color and are delimited by three blanks. The current (active) option is highlighted by the **SelColor** color (see Figure 15-3). The current command is specified by the **CurInd** variable. This variable points to the current keyword in the **ArrSt** array. If necessary, you can set an initially active option using the **CurInd** parameter by calling the **HMenu** function or by finding an active option where the **HMenu** exits. The **HMenu** returns True when you choose a particular command by pressing **ENTER**. If you press **ESC** it returns False.

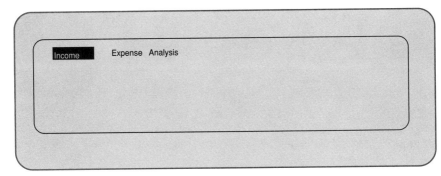

Figure 15-3
Horizontal Menu of the HomeFinances Program

Inside the **Hmenu** function you will find two auxiliary arrays with **ItemsMenu** elements: M and Xx. The M array has an **ABSOLUTE** specifier and is used to arrange access to the **ArrSt** array of arbitrary length. The Xx array contains the X-coordinates of keywords. The inner **TurnItem** procedure outputs a keyword on the screen. The **Ind** parameter specifies which keyword, the **Flag** parameter determines which color, either **SelColor** or **TxtColor**. Here's the **HMenu** function:

```
FUNCTION HMenu(VAR ArrSt; VAR CurInd: byte; Y,Size: byte) : boolean;
VAR
  M : array[1..ItemsMenu] of MenuStr absolute ArrSt; { menu lines }
  Xx : array[1..ItemsMenu] of byte;
  I, Cm, R : byte;

PROCEDURE TurnItem(Ind : byte; Flag : boolean);
BEGIN
  IF Flag THEN  SetCol(SelColor) { current menu element }
  ELSE  SetCol(TxtColor);
  WriteXY(M[Ind], Xx[Ind], Y);
END; { TurnItem }
```

```
BEGIN
  WrtHelp('ENTER select    ESC exit');
  SetCol(TxtColor);  gotoXY(1,Y);  ClrEol; { clears menu line }
  Cm := 3;                         { initial coordinate }
  FOR I := 1 TO Size DO BEGIN      { menu lines coordinates }
     Xx[I] := Cm;
     TurnItem(I, False);
     inc(Cm, 3+Length(M[I]));
  END;
  TurnItem(CurInd, True);          { current element }
  REPEAT
     Cm := Getkey;                 { get menu control command }
     CASE Cm OF
       mcExit : CurInd := 1;       { points first element }
         ELSE BEGIN
           TurnItem(CurInd, False);  { restores current element }
           CASE Cm OF
         mcLeft : IF (CurInd <> 1) THEN  CurInd := CurInd-1
            ELSE   CurInd := Size;
         mcRight : IF (CurInd <> Size) THEN CurInd :=    CurInd+1
               ELSE   CurInd := 1;
           mcEnd : CurInd := Size;
          mcHome : CurInd := 1;
            END;
           TurnItem(CurInd, True);   { new current element }
         END;
     END;
  UNTIL (Cm <= mcSelect);
  SetCol(NormColor);
  IF (Cm = mcExit) THEN BEGIN       { clears menu line }
     gotoXY(1,Y); ClrEol; WrtHelp('');
  END;
  Hmenu := (Cm = mcSelect);
END;  { Hmenu }
```

To use this function you must specify the keyword array and current command index. There is a working example of this at the end of the chapter.

Vertical Menu

The vertical menu is built on the same principles as the horizontal one. However, it differs from the horizontal one in the way its option list is formed as commands are placed on different lines (see Figure 15-4).

The list of the **VMenu** function parameters is extended by the X parameter, which specifies the first column of the vertical menu. Keywords are output by the **TxtColor**, and the current keyword by **SelColor**.

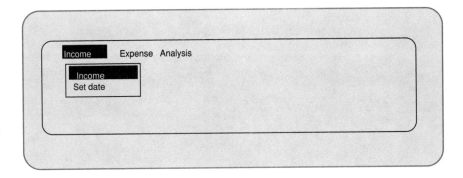

Figure 15-4
The Vertical Menu 'Income'

The **VMenu** returns **True** when you choose a particular option by pressing the ENTER key. It returns **False** if you press **ESC**.

In the **VMenu** you do not need to store coordinates of keywords - they are easily calculated by the X, Y, and **CurInd** parameters. This function also contains a section for calculating the maximum length of the keyword. In the **VMenu** function there is a blank string, **Fill**, that has a maximum length the same as the keyword length. This string puts an empty menu string on the screen before you enter the keyword. Here's the **VMenu** function:

```
FUNCTION VMenu (VAR ArrSt; VAR CurInd:byte; X,Y,Size:byte) : boolean;
VAR
 M : array[1..ItemsMenu] of MenuStr absolute ArrSt; { menu lines }
 Fill : MenuStr;
 I, Cm, Mlen : byte;
```

```
PROCEDURE TurnItem(Ind : byte; Flag : boolean);
BEGIN
 IF Flag THEN  SetCol(SelColor) { current menu element }
 ELSE  SetCol(TxtColor);
 WriteXY(' '+M[Ind]+Copy(Fill,1,Mlen-
                  Length(M[Ind])+1),X+1,Y+Ind);
END; { TurnItem }

BEGIN
 WrtHelp('ENTER select   ESC exit');
 Mlen := Length(M[1]);
 FOR I:= 2 TO Size DO
   IF (Length(M[I]) > Mlen) THEN  Mlen := Length(M[I]);
 FillChar(Fill, SizeOf(MenuStr), ' '); { blank string }
 Fill[0] := Chr(SizeOf(MenuStr)-1);
 I := FrameColor; FrameColor := TxtColor; { new frame color }
 Frame(X, Y, X+Mlen+3, Y+Size+1, '');{ draw frame }
 FrameColor := I; { old frame color }
 FOR I := 1 TO Size DO { output menu lines }
   TurnItem(I, False);
 TurnItem(CurInd, True); { current element }
 REPEAT
   Cm := Getkey; { get menu control command }
   CASE Cm OF
     mcExit : CurInd := 1; { point first element }
     ELSE BEGIN
           TurnItem(CurInd, False);{ restore current element }
           CASE Cm OF
         mcLeft   : IF (CurInd <> 1) THEN CurInd := CurInd-1
             ELSE  CurInd := Size;
         mcRight  : IF (CurInd <> Size) THEN CurInd      := CurInd+1
             ELSE  CurInd := 1;
         mcEnd    : CurInd := Size;
         mcHome   : CurInd := 1;
           END;
           TurnItem(CurInd, True); { new current element }
         END;
   END;
 UNTIL (Cm <= mcSelect);
 SetCol(NormColor);
 IF (Cm = mcExit) THEN BEGIN { clear menu window }
   Window(X, Y, X+Mlen+3, Y+Size+1);  ClrScr;
   Window(1, 1, 80, 25);  WrtHelp('');
 END;
 Vmenu := (Cm = mcSelect);
END; { Vmenu }
```

Service Unit Structure

Now that you understand all the unit components you can create a working program. We'll present its structure without including procedure and function texts:

```pascal
UNIT Service;
INTERFACE
USES Crt;
TYPE
  FrameChar = array[1..8] of char;
  MenuStr = string[20];
CONST
  MaxFrames = 2;
  ItemsMenu = 20;
  Frames : array[1..MaxFrames] of
  FrameChar = (' ┌ ┐|||└_┘ ')(' ╔ ═╗|||╚ ═╝ ');
VAR
  TxtColor, NormColor, HighColor, SelColor, FrameColor : byte;

PROCEDURE SetCol(Color : byte);
PROCEDURE MenuColors(Tc,Tbg, Nc,Nbg, Hc,Hbg, Sc,Sbg,
                          Fc,Fbg : byte);
PROCEDURE WriteXY(S : string; X,Y : byte);
PROCEDURE WriteXYc(S : string; X,Y,Color  : byte);
PROCEDURE WrtCenter(S : string; Y,Color  : byte);
PROCEDURE SetFrame(Ind : byte);
PROCEDURE Frame(X1, Y1, X2, Y2 : byte; Name : string);
PROCEDURE WrtHelp(S : string);
PROCEDURE AnyKey;
PROCEDURE WrtLabel(Name, Copyright : string);
PROCEDURE ExitProgram;
FUNCTION HMenu(VAR ArrSt; VAR CurInd: byte; Y,Size:
                          byte): boolean;
FUNCTION VMenu(VAR ArrSt; VAR CurInd:byte;
                      X,Y,Size:byte): boolean;

IMPLEMENTATION
```

```
CONST
  mcExit = 0;        mcSelect = 1;        mcLeft = 2;
  mcRight = 3;       mcHome = 4;          mcEnd = 5;
  mcNoComand = 6;
  NULL = #0;         Enter = #13;         Esc = #27;
  HomeKey = #71;     EndKey = #79;        UpKey = #72;
  DownKey = #80;     LeftKey = #75;       RightKey = #77;
  CopyAttr : byte = TextAttr;
VAR
  CurFrame : FrameChar;

{ source text procedure SetCol }
{ source text function ColorByte }
{ source text procedure MenuColors }
{ source text procedure WriteXY }
{ source text procedure WriteXYc }
{ source text procedure WrtCenter }
{ source text procedure SetFrame }
{ source text procedure Frame }
{ source text procedure WrtHelp }
{ source text procedure AnyKey }
{ source text procedure WrtLabel }
{ source text procedure ExitProgram }
{ source text function Getkey }
{ source text function HMenu }
{ source text function VMenu }

BEGIN   { Service }
  SetFrame(1);
  MenuColors(Black,LightGray,   LightGray,Blue,
           Yellow,Blue, Black,Green,  White,Blue);
END.    { Service }
```

Once you have compiled this program, create the **SERVICE.TPU** file, and all procedures and functions will now be accessible without any description. You can test this unit using the HomeFinances program. In this **Service** unit we have only presented a few routines, but you can of course include your own.

Using the Service Unit

We'll take the HomeFinances program as an example of how to use the **Service** unit. You will find the complete text of the HomeFinances program in Appendix A. It contains functions that process data from the **BASE.DTA** file and display them on the screen in the graphics mode. Here we will only look at part of the HomeFinances program, the part that deals with menu control and uses the **HMenu** and **VMenu** functions. We will also show you how to combine any menu command with a particular procedure (see the **NewDate** procedure). Note that in this instance we have used the standard unit **DOS** function **GetDate** to get the current system date.

```
PROGRAM HomeFinances;
USES Crt, Dos, Service;
CONST
  NamePro = 'WROX HOME FINANCES';
  CopyRight = 'Copyright (C) WROX 1992';
  Months: array[1..12] of MenuStr =
                        ('January','February','March','April','May',
                          'June','July','August','September',
                            'October','November','December');
  sMain = 3;   sInc = 2;   sExp = 7;     sAn = 2;
                  { description commands menu }
  aMain: array[1..sMain] of MenuStr = ('Income',
                              'Expense','Analysis');
  iMain: byte = 1; { index of current menu bar element}
  aInc: array[1..sInc] of MenuStr = ('Income', 'Set date');
  iInc: byte = 1; { index of current menu 'Income' element }
  aExp: array[1..sExp] of MenuStr =
        ('Food','Accommodation','Clothing',
            'Education','Medical care','Leisure','Other');
  iExp: byte = 1;    { index of current menu 'Expense' element }
  aAn: array[1..sAn] of MenuStr = ('Month', 'Year');
  iAn: byte = 1;     { index of current menu 'Analysis' element}
VAR
  cMonth, cYear, R: word;

FUNCTION GetReal(R: real; X, Y: byte; NameField, St: string): real;
{ Input value from the keyboard and display it at X,Y position }
VAR
  S: string;
  CopyR: Real;
  I: word;
BEGIN
  WrtHelp('ENTER exit');
  REPEAT
     CopyR := R;
     Frame(X, Y, X+35, Y+3, 'Enter '+NameField); { draw frame }
```

```
      WriteXYc('Old value: ', X+2, Y+1, NormColor);
      SetCol(HighColor);    Write(R:10:2);
      WriteXYc(St+' value: ', X+2, Y+2, NormColor);
      SetCol(HighColor);    Readln(S);    { enter numeric string }
      Val(S, CopyR, I);
      IF S = '' THEN BEGIN  { is string empty? }
         I := 0;   CopyR := 0;
      END;
      Window(X, Y, X+35, Y+3);
      SetCol(NormColor);    ClrScr; { clear window }
      Window(1, 1, 80, 25);
   UNTIL (I = 0);
   GetReal := CopyR;
END;  { GetReal }

PROCEDURE NewDate;
{ enter new date }
VAR
  M: byte;
  Y: word;
  St: string[4];
BEGIN
  Y := Round(GetReal(cYear, 15, 4, aAn[2], 'New'));
  IF ((Y = 0) OR (Y < 1990)) THEN   Y := cYear;
  Str(Y:4, St);
  Frame(15, 4, 40, 19, 'Enter month '+St);
  M := cMonth;
  IF VMenu(Months, M, 21, 5, 12) THEN BEGIN
     cMonth := M;   cYear := Y;
  END;
  Window(15,4,40,19);  SetCol(NormColor);  ClrScr;
                             { clear window }
  Window(1, 1, 80, 25);
END;  { NewDate }

BEGIN   { HomeFinances }
  GetDate(cYear, cMonth, R, R); { read system date }
  WrtLabel(NamePro, CopyRight);
  WHILE HMenu(aMain, iMain, 1, sMain) DO
     CASE iMain OF
         1: WHILE VMenu(aInc, iInc, 3, 2, sInc) DO
             IF iInc = 1 THEN   BEGIN END
                             { empty block }
             ELSE   NewDate;          { enter date }
         2: WHILE VMenu(aExp, iExp, 12, 2, sExp) DO
           BEGIN END;          { empty block }
         3: WHILE VMenu(aAn, iAn, 22, 2, sAn) DO
           BEGIN END;          { empty block }
     END;
  ExitProgram;
END.    { HomeFinances }
```

The menu system is made up of one horizontal menu and three vertical ones, as each horizontal menu command has its own corresponding vertical menu. Only one vertical menu command is implemented in this program, 'Set date'. It is combined with the **NewDate** procedure. Figure 15-5 shows the screen after the 'Set date' command:

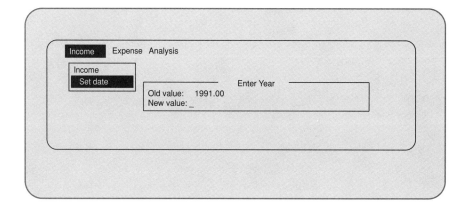

Figure 15-5
**'Set Date'
Command
Activation**

In this particular example there are no other commands implemented. To ensure that the computer compiles the program without errors in such cases, it is vital that instead of procedure calls which process a command, you specify empty operating blocks. In the above example the **BEGIN END** block fulfils this requirement. Of course, in the appendix you will find the complete HomeFinances program without any empty blocks.

CHAPTER
16

GRAPHICS

Graphics Mode

Commercial, scientific and other programs often need to be presented in graph and figure form. As graphics are an important topic, we will spend quite a lot of time on this mode. Obviously the ordinary character size is too big for drawing graphic images, which is why a pixel is used as the basic operating unit. A **pixel** is the smallest dot of light your monitor can display (see Figure 16-1). To compile the programs in this chapter you need to copy the **EGAVGA.BGI** file from the main Turbo Pascal system subdirectory.

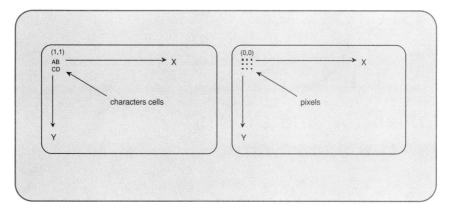

Figure 16-1
Coordinate Frames in the Text and Graphics Modes

Before drawing a pixel you have to determine where it will be placed on the screen. In the text mode this point is specified by the text cursor. In graphics modes however there is no cursor and the current output position is specified by an invisible **current pointer** (**CP**). Just as with the text cursor, you can also move the **CP** (procedures that move the **CP** are considered later).

There are several types of monitors (and corresponding chips, display adapters), each with different resolutions. The term resolution refers to the number of pixels in the vertical and horizontal lines.

The most widely used are **CGA (Color Graphics Adapter)**, **EGA (Enhanced Graphics Adapter)**, **VGA (Video Graphics Array)** adapters, see Table 16-1. For work with different adapters Turbo Pascal uses special **BGI (Borland Graphics Interface)** drivers. BGI drivers link particular graphics adapters to Turbo Pascal graphics procedures.

Adapter type	Mode constant	Resolution	BGI-file
CGA (1)	(CGAC0,CGAHI)	320x200 (640x200)	CGA.BGI
EGA (3)	(EGALo,EGAHI)	640x200 (640x350)	EGAVGA.BGI
VGA (9)	(VGALo,VGAHI)	640x200 (640x480)	EGAVGA.BGI

Table 16-1
Graphics Modes and Drivers

Turbo Pascal uses the **Graph** library to form graphic images. The **Graph** is included in the ordinary way using the **USES** command. You would be well advised to include the **Crt** module at once, as you will use it often:

```
USES Crt, Graph;
```

Initializing and Closing the Graphics Mode

From the moment you include the **Graph** module you can use all its routines. First you must call the **InitGraph** procedure which sets one of the graphics modes:

```
InitGraph(DriverVar,ModeVar,'C:/TP/GRAPH');
```

where **DriverVar** specifies the graphic driver and **ModeVar** specifies the graphic mode. You can set the **DriverVar** either by name or by number (the relevant numbers are shown in Table 16-1):

```
DriverVar := VGA;    DriverVar := 9;
```

The above two instructions are the same. If you don't know what type of monitor you have, you can use the **Detect** constant which automatically sets up the necessary driver:

```
DriverVar  :=  Detect;
```

Now **InitGraph** will automatically determine which graphics driver and mode should be used. The third parameter sets a path to get to the **Graph** module. Use the "- string if this module is in your current subdirectory. To sum up, here is a group of instructions which should help you avoid potential problems:

```
USES Graph;
VAR
  DriverVar, ModeVar: integer;
BEGIN
  DriverVar := Detect;
   InitGraph(DriverVar,ModeVar,'');
```

You can find out the current mode number using the **GetGraphMode** function:

```
VAR CurrentMode : integer;
...
  CurrentMode:=GetGraphMode;
...
```

There is one more procedure you'll need to use **CloseGraph**. It has no parameters and you call it when you want to leave the graphics mode for the text one and vice versa:

```
USES Graph;
VAR
  DriverVar, ModeVar: integer;
BEGIN
  DriverVar := Detect;
  InitGraph(DriverVar,ModeVar,'');
...
  CloseGraph;
END.
```

Processing Graphics Errors

Just like any other program, graphics programs can have errors, and you should do all you can to eliminate them. There are two functions you can use for this: **GraphResult** and **GraphErrorMsg**. **GraphResult** returns the value 0 if the most recent graphics operation was completed without error, or a number in the -15..-1 range if there was an error. All possible errors and their codes are shown in table 16-2.

Constant	Graph result	GraphErrorMsg
grOK	0	No error
grNoInitGraph	-1	Graphics not installed
grNotDetected	-2	Graphics hardware not detected
grFileNotFound	-3	Device driver file not found
grInvalidDriver	-4	Invalid device driver file
grNoLoadMem	-5	Not enough memory to load driver
grNoScanMem	-6	Out of memory of scan file
grNoFloodMem	-7	Out of memory in flood file
grFontNotFound	-8	Font file not found
grNoFontMem	-9	Not enough memory to load font
grInvalidMode	-10	Invalid graphics mode for selected driver
grError	-11	Graphics error (generic error)
grIOerror	-12	Graphics I/O error
grInvalidFont	-13	Invalid font file

Table 16-2
Graphics Error Messages

grInvalid FontNum	-14	Invalid font number
grInvalid DeviceNum	-15	Invalid device number

Table 16-2
*Graphics
Error
Messages
(continued)*

Look at the example below:

```
USES Graph;
VAR  ErrorNumber: integer;
BEGIN
  ErrorNumber := GraphResult;
```

The **ErrorNumber** variable contains the error code. You can use either the constant or the number of the error:

```
IF ErrorNumber <> grOK THEN Writeln('Error occurs!');
IF ErrorNumber <> 0 THEN  Writeln('Error occurs!');
```

The **GraphErrorMsg** function returns a description of the error which corresponds to the error code. For example, the instruction:

```
Writeln(GraphErrorMsg(ErrorNumber));
```

will produce the line: No error, which means that in our example the graphics mode has been set up correctly. The initialization of the graphics mode, and the checking of potential errors is conveniently organised by one procedure:

```
PROCEDURE Init;
{ Initiation procedure and analysis
                           of system errors.}
{ DriverVar and ModeVar are written into
                           the main program. }
BEGIN
  DriverVar := Detect;
  InitGraph(DriverVar,ModeVar,'');
  ErrorCode := GraphResult;
  IF ErrorCode <> grOK THEN BEGIN
      Writeln('Graphics system error: ',
        GraphErrorMsg(ErrorCode));
    Halt(1)
  END
END;
```

If you don't include this procedure then any initialization error will cause your PC to hang up and you will have to restart MS-DOS. Having read through all the preparatory stages, you can now start to work with some concrete graphics operations. We will consider the following major procedures: **PutPixel**, **Line**, **SetColor**, **SetBkColor** and a few others. At this stage, this is enough to give you an idea of working with graphics. When you need other procedures, turn to IDE Help for detailed information.

The Basic Procedures

All graphic images, no matter what they are, are made up of pixels. Pixels can create lines and curves and in theory you can use a pixel to create any graphics image, even a painting. The procedure **PutPixel** is used to output a pixel on the screen:

```
PutPixel (X,Y: integer; Color: word);
```

where **X**, **Y** are the coordinates and **Color** sets the color of the pixel. All possible color values are detailed in Table 13-2. For example:

```
FOR I:= 1 TO 10000 DO
   PutPixel(Random(640),Random(350),Random(16));
FOR I:= 1 TO 600 DO  PutPixel(I,1,Blue);
```

The first instruction will give you a sky scattered with stars, the second one will draw a blue line along the first screen line. To draw a line you only need one instruction:

```
Line (X1, Y1, X2, Y2: integer);
```

where **X1**, **Y1** are the start coordinates, and the **X2**, **Y2** are the end coordinates of line. For example:

```
Line(11, 600, 1, 200);
```

From time to time you will need to clear the screen, which you can do using the **ClearDevice** procedure. For example:

```
FOR I:= 1 TO 10000 DO
  PutPixel(Random(639),Random(199),LightGreen);
                             { fill the screen }
ClearDevice;   { clears the screen }
FOR I:= 1 TO 10000 DO
  PutPixel(Random(639),Random(199),LightRed);
                             { fill the screen }
ClearDevice;    { clears the screen }
```

Moving the Current Pointer

In the text mode, as you'll you remember, the cursor is moved by the **GoToXY** procedure. In the graphics mode there are a two similar procedures. The **MoveTo(X,Y)** procedure moves the CP to the position of the **X,Y** coordinates. For example:

```
MoveTo(200,100);
```

will move the **CP** to a position on the screen with the coordinates 200,100.

The procedure **MoveRel(dX,dY)** moves the CP to the **X+dX** position horizontally and to **Y+dY** vertically from the current position. For example:

```
MoveTo(200, 100); { CP coordinates are 200,100 }
MoveRel(5, 10);   { now CP coordinates
                        are 200+5, 100+10 }
```

Some programs will demand that you have constant control of the **CP** coordinates. For this you can use the **GetX** and **GetY** functions which return corresponding values of the **X** and **Y** coordinates of the **CP**:

```
VAR
  Xpos, Ypos : integer;
...
  Xpos := GetX;
  Ypos := GetY;
...
```

While operating the **CP** it can happen that the coordinates extend beyond the boundary limits. The following example shows quite clearly that the **MoveTo** procedure will not fit into the parameters:

```
X := 6000/10;
Y := 2000/2;
MoveTo(X,Y);
```

There are two functions however which will let you get round this: **GetMaxX** and **GetMaxY**. They return the maximum value of the **X** and **Y** coordinates for the current graphics mode:

```
X := 6000/10;
Y := 2000/2;
IF ((X > GetMaxX) OR (Y > GetMaxY)) THEN BEGIN
  OutText('Extends beyond range!');
  MarginHandling       { user procedure
                              error processing }
END;
...
```

Color and Background

As you will have realized already, the **Line** procedure does not have color parameters. This particular routine (and others too) uses a special procedure, **SetColor(Color)**, where **Color** defines a color from the Table 13-2. For example:

```
SetColor(Cyan);
Line(1, 1, 600, 1);
```

The **GetMaxColor** function returns the maximum valid color number for the current graphics mode:

```
SetColor(GetMaxColor);
```

If you use the **SetColor** to change the current output color and you want to change the screen background color, you can do this using the **SetBkColor(ForeColor)**, where **ForeColor** is the background color. Table 13-2 shows the parameters for this procedure. For example:

```
{ outputs bright green points on a lightblue
                                    background }
SetBkColor(Cyan);
FOR I:=1 TO 30000 DO
  PutPixel(Random(300),Random(200),LightGreen);
Delay(3000);
ClearDevice;
{ outputs bright red points on a green background }
SetBkColor(Green);
FOR I:=1 TO 30000 DO
  PutPixel(Random(300),Random(200),LightRed);
```

Text Output

Sometimes you'll need to accompany your graphic images with explanatory notes. You can do this in the graphics mode using the **OutText(St: string)** procedure. For example, if you wanted to output the message Press any key to continue... from the screen coordinates **60,320**, you would simply type in:

```
MoveTo(60, 320);
OutText('Press any key to continue...');
```

There is another procedure you can use which does not involve the **MoveTo** procedure:

```
OutTextXY (X, Y: integer; St: string);
```

where **X**, **Y** are the start coordinates and **St** is a constant or variable of the string type. Suppose we wanted to output the message "Press any key to continue..." from pixel **60,320**, it would look like this:

```
OutTextXY(60, 320, 'Press any key to continue...');
```

The biggest headache for novices in graphics is the output of numerical information, as the graphics mode isn't able to deal with such operations. The only way you can overcome this problem is to convert the digit into a string using the **Str** procedure, then include it in the output string using **+** :

```
Max := 34.56;
Str(Max:6:2, Smax);  { Max - real, Smax - string }
OutPutXY(400, 40, 'Max = ' + Smax);
```

To get a high quality display of text output on the screen you must use different fonts. The possible fonts are shown in Table 16-3. In order to set different fonts you use the procedure **SetTextStyle**:

```
SetTextStyle (Font: word; Direction: word;
                                    CharSize: word)
```

where **Font** is a closed font, **Direction** is a horizontal or vertical direction, and **CharSize** is the size of the output characters. Possible values of the first two parameters are shown in Tables 16-3, 16-4. As far as vertical output is concerned you should remember that if you do not specify starting points (using the **MoveTo** procedure) the output will start from the last bottom line up to the top. The size of output characters is set by the **CharSize** variable. If **CharSize** = **1** then an 8x8 matrix will be used, if **CharSize** = **2** then 16x16 and so on.

Constant	Value	Description
DefaultFont	0	Bit-mapped 8x8 font
TriplexFont	1	Stroked triplex font
SmallFont	2	Stroked small font
SansSerifFont	3	Stroked sans serif font
GothicFont	4	Stroked gothic font

Table 16-3
The Standard Graphics Text Fonts

Constant	*Value*	*Description*
HorizDir	0	Left to right
VertDir	1	Bottom to top

Table 16-4
Text Direction

As an example, we'll show you how to output a vertical and horizontal string with different character sizes by using the **DefaultFont**:

```
SetTextStyle(0, 1, 1); { standard letter size }
OutTextXY(200, 200, 'Vertical string');
SetTextStyle(0, 0, 2); { enlarged letter size }
OutTextXY(200, 220, 'Horizontal string');
```

When you are setting the font it is possible that an error will occur. All error codes are shown in Table 16-2. Error codes are returned by **GraphResult**:

```
IF GraphResult <> grOK THEN
              Writeln('Error in SetTextStyle!');
```

Quite often you will need to know the current setting of the output string. In this case, the **TextHeight(TextString: string)** and **TextWidth(TextString: string)** functions will return the height and the width in pixels of an output string.

Another frequent requirement is the need to justify one character in relation to another. For example, if you want to write X^2 the character **2** must be output above the character **X**. Justification is started from the current **CP** position.

The **SetTextJustify(Horiz, Vert: word)** procedure ensures horizontal and vertical text justification according to the **Horiz** and **Vert** values. Constants for text justification are shown in Table 16-5.

Horizontal justification		Vertical justification	
Constant	*Value*	*Constant*	*Value*
LeftText	0	BottomText	0
CenterText	1	CenterText	1
RightText	2	TopText	2

Table 16-5.
Graphics Text Justification

The example demonstrates how to output X^2:

```
SetTextJustify(CenterText, CenterText);
OutTextXY(100, 100, 'X');
SetTextJustify(CenterText,BottomText);
OutTextXY(108, 100, '2');
```

Using justification you can output any formula.

Graphic Windows

As in the text modes you can think of the whole graphic screen as one or more windows. You must remember however that a window performs all the functions of the full screen. When you define a window the remaining section of the screen disappears and you cannot use it for any input/output until the current window is active. If there is more than one window on the screen you have to switch between the windows yourself when inputting and outputting. By default, the active window covers the full screen. Windows are set by the following procedure:

```
SetViewPort (X1, Y1, X2, Y2: integer; Clip:boolean)
```

where **X1, Y1** are the top left corner coordinates and X2, Y2 are the bottom right corner coordinates. If **Clip = True** then output will be restricted outside the window, if **Clip = False** then the output will be extended beyond the boundaries of the window. In any window the top left pixel has internal coordinates **(0,0).**

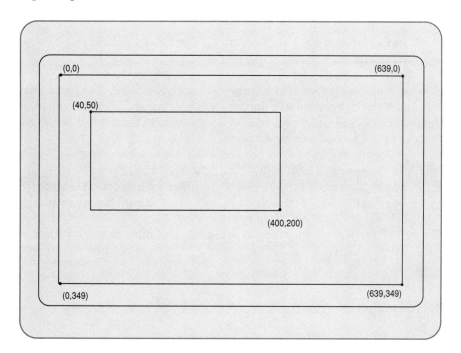

Figure 16-2
**SetViewPort
(40, 50, 400,
200)**

For example:

```
SetViewPort(40, 50, 400, 200, True);
```

The procedure **ClearViewPort** clears the current active window. All drawings are cleared and the **Current Pointer** is set on the pixel with **(0,0)** coordinates.

```
FOR I:= 1 TO 10000 DO
   PutPixel(Random(639),Random(199),LightGreen);
                                  { fill screen }
SetViewPort(40, 50, 400, 200, True);
                                  { set window }
ClearViewPort; { clearing only current window }
OutText('Output to the clearing window');
```

Remember that we are referring to the internal window coordinates here, not the screen one! The procedure **ClearDevice** restores the full screen window and clears it. You can perform the same action with the following statements:

```
SetViewPort(0, 0, GetMaxX, GetMaxY, True);
ClearDevice;
```

You should remember that unlike text windows the **SetBkColor** procedure sets a background color for the whole screen. In order to change the background of an active window only, you have to fill it with the **SetFillStyle** and **Bar** procedures:

```
SetViewPort(100, 50, 500, 200, True);
SetFillStyle(1, 3);      { choose background style }
Bar(100, 50, 500, 200);          { draw background }
```

The rest of the work with graphics windows is similar to work with text ones. As an example, here's a program that produces random sound and color effects:

```
PROGRAM DemoSetViewPort;
USES Crt, Graph;
VAR
  DriverVar, ModeVar, I: integer;
BEGIN
  DriverVar := Detect;
  InitGraph(DriverVar, ModeVar, '');
  SetViewPort(10, 10, 630, 320, True);      { choose window }
  I := 1;
  REPEAT
    I := I+1;
    Sound(Random(180)+40 +I);                 { generate random sound }
    Delay(Random(170));
    SetFillStyle(Random(4),Random(16));    {choose random fill style}
    Bar(10, 10, 630, 320);
    NoSound;                                   { break sound }
    Delay(100)
  UNTIL KeyPressed;
  Readln;
  CloseGraph;
END.
```

Switching Between Text and Graphics Modes

Turbo Pascal has two procedures that will ease the task of working with text and graphics modes at the same time.

SetGraphMode (CurrentMode) restores the graphic mode number **CurrentMode** and **RestoreCrtMode** restores last text mode. As an example test the following program:

```
PROGRAM DemoTextGraph;
USES Crt, Graph;
VAR
  DriverVar, ModeVar, CurrentMode: integer;
BEGIN
  ClrScr;
  Writeln('Text mode');
  ...
  Readln;
  DriverVar := Detect;
  InitGraph(DriverVar, ModeVar, '');
  OutTextXY(300, 250, 'Graphic mode');
  CurrentMode := GetGraphMode;
  ...
  Readln;
  RestoreCrtMode;
  Writeln('Text mode !');
  ...
  Readln;
  SetGraphMode(CurrentMode);
  OutTextXY(300, 250, 'Graphic mode !');
  ...
  Readln;
  CloseGraph
END.
```

Bar Drawing

Most of the other procedures are used for drawing various figures, such as rectangles, circles, ellipses, etc. The procedure **Rectangle** draws a rectangle:

```
Rectangle (X1, Y1, X2, Y2: integer);
```

where **X1, Y1** are coordinates of the left top angle, and **X2, Y2** are coordinates of the right bottom angle. This procedure is very useful for drawing various diagrams. Here's a small example which will output 100 dynamically changing rectangles:

```
SetColor(Green);
FOR I := 1 TO 100 DO BEGIN
  Rectangle(200, Random(300), 250, 300);
  Delay(50);
  ClearDevice
END;
```

In this example the rectangle's height changes at random (the second parameter is random 300). We can take it from an integer array (for example, the amount of a monthly payment). In this way we will display the dynamics of the data. This principle is used in many animation programs. Procedure **Bar (X1, Y1, X2, Y2: integer**) draws a rectangle and fills it with a particular style from Table 16-6. Fill style and its color is set by the **SetFillStyle** procedure. As an example we will draw a rectangle and fill it with the yellow **SlashFill** style:

```
SetFillStyle(SlashFill, Yellow);
Bar(10, 10, 50, 150);
```

Constant	Value	Description
EmptyFill	0	Background color
SolidFill	1	Solid fill
LineFill	2	Lines (—)
LtSlashFill	3	Slashes(///)
SlashFill	4	Slashes(///), thick

Table 16-6.
Fill Pattern

BkslashFill	5	Slashes (\\\\), thick
LtbkSlashFill	6	Slashes (\\\\)
HatchFill	7	Light crosshatch
XhatchFill	8	Heavy crosshatch
InterLeaveFill	9	Interleaving lines
WideDotFill	10	Wide-spaced dots
CloseDotFill	11	Close-spaced dots
UserFill	12	User-defined pattern

Table 16-6
*Fill Pattern
(continued)*

Procedure **Bar3D (X1, Y1, X2, Y2: integer; Depth: word; Top: boolean)** draws a more attractive 3-dimensional bar. The **Depth** parameter specifies the depth of the 3-dimensional rectangle, for example:

```
Depth := (X2-X1) DIV 4;
```

produces a good result. If **Top = True** the procedure draws the top of the bar. For example:

```
SetFillStyle(SolidFill, Green);
Bar3D(10, 10, 50, 100, 10, True);
```

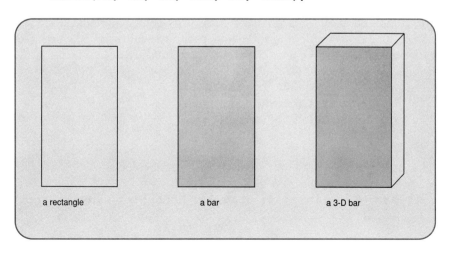

a rectangle   a bar   a 3-D bar

Figure 16-3
**The Results
of the
Procedures,
Rectangle,
Bar and
Bar3D.**

Circles, Arcs and Sectors

For drawing circles, arcs and ellipses you need to set the following parameters: center coordinates, radius and angles (see Figure 16-4).

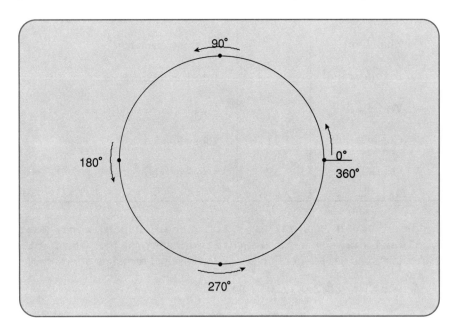

Figure 16-4
**Polar
Coordinate
System**

Using various circles and pie charts will make your business program more understandable and more attractive to look at. The procedure **Circle (X, Y: integer; Radius: word)** draws a circle using the current color. Parameters **X, Y** are coordinates of its center and **Radius** sets its radius. For example, the following program will draw 100 circles of random colors with central coordinates of **300, 150**:

```
FOR I:= 1 TO 100 DO BEGIN
  SetColor(Random(16));
  Circle(300, 150, 100-I)
END;
```

The procedure **Arc** draws an arc with the current color:

```
Arc (X, Y: integer; StAngle, EndAngle, Radius: word)
```

where **X,Y** are center coordinates, **StAngle** is the start angle, **EndAngle** is the end angle and **Radius** is its radius. It is quite clear that the **Arc** procedure with **StAngle = 0** and **EndAngle = 360** will draw a circle. As an example we will a draw red arc with **StAngle = 0**, **EndAngle = 90** in the circle:

```
SetColor(LightGreen);
Circle(450, 100, 50);
Setcolor(LightRed);
Arc(450, 100, 0, 90, 50);
```

Procedure **Ellipse** draws an ellipse:

Ellipse(X, Y:integer; StAngle, EndAngle:word; Xr, Yr: word)

where **X,Y** are center screen coordinates, **Xr** and **Yr** specify the width and height of the ellipse, respectively. Ellipses are drawn from **StAngle** to **EndAngle**. Settings **StAngle = 0** and **EndAngle = 360** will result in a complete ellipse being drawn. The following statement draws a complete light cyan ellipse:

```
SetColor(LightCyan);
Ellipse(100, 100, 0, 360, 60, 30);
```

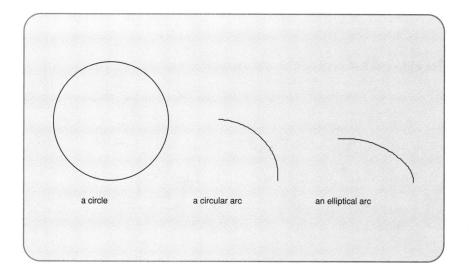

a circle   a circular arc   an elliptical arc

Figure 16-5
**The Results
of the
Procedures,
Circle, Arc
and Ellipse**

The procedure **Ellipse** does not change the background color inside the ellipse. To do this you have to use the **FillEllipse** procedure:

```
FillEllipse (X, Y: integer; Xr, Yr: word)
```

where **X,Y** are the ellipse center coordinates, and **Xr** and **Yr** are the width and height of the oval. The fill style is set by the **SetFillStyle** procedure:

```
SetFillStyle(WideDotFill, Green); { style setting }
SetColor(LightRed);               { color of style }
FillEllipse(300, 150, 60, 30);
```

In this example the ellipse is drawn in red and filled in using the standard **WideDotFill** style (see Table 16-6).

While making diagrams you will often need to draw a sector of a circle, for which you use the procedure **PieSlice**:

```
PieSlice(X, Y: integer; StAngle, EndAngle, Radius: word)
```

where **X,Y** are center coordinates, the sector is drawn from the **StAngle** to the **EndAngle**. The sector outline is the current color and is filled in by the current fill style:

```
SetFillStyle(10, LightGreen); { set fill style }
SetColor(12);                 { set color }
PieSlice(100, 100, 0, 90, 50);
```

The ellipse sector is drawn by the **Sector** procedure:

```
Sector (X, Y: integer; StAngle, EndAngle, Xr, Yr: word)
```

The parameters are identical to and have the same effects as the parameters for **Ellipse**. The sector is filled by the current fill style:

```
SetFillStyle(CloseDotFill, LightBlue);
                             { set fill style }
SetColor(LightMagenta);  { set color }
Sector(300, 150, 180, 135, 60, 70);
```

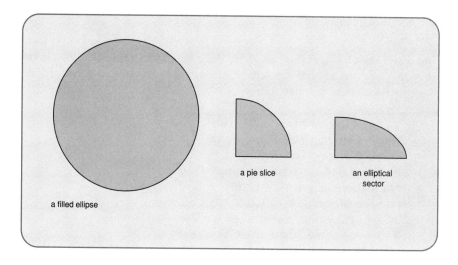

a pie slice

an elliptical
sector

a filled ellipse

Figure 16-6
**The Results
of the
Procedures,
FillEllipse,
PieSlice and
Sector.**

Circles, arcs and pie slices may not appear to be round for different types of graphics devices. The aspect ratio is the ratio of horizontal pixels to vertical pixels allowing you to draw a properly proportioned graphic display. The procedure:

```
GetAspectRatio (VAR Xasp, Yasp: word)
```

returns two word values, **Xasp** and **Yasp**. You may divide **Xasp** by **Yasp** to determine the ratio for your equipment. The example below (see the **Pie** procedure) shows how to use **GetAspectRatio**.

We'll now put these graphics procedures into practical implementation. There are two sorts of graphics programming: **traditional** and **object-oriented**. So that we don't put off any inexperienced programmers, we'll only consider the former, traditional way.

Business Graphics

Commercial and scientific applications usually contain a lot of various different tables, graphs and diagrams which make explanations more understandable and attractive looking. Tables are usually drawn in the text modes, but for high-quality graphs and diagrams you obviously need to use the graphics mode.

The Coordinate System

The **coordinate system** provides the base of all graphs, so it's a good idea to design a special **Coord** procedure for drawing the coordinate system. Its parameters are as follows:

start point coordinates (X0, Y0);
graduation step size in pixels on X (Sx);
number of steps on X (Cx);
integer value for first step on X (Vx);
graduation step size in pixels on Y (Sy);
number of steps on Y (Cy);
integer value for first step on Y (Vy);
X, Y axes names (NameX, NameY);
axis color and axis names color (ColorC, ColorN).

The named parameters completely defined the **two-dimensional coordinate system**. The only problem is to customize the graduation size of the pixels to a particular graphics driver. The procedure **Coord** is rather simple:

```
PROCEDURE Coord(X0, Y0, Sx, Cx, Vx, Sy, Cy, Vy: integer;
                NameX, NameY: string; ColorC, ColorN: word);
VAR
  St: string[6];
  I, J: word;
BEGIN
  SetColor(ColorC);       { set the color of the X and Y axes }
  Line(X0, Y0, X0+Sx*Cx, Y0);              { outputs X axis }
  SetTextJustify(CenterText, TopText);
  FOR I:=1 TO Cx DO BEGIN              { graduates the X axis }
    J := X0+Sx*I;   Line(J, Y0-2, J, Y0+2);
    Str(Vx*I, St);       { convert the number into a string }
    OutTextXY(J, Y0+8, St);
  END;
  Line(X0, Y0, X0, Y0-Sy*Cy);              { outputs the Y axis }
  SetTextJustify(RightText, CenterText);
  FOR I:=1 TO Cy DO BEGIN              { graduates the Y axis }
    J := Y0-Sy*I;   Line(X0-2, J, X0+2, J);
    Str(Vy*I, St);       { convert the number into a string }
    OutTextXY(X0-4, J, St);
  END;
```

```
   SetColor(ColorN);                   { set the color of the name }
   IF (TextWidth(NameY) DIV 2) >= X0 THEN BEGIN
     I := LeftText;
     J := 1;   END
   ELSE BEGIN
     I := CenterText;
     J := X0;
   END;
   SetTextJustify(I, CenterText);     { output the axes names }
   OutTextXY(J, Y0-Sy*Cy-20, NameY);
   SetTextJustify(LeftText, CenterText);
   OutTextXY(X0+Sx*Cx+10, Y0, NameX);
 END;    { Coord }
```

In order to simplify the program we have omitted the testing of input parameters. So you have to be careful when using this procedure. We will show an example with **Coord** call in the **DemoChart** sections later.

Drawing Bar Charts

The simplest **bar chart** is made up of columns, and to draw these you use **Bar** and **Rectangle** procedures. The first column should ideally have **X+n, Y** coordinates so that it does not cover the **Y** axis. We will design a special procedure **Chart** for drawing a bar chart. Its parameters are as follows:

> bar chart start point (X0,Y0);
> graduation size in pixels on X (Sx);
> number of graduations on X (Cx);
> column width in pixels on X (Wx) ;
> graduation size in pixels on Y (Sy);
> array of column Y coordinates (Values);
> column color (ColorBar);
> column fill style (FillCode).

The **Coord** and **Chart** procedures have the same parameters because they must correspond to each other on the screen. The **Wx** parameter allows you to place more than one column in each graduation on the X axis. The procedure **Chart** will look like this:

```
PROCEDURE Chart(X0, Y0, Sx, Cx, Wx, Sy, Vy: integer;
             VAR Values; ColorBar, FillCode: word);
VAR
  ArrY: array[1..50] of integer ABSOLUTE Values;
  I, X2, Y2: integer;
BEGIN
  SetFillStyle(FillCode, ColorBar);
  SetColor(ColorBar);
  FOR I := 1 TO Cx DO BEGIN
    IF ArrY[I] > 0 THEN BEGIN
      X2 := X0+Wx;
      Y2 := Y0-Trunc((ArrY[I]/Vy)*Sy);
      Bar(X0, Y0, X2, Y2);
      Rectangle(X0, Y0, X2, Y2);
    END;
    X0 := X0+Sx;
  END;
END; { Chart }
```

Here we used the **ArrY** array as an untyped values array. **ArrY** is allocated in the same place as the **Values** array, which is achieved using the **ABSOLUTE** specifier. The **ColorBar** and **FillCode** parameters allows you to display various diagrams in different colors at the same time. As an example you could create some bar charts for our HomeFinances program:

```
PROGRAM DemoChart;
USES Graph;
CONST
  Cx = 12;     { 12 months }
  Cy = 10;   Max = 10000;
  NameX = 'X month';   NameY = 'sum Y';
TYPE  ArrInt = array[1..Cx] of integer;
```

```
CONST
  InData : ArrInt = (7000,7000,7500,7500,8500,7500,
     7000,7500,9000,8000,7000,8500);
  ExpData : ArrInt = (6000,6500,7000,7000,9000,5000,
      6500,6000,6500,6500,6000,6000);
VAR
  X0, Y0, Sx, Wx, Sy, Vy, J,
  DriverVar, ModeVar, X, Y, W, H: integer;

{ source text of the Coord procedure }
{ source text of the Chart procedure }

BEGIN   { DemoChart }
  DriverVar := Detect;
  InitGraph(DriverVar, ModeVar, '');
  Vy := Max DIV Cy;
  J := TextHeight('N');
  Y0 := GetMaxY -J*6;   X0 := GetMaxX DIV 12;
  Sx := (GetMaxX -X0*5) DIV Cx;
  Sy := (GetMaxY -J*(6+12+4)) DIV Cy;
  { output system coordinates }
  Coord(X0, Y0, Sx, Cx, 1, Sy, Cy, Vy,
            NameX, NameY, Cyan, LightRed);
  Wx := (Sx -12) DIV 2;                { column width }
  Chart(X0+4, Y0, Sx, Cx, Wx, Sy, Vy,
            InData, LightCyan, LtSlashFill);
  X := X0 +Sx*Cx+10;   Y := Y0 -Sy*(Cy-2);
  W := 40;  H := J*2;
  Bar(X, Y, X+W, Y+H);  Rectangle(X, Y, X+W, Y+H);
  SetTextJustify(LeftText, CenterText);
  OutTextXY(X+W+4, Y +H DIV 2, 'Income');   { output the name }
  Chart(X0+8+Wx, Y0, Sx, Cx, Wx, Sy, Vy,
                ExpData, LightGreen, SolidFill);
  Y := Y +H +J;
  Bar(X, Y, X+W, Y+H);  Rectangle(X, Y, X+W, Y+H);
  SetTextJustify(LeftText, CenterText);
  OutTextXY(X+W+4, Y +H DIV 2, 'Expense');  { output the name }
  Readln;
  CloseGraph;
END.   { DemoChart }
```

Figure 16-7 shows the result of **DemoChart** execution:

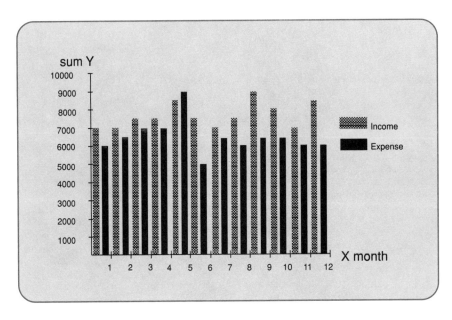

Figure 16-7
Two-Dimensional Bar Chart

The HomeFinances program (see Appendix A) contains the **DrawChart** procedure which is similar to the **DemoChart** program considered above. The only difference is that **DemoChart** uses constants as input data and **DrawChart** reads data from **BASE.DTA** file. You can use the **Bar3D** procedure instead of the **Bar** and **Rectangle**, in which case you will get a 3-dimensional column. The only problem is placing the columns in order to produce a 3-dimensional effect.

Drawing Pie Charts

There is yet another way you can approach sector diagrams for representing information. Sometimes you will want to divide an object into parts and display information in percentages. In this case the whole object will be displayed by the circle and its components will be shown as a sector of corresponding size. The sector size is directly proportional to the component. The **sector diagram** will be drawn by the **Pie** procedure and its parameters are as follows:

> starting point coordinates (X,Y);
> sector radius in pixels (Radius);
> number of sector or components (Count);

array of percentage of each component (Percents);
array of component names (Names).

Each sector will be drawn with its own color and fill style. On the right hand side of the diagram an identification column will be displayed. Here is the text of the **Pie** procedure:

```
PROCEDURE Pie(X, Y, Radius, Count: integer; VAR Percents, Names);
CONST  MaxValues = 30;
VAR
   ArrPer: array[1..MaxValues] of byte ABSOLUTE Percents;
   ArrNames: array[1..MaxValues] of MenuStr ABSOLUTE Names;
   MaxColor, FillPie, ColorPie, Xasp, Yasp,
   Angle, AngleMed, AngleCur: word;
   Xb, Yb, Wb, Hb, Xp, Yp, Psum, I: integer;
   Radians: real;
   St : string[5];
BEGIN
   Angle := 0;    { the first corner of the diagram }
   FillPie := SolidFill;   ColorPie := Blue; { first values }
   GetAspectRatio(Xasp, Yasp); { relational X and Y coordinates }
   MaxColor := GetMaxColor;   Psum := 0;
   Xb := X+Radius+30;
   Yb := Y -Round(Radius*Xasp/Yasp) +30;
   Wb := 50;   Hb := TextHeight('N')*2;
   FOR I := 1 TO Count DO BEGIN
     IF I = Count THEN BEGIN    { final sector }
       ArrPer[I] := 100 -Psum;
       AngleCur := 360 -Angle;  END
     ELSE
       AngleCur := Round(ArrPer[I]*3.6); { reorganizes }
     AngleMed := AngleCur DIV 2 +Angle; { middle corner sector }
     Radians := AngleMed*Pi/180;
     SetFillStyle(FillPie, ColorPie);
     PieSlice(X, Y, Angle, Angle+AngleCur, Radius);
     Angle := Angle +AngleCur;
     Psum := Psum +ArrPer[I];
     { calculates the boundary coordinates of the sector
                            and outputs the percentage }
     Xp := X +Round(Cos(Radians) *Radius);
     Yp := Y -Round((Xasp/Yasp)*Round(Sin(Radians) *Radius));
     IF AngleMed < 90 THEN
       SetTextJustify(LeftText, BottomText)
     ELSE IF AngleMed < 180 THEN
       SetTextJustify(RightText, BottomText)
     ELSE IF AngleMed < 270 THEN
       SetTextJustify(RightText, TopText)
     ELSE  SetTextJustify(LeftText, TopText);
     Str(ArrPer[I], St);
     OutTextXY(Xp, Yp, St+' %');
```

```
      IF FillPie < CloseDotFill THEN   Inc(FillPie);
      IF ColorPie < MaxColor THEN   Inc(ColorPie);
      { outputs the sector name }
      Bar(Xb, Yb, Xb+Wb, Yb+Hb);
      Rectangle(Xb, Yb, Xb+Wb, Yb+Hb);
      SetTextJustify(LeftText, CenterText);
      { output the name }
      OutTextXY(Xb+Wb+4, Yb+ Hb DIV 2, ArrNames[I]);
      Yb := Yb+Hb*2;
    END;
END;  { Pie }
```

Here we have use of the **ABSOLUTE** specifier to set the untyped arrays
Percents and **Names**. MenuStr type was defined in the **Service** unit
(see Chapter 15), and will be used in the HomeFinances program (see
Appendix A). You should also remember that we have omitted testing
the input parameters in this procedure.

As an example of how the **Pie** procedure is used we will demonstrate
the **DemoPie** program. The input data for this program will be items of
monthly expenditure. This data can easily be presented as a percentage
of the whole sum. The **DemoPie** program look like this:

```
PROGRAM DemoPie;
USES Graph;
TYPE  MenuStr = string[20];
CONST
  sExp = 7;
  aExp: array[1..sExp] of MenuStr = ('Food','Accommodation',
    'Clothing','Education','Medical care','Leisure','Other');
  Percents: array[1..sExp] of byte = (20, 45, 10, 10, 5, 5, 5);
VAR
  DriverVar, ModeVar, X, Y, Radius : integer;

{ source text of the Pie procedure }

BEGIN   { DemoPie }
  DriverVar := Detect;
  InitGraph(DriverVar, ModeVar, '');
  Y := GetMaxY DIV 2;
  X := GetMaxX DIV 2 - GetMaxX DIV 6;
  Radius := GetMaxX DIV 4;
  SetColor(GetMaxColor);
  Pie(X, Y, Radius, sExp, Percents, aExp);
  Readln;
  CloseGraph;
END.   { DemoPie }
```

Figure 16-8 shows the result of **DemoPie** execution:

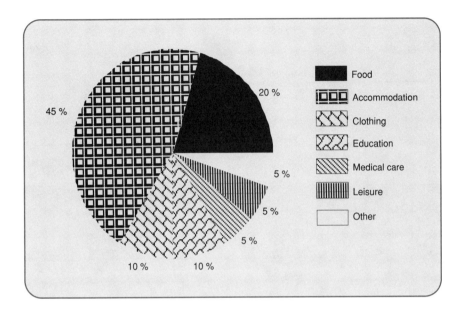

Figure 16-8
Pie chart

The HomeFinances program contains the **DrawPie** procedure which is similar to the condensed **DemoPie** one. The only difference is that **DrawPie** reads data from the **BASE.DTA** file.

All the business graphics techniques that we have looked at will mean that you can add good illustrations to various commercial and scientific applications.

CHAPTER 17

OBJECT ORIENTED PROGRAMMING

Introduction

What we have looked at so far can be characterized as traditional structured programming. It is based on the sequential completion of steps, dealing with data which corresponds to given algorithms. These steps are carried out according to specific rules and given operators: **BEGIN..END, IF..ELSE, WHILE..DO, FOR..DO, REPEAT..UNTIL.** Actions that are repeated frequently can be grouped into separate procedures and functions. Complex data types can be presented in the form of records, which correspond to a higher level-data abstraction.

Nowadays, the complexity of programs increases at such a fast rate, that we need to be able to modify our procedures and functions accordingly. This obviously takes a lot of time, and is very expensive, which is one of the reasons why **object-oriented programming (OOP)** was developed. The first languages to use OOP features such as Simula 67 and Smalltalk, laid down the foundations for developing programming languages in general.

There are three main features to object-oriented programming:

    Encapsulation: the linking of records with procedures and functions which are called **methods**, to create a new type of data - **object**.

    Inheritance: the use of a particular object to build a hierarchy of similar objects which are all descendants of data and methods from one ancestor.

    Polymorphism: this feature allows you to create an object which can take on the form of other objects within the hierarchy. This object is known as a **polymorphal object**.

Now, instead of having to recreate a program from the beginning, using OOP you can select certain objects, data and methods which are more or less suited to the task in hand. Once you have done this you simply need to expand the relevant objects to complete your work.

It is these features which allow OOP to make a programmer's work more effective, in as much as you are only required to develop new objects, and don't need to waste time re-working the old ones. In this chapter, and the next one, we will demonstrate how easy it is to follow the characteristics of one object to create a new one.

Turbo Pascal has a unique characteristic which allows you to use OOP to its full capability. The features which support OOP in Turbo Pascal are so well developed, that if you need to use another language for some reason, you will always be able to recognize OOP features by drawing on your knowledge of Turbo Pascal.

This chapter is intended to help you understand how OOP works, and to prepare you for working with the object-oriented library Turbo Vision (see Chapter 18). Remember that OOP is becoming more and more influential (evidence of this can be taken from the appearance of new OOP versions of popular compilers). This isn't just a passing phase, OOP is the future as far as programming is concerned. So, don't put off getting to grips with OOP - now's your chance!

It remains to add that the material given in previous chapters by no means excludes the use of OOP. The choice of which programming technique you employ is up to you.

Objects

Object type data allows you to operate both with data and with the functions that process the data. You define an object type using the reserved words **OBJECT** and **END**. Objects are similar to standard records, but they also have their own procedures and functions called **methods**.

This unification of data fields, procedures and functions is called **encapsulation**. Encapsulation sets fixed ties between data and its processing within the object. This is one of the most important features of OOP.

```
TYPE
  NameStr = string[25];
  CompStr = string[30];
  PersonType = OBJECT
    Name : NameStr;
    Company : CompStr;
    PROCEDURE Init(Nm:NameStr; Cmp:CompStr);
    PROCEDURE Show;
    FUNCTION GetName : NameStr;
  END;
```

Here, **PersonType** is an object type. It has **Name** and **Company** data fields and **Init**, **Show** and **GetName** methods. The **Init** method sets the **Name** and **Company** fields, the **Show** method displays the object fields on the screen and the **Getname** method gets the **Name** field value.

```
TYPE
  PhoneStr = string[15];
  PhoneType  = OBJECT(PersonType)
    Phone : PhoneStr;
    PROCEDURE Init(Nm:NameStr;
                   Cmp:CompStr; Ph:PhoneStr);
    PROCEDURE Show;
    FUNCTION GetPhone : PhoneStr;
  END;
```

The **PhoneType** object type is based on **PersonType**. This is made clear by the fact that the **PersonType** appears in parentheses after the reserved word **OBJECT**. The **PhoneType** inherits all the **PersonType** definitions (see Figure 17-1) and has its own **Phone** data field and **GetPhone** method. The new **GetPhone** method gets the **Phone** field value.

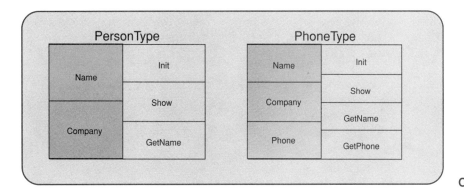

Figure 17-1
**PersonType
and
PhoneType
Object Types**

Now you can declare an object or a type instance. This type of declaration is similar to ordinary variable declaration:

```
VAR
  WorkPerson : PersonType;
```

The **WorkPerson** object is now allocated in the memory and you can access its fields just as you would access record fields. The **WITH** statement can also be used.

```
WorkPerson.Name := '';
WITH WorkPerson DO BEGIN
  Name := 'Bill Bricks';
  Company := 'Housing International';
END;
```

You should be aware, however, that this method of direct access is not the best way of initializing the object fields. Direct access puts objects on the same level as records, which narrows its application area. One of the basic principles of OOP is that object operating is mostly determined by methods. According to this principle, the **Init** method performs object field initialization, and the **GetName** and **GetPhone** methods return field values. Programming this way, you can avoid direct access to the object fields.

Methods

The procedures and functions which are used for operating object data fields are called **methods**. You declare method titles in the object type in the same way as you declare ordinary procedures and functions in the **INTERFACE** section for units.

Different object types may have methods with similar names, so to avoid confusion, the object type is specified first. Type and name are separated by a full stop:

```
PROCEDURE PersonType.Init (Nm:NameStr; Cmp:CompStr);
BEGIN
  Name := Nm;
  Company := Cmp;
END;    { Init }

PROCEDURE PersonType.Show;
```

```
BEGIN
  Writeln;
  Writeln('NAME: ', Name);
  Writeln('COMPANY: ', Company);
END;    { Show }


FUNCTION PersonType.GetName : NameStr;
BEGIN
  GetName := Name;
END;    { GetName }
```

The notation **PersonType.Init** shows the compiler that the **Init** method belongs to the **PersonType** object type. Inside the method, you can access object fields without type specification, as ordinary variables. In reality Turbo Pascal uses a pseudo-variable **Self** for object type specification. So, the text of the **Init** procedure will look like this:

```
PROCEDURE PersonType.Init (Nm:NameStr; Cmp:CompStr);
BEGIN
  Self.Name := Nm;
  Self.Company := Cmp;
END;    { Init }
```

When you perform the **Init** method:

WorkPerson.Init('Bill Bricks', 'Housing International');

the compiler will replace the pseudo-variable **Self** with the concrete **WorkPerson** instance specification and initialize its fields. In most cases you can omit the **Self** specification and the compiler will insert it automatically. However, you will sometimes have to use **Self** in order to avoid ambiguity. For example, when you have a field and variable with similar names:

```
VAR
  Name : string[80];              { global variable }

PROCEDURE PersonType.Init (Nm:NameStr; Cmp:CompStr);
BEGIN
  Self.Name := Nm; {use Self to resolve
                            identifier conflict}
  Company := Cmp;
END;    { Init }
```

Inheritance

An object that inherits characteristics of another object is called a **descendant**; the parent object is called an **ancestor**. In our example the **PhoneType** object type is an **immediate descendant** of the **PersonType** object type. If we then create the **ConnectionType** type based on the **Phonetype**, this new type will also be a descendant of the **PersonType**, but not an immediate descendant. Using one parent type you can create a whole family tree. For example:

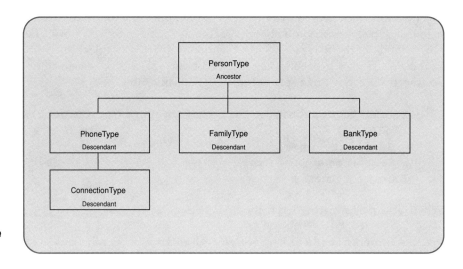

Figure 17-2
The Object Tree of the PersonType Type

There are two kinds of inheritance: **field inheritance** and **method inheritance**. As far as field inheritance is concerned, remember that every descendant inherits all its ancestor's fields without any additional definition. As we have already mentioned, the **PhoneType** inherits the **Name** and **Company** fields from the **PersonType**.

Method inheritance is not so simple. The **PhoneType** inherits 3 methods from the **PersonType**: **Init**, **Show** and **GetName**. By definition the **Init** method initializes two fields of the **PersonType**, the **Show** method outputs their values on the screen, and the **GetName** returns the **Name** value. While working with the **PhoneType** you will have to operate with one more field, the **Phone**, which means that you will have to alter the initialization and output methods. You can rewrite them like this:

```
PROCEDURE PhoneType.Init(Nm:NameStr;
                         Cmp:CompStr; Ph:PhoneStr);
BEGIN
  PersonType.Init(Nm, Cmp); { initialization
                        of PersonType fields }
  Phone := Ph;
END;    { Init }


PROCEDURE PhoneType.Show;
BEGIN
  PersonType.Show;
  Writeln('PHONE: ', Phone);
END;    { Show }
```

In your text you should use calls that correspond to the parent methods of the **PersonType**. You can also include new methods for the **PhoneType**:

```
FUNCTION PhoneType.GetPhone : PhoneStr;
BEGIN
  GetPhone := Phone;
END;    { GetPhone }
```

The **Getname** method is unchangeable when it is inherited. Now you need to declare the object variable:

```
VAR
 WorkPhone : PhoneType;
```

and use its methods:

```
WorkPhone.Init('Bill Bricks',
         'Housing International','111-111-1111');
WorkPhone.Show;
```

This example shows another characteristic feature of OOP. Method inheritance implies the inheritance of certain logic functions without actually showing concrete implementation. For example, we use the **Init** method for field initialization in both the **PersonType** and **PhoneType** objects. The **Init** method for these two types has a similar name and logic function, but is implemented differently.

Object Application in Units

Unit structure is very useful for the representation of object hierarchy. Object types will be defined in the **INTERFACE** section, and methods will be described in the **IMPLEMENTATION** section. There are some common rules you should be aware of when creating objects in units:

1. All object types that you intend to use in a unit should be declared in the **INTERFACE** section.

2. All object types for internal use should be declared and placed in the **IMPLEMENTATION** section.

3. If B unit uses A unit, you can create descendants of any A object type in the B unit.

In the following example we'll assemble the **PhoneType** and the **PersonType** definition in the **ObjPhone** unit:

```
UNIT  ObjPhone;
INTERFACE
TYPE
   ...
   < the definition for PersonType and PhoneType>
   ...
IMPLEMENTATION
   ...
   < method definition for  PersonType
                                  and  PhoneType>
   ...
BEGIN
END.
```

The program that was used to activate the above methods looks like this:

```
PROGRAM  Phones;
USES  ObjPhone;
VAR
   WorkPerson  :  PersonType;
   WorkPhone   :  PhoneType;
```

```
BEGIN
  WorkPerson.Init('Bill Bricks','Housing International');
  WorkPerson.Show;
  WITH WorkPhone DO BEGIN
   Init('Bill Bricks','Housing International', '111-111-1111');
    Show;
    Writeln(GetPhone, '    ', GetName);
  END;
END.
```

When including the **ObjPhone** unit you gain access to any object type declared in the **INTERFACE** section. There is no need for you to study the method body in the **IMPLEMENTATION** section, it is quite enough for you to deal with method declaration in the **INTERFACE** section, and determine whether a method is suitable for solving a particular task. This kind of approach is characteristic of OOP programming.

NAME: Bill Bricks
COMPANY: Housing International

NAME: Bill Bricks
COMPANY: Housing International
PHONE: 111-111-1111
111-111-1111   Bill Bricks

Figure 17-3
**Result of the
Phones
Program**

Private Directive

The **PRIVATE** directive which limits the access rights to fields and methods first appeared in Turbo Pascal 6.0. Fields and methods are declared with the reserved word **PRIVATE** and are only accessible within the unit where the object is declared. These fields and methods are consequently called **private**, all the others are called **public**. Private declarations are always placed after public ones. The example below shows how you can change the **PersonType** definition:

```
TYPE
   PersonType = OBJECT { public definition }
      Name : NameStr;
      Company : CompStr;
      PROCEDURE Init(Nm:NameStr; Cmp:CompStr);
      PROCEDURE Show;
      FUNCTION GetName : NameStr;
      FUNCTION IsUpperCase : boolean;
   PRIVATE { private definition }
      FlagUpperCase : boolean;
      FUNCTION UpString (St : string) : string;
   END;
```

The **UpString** method converts a string to the upper case. The **FlagUpperCase** is a flag for the **Show** method. The **UpString** and **FlagUpperCase** are private, and they are only accessible in the unit where they were defined. **IsUpperCase** is a public method and it returns the current value of the local **FlagUpperCase** field. So, you can think of the **FlagUpperCase** as being a "read only" field. We'll now rewrite the **ObjPhone** text so that the new version will only contain new and altered methods:

```
UNIT ObjPhone;
INTERFACE
TYPE
  < type definitions >
  ...
IMPLEMENTATION
  ...
  < method definitions >
  ...
PROCEDURE PersonType.Init (Nm: NameStr;
                                 Cmp: CompStr);
BEGIN
  Name := Nm;
  Company := Cmp;
  { set FlagUpperCase - the method Show
                          will output fields }
  { in the upper case }
  FlagUpperCase := True;
END;    { Init }
```

```
FUNCTION PersonType.IsUpperCase : Boolean;
BEGIN
  IsUpperCase := FlagUpperCase;
END;    { IsUpperCase }

PROCEDURE PersonType.Show;
BEGIN
  Writeln;
  Write('NAME: ');
  IF FlagUpperCase THEN Writeln(UpString(Name))
  ELSE Writeln(Name);
  Write('COMPANY: ');
  IF FlagUpperCase THEN Writeln(UpString(Company))
  ELSE Writeln(Company);
END; { Show }

FUNCTION PersonType.UpString(St : string) :
string;
  { converts string letters to upper case }
VAR  J : byte;
BEGIN
  FOR J := 1 TO Length(St) DO
    St[J] := UpCase(St[J]);
  UpString := St;
END;    { UpStr }
  . . .
  < old method definitions >
  . . .
BEGIN
END.
```

Now when you call the **Phones** program, the string fields will be displayed in upper-case letters (see Figure 17-4).

```
NAME:  BILL BRICKS
COMPANY: HOUSING INTERNATIONAL

NAME: BILL BRICKS
COMPANY: HOUSING INTERNATIONAL
PHONE: 111-111-1111
111-111-1111    BILL BRICKS
```

Figure 17-4
The Phones Program with the New ObjPhone Unit

This action is determined by the value of the private **FlagUpperCase** field. The value is assigned in the **PersonType.Init** method. The **FlagUpperCase** field is only visible in the **ObjPhones** unit, in the same way that any variable declared in the **IMPLEMENTATION** section (see Figure 17-5) is only visible in that section. If you try to access the **FlagUpperCase** field the compiler will generate an error message. Note that you can only operate the **FlagUpperCase** field within **PersonType** methods.

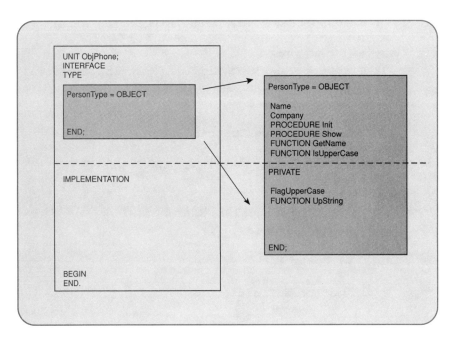

Figure 17-5
Access Rights in the ObjPhone Unit

Here are some reminders for the application of **PRIVATE** directives:

1. Try to declare only inner variables and functions that deal with this particular object type as private.

2. Declare all fields that you want to make "read-only" as private. Of course, you will have to create a public method to read this field. For example, the private **FlagUpperCase** field is read using the public **IsUpperCase** method.

Static Method

All the objects considered above are **static**, and the compiler allocates them in the memory as ordinary variables. The methods of such objects are also static. Static methods are closely linked with certain object types.

While defining an object type you should organize its methods as you would an ordinary procedural type. Each static method corresponds to a certain pointer in the object, and during the compilation process this pointer is placed on the method code. If an immediate object has no such method, the compiler looks for it on a higher level in the hierarchy, in the ancestor. Finally, if the root object has no such method, the compiler generates an error message.

To activate the ancestor method you have to write the ancestor type and method name separated by a full stop. For example, in the **PhoneType** object you can activate the **Init** method of the **PersonType** using the **PersonType.Init** notation.

Object Type Compatibility

The principles of object compatibility are very similar to the principles of inheritance. Each descendant inherits all the fields and methods of its ancestor. So, you can define all fields and methods of the **WorkPerson** object from those of the **WorkPhone's**. However, this does not work the other way round:

```
WorkPerson := WorkPhone; { it is right }
WorkPhone  := WorkPerson;{ it is wrong, Phone field  }
                         { cannot be defined }
```

Of course, it looks strange because you are assigning the greater object to the lesser one. Try to accept it though, you'll come across stranger things than this in OOP.

Polymorphism

Polymorphism is a term which is used to refer to the process which allows descendants to redefine the methods of parent objects. Object instances that take various representational forms during program execution are called **polymorphal objects**.

Polymorphism is implemented by **virtual methods** (all the methods we discussed above were static). You declare virtual methods using the reserved word **VIRTUAL**, for example:

```
PROCEDURE Show; VIRTUAL;
```

If the method is defined as virtual it can be redefined in any descendant of the parent object. Virtual methods usually perform the same logic actions although the implementation is different in each level of object hierarchy. For example, the virtual method **Show** performs the same actions for both **PersonType** and **PhoneType**, it outputs field values.

You must remember that when you are declaring a virtual method it has to be defined as virtual in all the descendants. If you don't do this, a compiling error will occur. There are some special actions which you must perform before using virtual methods. Object instance and static methods are bound during compilation (**early binding**), which is why any static method is automatically performed any time you call it in the program. Virtual methods are bound with the instance only during program execution (**late binding**). A special method called a **constructor** performs the actions necessary for the initialization of an object containing the virtual method. You have to activate the constructor before any other virtual methods.

The constructor sets the binding between the object instance and the virtual method with the help of a special internal table called the **Virtual Methods Table** (**VMT**). The VMT is created during the compilation of each object type which contains virtual methods. The VMT contains pointers to the executable code of the virtual methods. The constructor binds the object instance with the corresponding VMT. So, while calling virtual methods you first turn to the VMT and then to the method code (see Figure 17-6). The reason for this complex structure is that it enables you to use one of the most powerful tools of OOP, polymorphism.

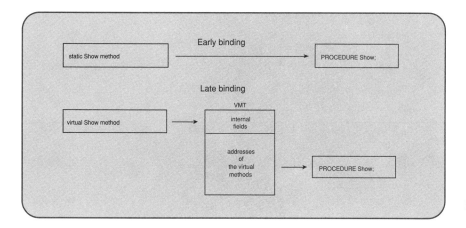

Figure 17-6
Early and Late Binding

We'll take a simple example of polymorphism. Here, you add the new **ShowToClearScr** method to the **PersonType**. This method clears the screen (using the standard **Crt** function **ClrScr**) and outputs the object fields:

```
PROCEDURE   PersonType.ShowToClearScr;
BEGIN
    ClrScr;
    Show;
END;          {  ShowToClearScr  }
```

Now we activate the new method:

```
WorkPhone.ShowToClearScr;
```

To everyone's astonishment, instead of the **PhoneType** field values, the **PersonType** fields values will be output. The **ShowToClearScr** method activates the **Show** method, which corresponds to the **PersonType** object.

If we declare the **Show** method virtual it will automatically be linked with the current object type (**PhoneType** in this case). Now the **WorkPhone** fields will be output on the screen. When the **Show** method is activated, the object type is automatically identified. Here the **PersonType** and the **PhoneType** can be considered as polymorphic. Note that virtual methods require a stricter declaration procedure. Their names and parameter list cannot be changed within the whole hierarchy.

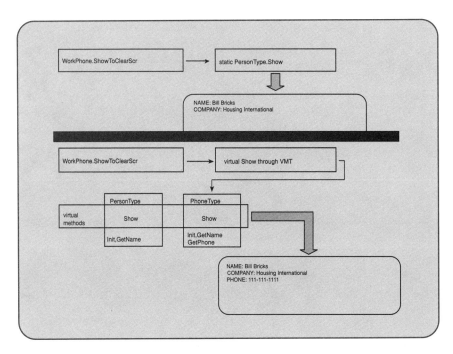

Figure 17-7
**Example of
Polymorphism**

Dynamic Objects

Object pointers are declared in the same way as ordinary pointers:

```
TYPE
  PersonTypePtr = ^PersonType;
  PhoneTypePtr  = ^PhoneType;
VAR
  PersonPtr : PersonTypePtr;
  PhonePtr : PhoneTypePtr;
```

Of course, you must allocate the **PersonPtr** and the **PhonePtr** variables
in the Heap first. Pointers compatibility is the same as object instance
compatibility. The **PersonPtr** can point to both **PersonType** and
PhoneType objects:

```
PhonePtr := PersonPtr;      { it is not right }
PersonPtr := PhonePtr;      { right }
```

The standard **New** procedure can allocate the memory for the object addressed by **PhonePtr** in the Heap:

```
New(PhonePtr);
```

Now you can use the **PhonePtr** to access this instance. To do this you must first activate the **Init** method to initialize the **PhonePtr** object fields:

```
PhonePtr^.Init('Bill  Bricks',
          'Housing  International',
          '111-111-1111');
```

You can unite these two operations, because the **New** procedure can have a second parameter, the constructor. As we said in our explanation of polymorphism, the constructor binds the object with the VMT. It is common practice to declare the constructor as an initialization procedure:

```
TYPE
  PersonTypePtr = ^PersonType;
  PersonType = OBJECT
        Name : NameStr;
        Company : CompStr;
        CONSTRUCTOR Init(Nm:NameStr; Cmp:CompStr);
        DESTRUCTOR Done; VIRTUAL;
        PROCEDURE Show; VIRTUAL;
        FUNCTION GetName : NameStr;
        PROCEDURE ShowToClearScr;
  END;
  PhoneTypePtr = ^PhoneType;
  PhoneType = OBJECT(PersonType)
    Phone : PhoneStr;
    CONSTRUCTOR Init(Nm:NameStr; Cmp:CompStr;
                            Ph:PhoneStr);
    DESTRUCTOR Done; VIRTUAL;
    PROCEDURE Show; VIRTUAL;
    FUNCTION GetPhone : PhoneStr;
  END;
```

The word **PROCEDURE** in the **Init** method is replaced by the word
CONSTRUCTOR. Now you can allocate memory using simultaneous field
initialization:

```
New(PhonePtr,  Init('Bill  Bricks',
          'Housing International', '111-111-1111'));
```

or

```
PhonePtr  :=  New(PhoneTypePtr,Init('Bill  Bricks',
          'Housing International', '111-111-1111'));
```

Note that in the second variant we refer to the **New** procedure as a function.
Its result will be the pointer to the allocated object. The first parameter
specifies the object type for the pointer.

In the previous example you'll see a new virtual method, **Done** which
is called a **destructor**. Destructors reallocate dynamic objects. Destructors
are declared using the reserved word **DESTRUCTOR** and they are used
as the second parameter of the standard **Dispose** procedure:

```
Dispose(PhonePtr,  Done);
```

If you name a procedure as a destructor, the compiler will automatically
add the necessary instructions for memory reallocation, which means
that the destructor can be empty:

```
DESTRUCTOR  PersonType.Done;
BEGIN
END;

DESTRUCTOR  PhoneType.Done;
BEGIN
END;
```

We strongly recommend that you declare destructors as virtual, to be
sure that the correct one will be called for any polymorphic object. For
an example of this see program **Phones2** at the end of this chapter.

If you need to, you can also put instructions in the destructor's body.
These will be performed before the object is deleted from memory.

If you include all the above mentioned changes the **ObjPhon2** unit will look like this:

```
UNIT ObjPhon2;
INTERFACE
USES Crt;
TYPE
 NameStr = string[25];
 CompStr = string[30];
 PhoneStr = string[15];
 PersonTypePtr = ^PersonType;
 PersonType = OBJECT
   Name : NameStr;
   Company : CompStr;
   CONSTRUCTOR Init (Nm:NameStr; Cmp:CompStr);
   DESTRUCTOR Done; VIRTUAL;
   PROCEDURE Show; VIRTUAL;
   FUNCTION GetName : NameStr;
   PROCEDURE ShowToClearScr;
 END;
 PhoneTypePtr  = ^PhoneType;
 PhoneType  = OBJECT(PersonType)
   Phone : PhoneStr;
   CONSTRUCTOR Init(Nm:NameStr; Cmp:CompStr; Ph:PhoneStr);
   DESTRUCTOR Done; VIRTUAL;
   PROCEDURE Show; VIRTUAL;
   FUNCTION GetPhone : PhoneStr;
 END;

IMPLEMENTATION

CONSTRUCTOR PersonType.Init (Nm:NameStr; Cmp:CompStr);
BEGIN
 Name := Nm;
 Company := Cmp;
END;      { Init }

DESTRUCTOR PersonType.Done;
BEGIN
END;      { Done }

PROCEDURE PersonType.Show;
BEGIN
 Writeln;
 Writeln('NAME: ', Name);
 Writeln('COMPANY: ', Company);
END;      { Show }
```

```
FUNCTION  PersonType.GetName  :  NameStr;
BEGIN
    GetName  := Name;
END;        {  GetName  }


PROCEDURE  PersonType.ShowToClearScr;
BEGIN
    ClrScr;
    Show;
END;        {  ShowToClearScr  }


CONSTRUCTOR  PhoneType.Init  (Nm:NameStr;
                                Cmp:CompStr;  Ph:PhoneStr);
BEGIN
    PersonType.Init(Nm,  Cmp);
      {  initialization  of  PersonType  fields  }
    Phone  :=  Ph;
END;        {  Init  }


PROCEDURE  PhoneType.Show;
BEGIN
    PersonType.Show;
    Writeln('PHONE:  ',  Phone);
END;        {  Show  }


FUNCTION  PhoneType.GetPhone  :  PhoneStr;
BEGIN
    GetPhone  :=  Phone;
END;        {  GetPhone  }


DESTRUCTOR  PhoneType.Done;
BEGIN
END;        {  Done  }


BEGIN       {  ObjPhone  }
END.
```

At last we'll show you the program text:

```
PROGRAM Phones2;
USES ObjPhon2;
VAR
  WorkPhone : PhoneType;
  PersonPtr1, PersonPtr2 : PersonTypePtr;
  PhonePtr : PhoneTypePtr;
BEGIN
  WorkPhone.Init('Bill Bricks', 'Housing International',
                                         '111-111-1111');
  { this method will activate Show method of PhoneType object }
  WorkPhone.ShowToClearScr;
  New(PhonePtr,Init('Bill Bricks', 'Housing International',
                                         '111-111-1111'));
  WITH PhonePtr^ DO
    Writeln(GetPhone, '    ', GetName);
  PersonPtr2 := New(PersonTypePtr,Init('Richard Gardener',
                                         'Landscapes Ltd.'));
  PersonPtr1 := PersonPtr2;
  PersonPtr1^.Show;         { call Show method of PersonType }
  PersonPtr1 := PhonePtr;
  PersonPtr1^.Show;          { call Show method of PhoneType }
  { dispose dynamic object of PhoneType }
  Dispose(PersonPtr1, Done);
  { dispose dynamic object of PersonType }
  Dispose(PersonPtr2, Done);
END.
```

The polymorphism of the **PersonType** and **PhoneType** objects works in the following way: the program **Phones2** uses two virtual **Show** method calls for the dynamic **PersonPtr1^** object. In the first case, **PersonPtr1** points to the   **PersonType** object; in the second case it points to the **PhoneType** object. In each case the **Show** method belongs to the object pointed to and it displays the fields of this object. This happens because the **Show** method is presented as virtual. For this reason, the **WorkPhone.ShowToClearScr** method will activate the **Show** method, which corresponds to the current object type.

We'll now explain the process of disposing the dynamic objects from the Heap. When the **Dispose** procedure is addressed for the first time, the dynamic object **PersonPtr1**^ is the **PhoneType** object. Therefore, in order to free **PersonPtr1**^ from the Heap, you must call the **PhoneType.Done** destructor.

When the **Dispose** procedure is addressed the second time, the dynamic object **PersonPtr2**^ is the **PersonType** object. In this case, to free **PersonPtr2**^ from the Heap you need to call the **PersonType.Done** destructor. However, since the **Done** destructor is declared as virtual, you don't need to worry about the current type of polymorphic object. The correct destructor is automatically called and the relevant dynamic object is cleared from the Heap.

Figure 17-8
Result of the Phones2 Program

```
NAME: Bill Bricks
COMPANY: Housing International
PHONE: 111-111-1111
111-111-1111    Bill Bricks

NAME: Richard Gardener
COMPANY: Landscapes Ltd.

NAME: Bill Bricks
COMPANY: Housing International
PHONE: 111-111-1111
```

TURBO VISION BEGINNING

Introducing Turbo Vision

In the previous chapter we dealt with OOP, which offers a new way of approaching application program design. Turbo Vision is a powerful tool which uses this approach for windowing programs. Turbo Vision is a set of object-oriented units based on the common OOP ideology. It contains sources for creating all types of menus and windows, dialog boxes, mouse support and many other useful things. The developers of Turbo Pascal used Turbo Vision to write the new IDE which is probably the best advertisement this framework could have!

Object definitions are contained in the Turbo Vision interface modules. Using inheritance you can easily create your own objects on the basis of the Turbo Vision ones. Unlike traditional structured programming, you alter Turbo Vision by extending it. This is Turbo Vision's main advantage, it saves you time and effort.

Fundamentals

Turbo Vision consists of **views, events** and **mute objects**, each of which is made up of several different objects. The identifiers for these objects have meaningful names which you will find easy to understand. Moreover, the Turbo Pascal 6.0 help system is extended by a description of objects, variables and constants of Turbo Vision.

Views

Views define all visible elements on the screen. For example, menu bars, frames and control fields are views. Views in turn can be combined to form more complex objects - windows, for example. These complex objects are called **groups** and they can be processed as a single view.

Views are always displayed on the screen in the form of a rectangle. A special internal control system processes every action within this rectangle, for example mouse clicking on the scrolling bar. The whole screen of each Turbo Vision program is considered to be a view. Naturally, this view contains other views: menu bar, status line, etc. Every view is a descendant of the basic **TView** object. It contains fields and methods that define the views' behavior on the screen. The **TView** object is the base of view hierarchy:

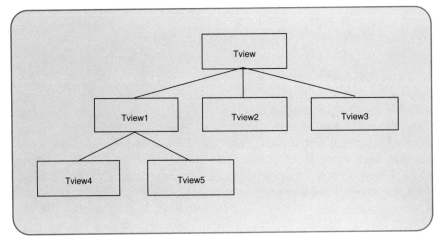

Figure 18-1
**View
Hierarchy
Based on the
TView Object**

Views are defined as follows:

```
View1  =  OBJECT(TView)
   ...
END;
```

The main characteristic of a view is that it knows how to output itself on the screen. For example, if you want to create a menu system, you only need to specify the necessary keywords and the inner Turbo Vision mechanisms will do the rest. It is not advisable to use the standard **Write** and **Writeln** functions, because the output text will not be a view and the entire Turbo Vision view system will be ruined.

Events

In Turbo Vision, **events** deal with all external actions which the program must process. Sources for events are the keyboard, a mouse or other parts of Turbo Vision.

Each event is placed in a queue as it occurs and is processed by an event handler. The substance of each program is an object of the **TApplication** type and it is this object that contains the **event handler**. The **TApplication** object is a group of nested views, something like a binary tree. The events that are not serviced by the **TApplication** event handler (i.e. views) are moved to other views according to an object hierarchy. If the event does not find a corresponding view an abandoned event error occurs.

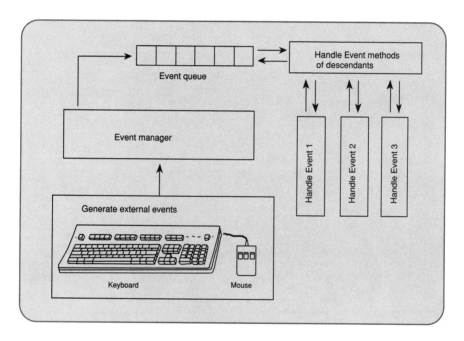

Figure 18-2
**Event
Handling in
Turbo Vision**

Unlike views, events are not objects, because they do not perform any actions. The events contain information for objects and are represented in the form of records. The kernel of such a record is the **What** field. It has word type and describes the form of events. The record also contains some special information about the events: scan code, mouse position, etc.

Mute Objects

Mute objects are program elements that do not output anything on the screen. In short, any program object that is not a view is a mute object. They are mute because they do not output anything on the screen. They perform various calculations, communicate with peripheral devices and do other work for the application program. If the mute object wants to display something on the screen it has to connect with the view. Remember that only views can be output on the screen!

Program Design

Turbo Vision provides standard mechanisms for screen design. Figure 18-3 shows the main objects that might appear as part of an application program in Turbo Vision.

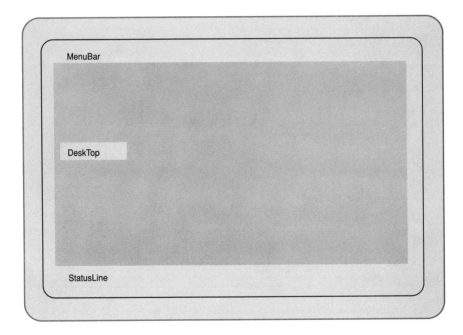

Figure 18-3
Turbo Vision Objects on Screen

The **desktop** is shaded with a background color, the **menu bar** is at the top of the screen and the **status line** is at the bottom. All three of these elements are objects and their functions are similar to the functions of the corresponding IDE elements. For example, if you create a menu bar you can activate the menu options like main IDE menu options.

In Turbo Vision, an application program interacts with the user by means of windows and dialog boxes that appear in the desktop. You control these windows and boxes using the keyboard and a mouse.

Turbo Vision application programs are built with the help of the unique, abstract **TApplication** object, which is defined in the **APP.TPU** unit. When you want to create a new object type you must use **TApplication** as a base. Your new type inherits the standard characteristics of a Turbo Vision program from **TApplication**. You can then extend it by adding methods and fields which you might need for a particular program.

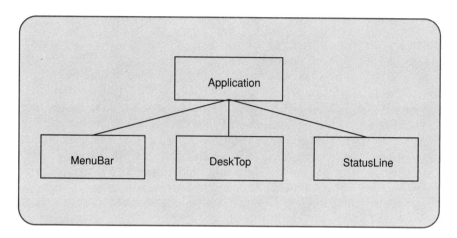

Figure 18-4
**Global
Tree of
Application
Views**

You should realize that with this kind of design you won't need to waste much time creating an interface and can therefore concentrate your efforts on solving specific application tasks.

In this chapter we'll look at our old friend the HomeFinances program (see Chapter 15), but this time we will design it with the help of Turbo Vision. The **TpAppl** object, based on **TApplication** will be the basis of the program. The example below shows the simplest form, in which the **TpAppl** type does not contain any additional codes:

```
USES App;
TYPE
   TpAppl = OBJECT(TApplication) { without
                         additional descriptions }
   END;
VAR
   wApp : TpAppl; { instance of the
                         TpAppl object type }
```

Below we have declared the **wApp** instance of the **TpAppl** type. As you can see the program text is quite simple:

```
BEGIN
  wApp.Init;    { init application }
  wApp.Run;     { run application }
  wApp.Done;    { close application }
END.
```

When you execute this program, you will get the screen image shown in Figure 18-3. The status line will contain the usual IDE prompt **Alt-X Exit** which tells you how to exit the program. As a rule, the current status line should prompt how to move backwards and forwards within a program, and how to exit it. This example shows how the inheritance mechanism works. You get display images of the main elements without changing the parent **TApplication** type. The **Init** and **Done** methods conventionally represent the constructor and destructor of the **wApp** object respectively. All these methods are inherited from **TApplication** and are activated in the following order:

> **Init** - initialize application program
> **Run** - execute application program
> **Done** - exit application program

The Init Method

The **wApp** object inherits virtual methods, so you must activate the constructor before using any of them. All constructors in Turbo Vision are named **Init**. The **TpAppl.Init** method clears the screen, initializes internal variables, fills the desktop of the screen, and outputs the status line and menu bar. The **Init** method also activates the internal constructors of other objects.

The Run Method

The **Run** method is the main working method of an application program. You can think of it as a large **REPEAT..UNTIL** loop:

```
REPEAT
  < wait for event >
  < process event >
UNTIL   < event that exits the program >
```

The loop will repeat until another event occurs within the program.

The Done Method

The **Done** method is a destructor and, as with all Turbo Vision destructors, it is virtual. It secures the activation of the correct destructor for any polymorphal object.

The **Done** method performs the direct opposite of any action which **Init** performs. Consequently it deletes the standard Turbo Vision objects: menu bar, status line, desktop, mute Turbo Vision drivers, error handler.

A New Approach

In Chapter 15 we looked at the **Service** unit which provides a set of useful procedures and functions for program design. However, it would be wrong to think of Turbo Vision as simply a large library for windowing programs, as it is based on new OOP techniques.

In traditional structured programming you have to change the codes every time you want to change the program logic. This involves rewriting procedures and functions, declaring new variables, deleting old ones and so on. Naturally, you'll probably make quite a few mistakes doing this. In Turbo Vision, however, you never touch the initial code, instead you change it by extending it. The **TApplication** type remains unchangeable inside the **APP.TPU** unit, and you create new types by adding the necessary definitions and overwriting inherited methods with new ones. This is one of the main advantages of Turbo Vision.

Don't forget that Turbo Vision is made up of a complex hierarchy of objects, so you cannot just include a part of Turbo Vision - you always inherit the entire system. So don't despair when your small, modest programs generate large **.EXE** files. Most modern PCs can cope with it and it means that you can dramatically improve your program design.

Basic Objects

Each Turbo Vision program begins with the creation of an object instance based on **TApplication** which you can then extend by adding new fields and methods.

We'll use the following standard Turbo Vision objects for creating menus:
TView, TMenuView, TMenuBar, TMenuBox, TStatusLine, TGroup,

TDeskTop. We won't go into these objects in detail here as they would take quite a long time to explain. Our aim is rather to explain how to actually use these objects. More complete information about Turbo Vision objects is given in your Turbo Vision Guide or IDE Help.

As their names imply, **InitDeskTop**, **InitMenuBar** and **InitStatusLine** objects of the **TApplication** type are used for creating the desktop, menu bar and status line. They are virtual and as such are activated by the **TApplication.Init** constructor, so you don't need to call them directly. **InitDeskTop**, **InitMenuBar** and **InitStatusLine** methods initialize the global **DeskTop**, **MenuBar** and **StatusLine** variables.

If you want to create your own **Init** method for the **TpAppl** type you have to activate the parent **Init** method first:

```
PROCEDURE TpAppl.Init;
BEGIN
  TApplication.Init; { activate parent method }
  ...
  < code of initialization >
END;
```

In order to operate menus, status line and standard key definitions you have to include **Objects**, **Drivers** and **Menus** units.

Status Line

The **TApplication.InitStatusLine** method sets the **TStatusLine** view and initializes the **StatusLine** variable. It defines hotkeys and displays the corresponding help items. These hotkeys are bound to the commands, and the help items are clicked on with a mouse.

You can create your own status line by rewriting the standard **TApplication.InitStatusLine** method like this:

```
TYPE
    TpAppl = OBJECT(TApplication)
      PROCEDURE InitStatusLine; VIRTUAL;
                        {VIRTUAL - very important!}
    END;
```

```
PROCEDURE TpAppl.InitStatusLine;
VAR  R: TRect; { object for rectangle }
BEGIN
 GetExtent(R);      { sets status line boundaries }
 R.A.Y := pred(R.B.Y);    { bottom line }
 StatusLine := New(PStatusLine, Init(R,
  NewStatusDef(0, $FFFF,
    NewStatusKey('~F5~ Month', kbF5, cmMonth,
    NewStatusKey('~F6~ Year', kbF6, cmYear,
    NewStatusKey('~F10~ Menu', kbF10, cmMenu,
    NewStatusKey('~Alt-X~ Exit', kbAltX,
                                    cmQuit, nil)))),
 nil)));
END; { InitStatusLine }
```

The **TRect** object represents a rectangle. Its fields **A** and **B**, which are **TPoint** objects, define the top left and bottom right boundaries. The **TPoint** object contains **X** and **Y** fields and defines a point on the screen. Although the **TRect** objects themselves are not views, all views use the R parameter of the **TRect** type in their **Init** constructors to get the size of the view rectangle. The **GetExtent** method assigns the coordinates of the rectangle that covers the active view, to the **R** argument of **TRect** type. In our example,   it is assigned with full screen coordinates.

The first two arguments of the **NewStatusDef** procedure define the range of help contexts from 0 through $FFFF. Any view can be binded with a **help context number**, and using these numbers you can organize a complete help context system. If you do not want to set a number to the view, use the **NoContext** constant.

The status line is built using nested calls according to the standard **NewStatusDef** and **NewStatusKey** functions. First a range of help contexts (0 - $FFFF) is specified, then the nested **NewStatusKey** calls bind commands with certain hotkeys. The **Nil** pointer is then used to end the sequence of calls.

All standard Turbo Vision commands begin with the letters cm-. Numbers 0-99 and 256-999 are reserved for predefined Turbo Vision commands, others (up to 65535) can be user-defined. In the **InitStatusLine** method you will notice new user-defined commands: **cmMonth**, **cmYear**, and inner predefined commands: **cmMenu**, **cmQuit**. The **cmMenu** command activates the menu bar, and **cmQuit** exits the program.

User-defined commands are declared as constants:

```
CONST
     cmAbout= 100;              { about command }
     cmIncome= 101;            { changes income value }
     cmFood= 102;               { changes expenses value
                                         for food}
     cmAccommodation=103;   { changes expenses value
                                    for accommodation }
     cmClothing= 104;         { changes expenses value
                                         for clothing }
     cmEducation= 105;        { changes expenses value
                                      for education }
     cmMedicalCare= 106;      { changes expenses value
                                    for medical care}
     cmLeisure= 107;          { changes expenses value
                                       for leisure }
     cmOther= 108;             { changes expenses value
                                        for other}
     cmSetDate= 109;          { sets date }
     cmMonth= 110;             { month analysis }
     cmYear= 111;              { year analysis }
```

In the **NewStatusKey**, each command is bound by certain constants beginning with the letters **kb-**. These constants define various key combinations, and their identifiers have meaningful names. For example, constant **kbF5** is bound with the F5 key. You can find a list of all **kb-** and **cm-** constants in your Turbo Vision reference.

Each command can be bound further with a key string, such as **~F5~ Month**. The part of the string which is enclosed by tildes (~) will be highlighted on the screen. If the command is currently disabled the status item is not highlighted and clicking has no effect.

Note that the new **InitStatusLine** method doesn't activate the parent method, and it overrides the **TApplication.InitStatusLine**. There is no reason for such activation because both methods assign the same **StatusLine** variable and cover the same range of help context. So there is nothing useful to the new method in the parent method. As a result of the **TpAppl** extension there will be a new status line.

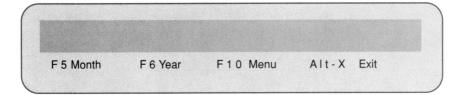

Figure 18-5
**StatusLine
of TpAppl
Object**

The Menu Bar

Menu bar initialization consists of a sequence of nested calls to standard Turbo Vision functions: **NewMenu**, **NewSubMenu**, **NewItem** and **NewLine**. The result of initialization is a **MenuBar** variable. If this variable is assigned, the menu bar has already been created.

If you want to create your own menu bar you will have to override the **TApplication.InitMenuBar** method. First insert the new definitions:

```
TYPE
  TpAppl = OBJECT(TApplication)
    PROCEDURE InitMenuBar; VIRTUAL;
    PROCEDURE InitStatusLine; VIRTUAL;
  END;
```

We will explain the method body part by part:

```
PROCEDURE TpAppl.InitMenuBar;
VAR  R : TRect;
BEGIN
 GetExtent(R);
 R.B.Y := succ(R.A.Y); { top screen line }
 MenuBar := New(PMenuBar, Init(R, NewMenu(
   NewSubMenu('~≡~', hcNoContext,
                          NewMenu( { submenu About }
     NewItem('~A~bout...', '', 0, cmAbout, hcNoContext,
     nil)),
```

Menu bar initialization starts with the **NewMenu** call which forms a menu bar. First the submenu ≡ is made by a nested **NewSubMenu** function call. You can now consider this submenu as being a new menu and call the **NewMenu** again. The **NewMenu** function displays the ≡ submenu options (in our case there is only one option - ~A~about) using the **NewItem** call. The **Nil** pointer ends the sequence of calls. Figure 18-6 shows how this works:

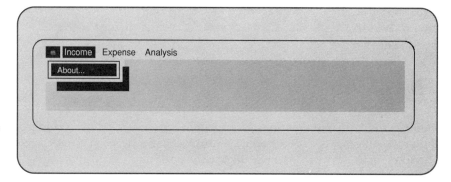

Figure 18-6
**Submenu "≡"
of TpAppl
Object Type**

The **NewItem** function will also bind a new menu item with the user-defined command **cmAbout**. This command will display help information about the program. The standard **hcNoContext** identifier shows that there is no help context for this menu item. The next empty string parameter informs that no hotkeys have been defined for the item. The letter ≡ enclosed by tides (~) indicates that if you press the ≡ key you will gain direct access to the ≡ submenu.

It's a good idea to justify all nested calls of the same level on the same left boundary as it will make your program text more understandable.

Next, the **NewSubMenu** call opens the new submenu Income:

```
NewSubMenu('~I~ncome', hcNoContext,
                    NewMenu( {submenu Income}
  NewItem('~I~ncome', '', 0, cmIncome,
                          hcNoContext,
  NewItem('~S~et date', '', 0, cmSetDate,
                          hcNoContext,
  NewLine(
  NewItem('~E~xit', 'Alt-X', kbAltX, cmQuit,
                          hcNoContext,
  nil))))),
```

The Income submenu has two items, each of which is defined by the **NewItem** call. All menu items are built in this way and are bound with certain commands.

The **NewLine** function delimits the submenu items with a horizontal line. Figure 18-7 shows the Income submenu:

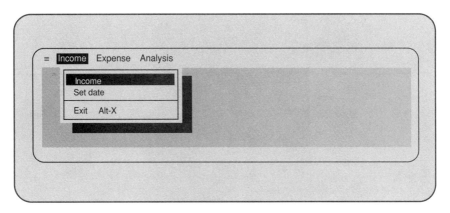

Figure 18-7
**The
"Income"
Submenu**

The last **NewItem** call binds the Exit item of the Income submenu with the standard **cmQuit** command, **kbAltX** hotkey and **Alt-X** help string. There are three different ways in which you can perform this command:

1   Choose the necessary menu item using the cursor or a mouse.

2   Press the hotkey **ALT-X**.

3   Click on the status line item.

```
NewSubMenu('~E~xpense',hcNoContext,NewMenu({submenu
                                        'Expense'}
    NewItem('~F~ood', '', 0, cmFood, hcNoContext,
    NewItem('~A~ccommodation', '', 0,
                    cmAccommodation, hcNoContext,
    NewItem('~C~lothing', '', 0, cmClothing,
                                        hcNoContext,
    NewItem('~E~ducation', '', 0, cmEducation,
                                        hcNoContext,
    NewItem('~M~edical care', '', 0, cmMedicalcare,
                                        hcNoContext,
    NewItem('~L~eisure', '', 0, cmLeisure,
                                        hcNoContext,
    NewItem('~O~ther', '', 0, cmOther, hcNoContext,
        nil)))))))),
```

The Expense submenu has 7 items, each of which is defined by a particular nested **NewItem** call. Figure 18-8 shows the Expense submenu:

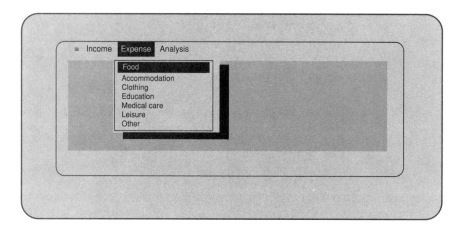

Figure 18-8
The "Expense" Submenu

```
NewSubMenu('~A~nalysis', hcNoContext,
                    NewMenu(  { Analysis }
        NewItem('~M~onth', 'F5', kbF5, cmMonth,
                            hcNoContext,
        NewItem('~Y~ear', 'F6', kbF6, cmYear,
                            hcNoContext,
        nil))),
   nil)))))));
END;  { InitMenuBar }
```

At last we've come to the Analysis submenu definition. Menu items are bound with corresponding **cmMonth** and **cmYear** commands, and the hotkeys **F5** and **F6**. Figure 18-9 shows the Analysis submenu.

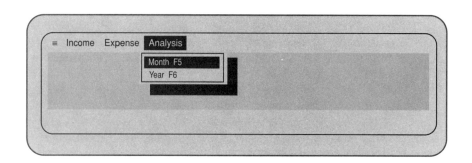

Figure 18-9
The "Analysis" Submenu

The **InitMenuBar** method defines the menu bar for the program. The menu is now a complete system for activating several commands. The final thing you need to do is to write the processing procedures for these commands. Unlike traditional programming, you can separate the interface part (menu system) from the processing part. This means that you can now design the program as a set of independent functional blocks, which is an important step forward in program design.

Now if you want to change the menu bar, there is no need for you to touch the processing part, as the interface part and processing part work independently and do not influence one another.

Event Handler

Once you have created the menu bar you can generate menu commands. You can then bind each command with a processing procedure using the **event handler**. The event handler is contained in **HandleEvent** method of the **TApplication** object.

The event handler processes the event queue. Each event in this queue is defined by the variant record - **TEvent**, and the **What** field of this record specifies which kind of event:

> **outside event**   - generated by mouse, keyboard, etc.
> **command event**   - generated by views.

If **TEvent.What** = **evCommand** constant, then the event is a command. If the event is a command, then its code is specified by the **Command** field. If you want to handle commands generated by your own views (for example, menu bar, status line) you have to override the parent **TApplication.HandleEvent** method. First include it in the definition of the **TpAppl** object:

```
TYPE
  TpAppl = OBJECT(TApplication)
    PROCEDURE HandleEvent(VAR Event : TEvent);
                                        VIRTUAL;
    PROCEDURE InitMenuBar; VIRTUAL;
    PROCEDURE InitStatusLine; VIRTUAL;
    PROCEDURE AboutSystem;    { method for the
                                 command cmAbout }
  END;
```

We have added the **AboutSystem** method here. It corresponds to the **cmAbout** command and is used for outputting help information about the program. Now we can override the parent **HandleEvent** method:

```
PROCEDURE TpAppl.HandleEvent (VAR Event: TEvent);
BEGIN
   TApplication.HandleEvent(Event); { activate parent
                                    method }
   IF (Event.What = evCommand) THEN BEGIN {if the
                           command is entered}
     CASE (Event.Command) OF      { user command }
     cmAbout: AboutSystem; { help about the program }
         ELSE   Exit;       { end of event handling }
     END;
     ClearEvent(Event); { event is successfully
                                    handled }
   END;
END;  { HandleEvent }
```

With this method, the parent **TApplication.HandleEvent** method is called to inherit standard Turbo Vision handling. Then the **TEvent.What** field is tested. If **What** = **evCommand**, then this event really is caused by a view. In the **CASE** statement, the **Command** field is tested and the corresponding procedure for event processing is chosen. When the event is handled it has to be cleared from the queue using the **ClearEvent(VAR Event: TEvent) method.**

In the above program we add the handling of the About view. Later it will be handled by the **AboutSystem** method (see Windows and Dialog Boxes). You should note that when you start working with views here you have to include the **Views** unit in your program:

```
USES Objects, Drivers, Views, Menus, App;
```

Now that we have changed the example take a look at the new methods that we'll need for our program.

Desktop

As a rule, all user commands deal with data output. The new **TpAppl** method will output text information on the screen. We stated earlier in this chapter that any output in Turbo Vision is defined by views or by a group of views. For example, **TDeskTop** object is a group of views that operates with user windows.

Desktop is defined by the **TDeskTop** object. The **InitDeskTop** method creates the **TDeskTop** object and assigns its pointer to a global **DeskTop** variable. We will leave these actions as they are by inheriting the parent **InitDeskTop** method, and activate the parent method automatically in the **TApplication.Init** method.

The **TDeskTop** object is a group of views. Initially there is only one view in it, the **TBackGround** object which forms a background on the screen, but you can add any views you like, for example, windows. To add new views use the **Insert**(P: PView) method (where **PView** is the pointer to the **TView** object):

```
WITH DeskTop^ DO BEGIN
  Insert(Window1); { Window1, Window2,Window3 are }
  Insert(Window2);   { pointers to window object }
  Insert(Window3);
END;
```

The Desktop group will now look like this:

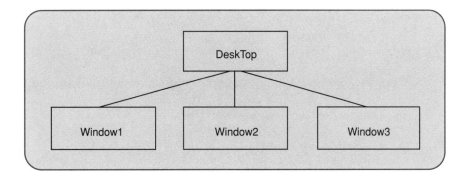

Figure 18-10
**Desktop
Group of
Views**

Windows will be displayed on the screen in the same order as they were inserted by the **Insert** method:

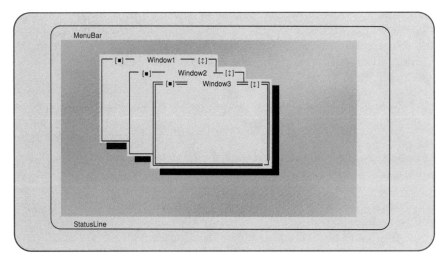

Figure 18-11
**Desktop
Group of
Windows on
the Screen**

Windows

Windows are among the most important objects of Turbo Vision. Their control is automatic which means that when you define a window in the program you can operate with it easily: open, close, move, etc. The window is defined by the **TWindow** object which is a special group of views that contains standard Turbo Vision views:

> **TFrame** - draws frames around windows.
> **TScroller** - sets up and down scrolling (holds a scrollable array of text).
> **TScrollBar** - provides scroll bar control (horizontal and vertical).

To add your own views into the **TWindow** group, follow this algorithm:

> 1 Define the window of **TWindow** type.

> 2 For all views of **TWindow** group:
>   define view.
>   add view to **TWindow** group using **Insert** method.

> 3 Add **TWindow** group to **TDeskTop** group using **Insert** method.

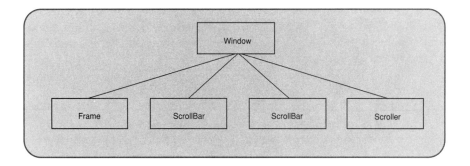

Figure 18-12
**Window
Group of
Standard
Views**

As an example we'll show you how to make the About window. This
window is displayed by the **cmAbout** command from the About menu.
When you call the command, the window will appear in the middle of
the screen. First we'll define **TWindow** object:

```
TYPE
   PAboutWindow = ^TAboutWindow;
   TAboutWindow = OBJECT(TWindow)
     CONSTRUCTOR Init(R : TRect; Wname : string;
                                    Wnumber : word);
   END;
```

The new **TAboutWindow** type is a descendant of the standard **TWindow**.
It overrides the parent **Init** method that sets the size, position, title and
number of the window. Now we'll define the view that we'll add to the
TWindow group later:

```
TYPE
    PInterior  =  ^TInterior;
    TInterior  =  OBJECT(TView)
        CONSTRUCTOR  Init(VAR  R  :  TRect);
        PROCEDURE  Draw;  VIRTUAL;
    END;
```

The new **TInterior** type outputs text strings in the window. As we
explained earlier, the strings are defined by the following constants (see
Chapter 15):

```
CONST
    NamePro  =  'WROX  HOME  FINANCES';
    CopyRight  =  'Copyright  (C)  WROX  1992';
```

As with all descendants of the standard **TView** type, **TInterior** is a view. It overrides two of the parent type methods: the **Init** constructor and **Draw** method which define the output mechanism. You can extend type definitions in any way you like:

```
CONSTRUCTOR TInterior.Init(VAR R: TRect);
BEGIN
  TView.Init(R);                { initialize view }
  GrowMode := gfGrowHiX +gfGrowHiY; { set mode of
                                 view output }
END;  { Init }

PROCEDURE TInterior.Draw;
BEGIN
  TView.Draw;                        { draw view }
  WriteStr(8, 2, NamePro, 2);{ output
                               information }
  WriteStr(9, 4, CopyRight, 2);
END;  { Draw }
```

The **TInterior.Init** method initializes the **TInterior** view. The parameter of the   **Init** method specifies the coordinates of the rectangle. It has **TRect** type. You can also use the **Init** method to set options that determine the output mode of the view. These options will be used by the **TView.Draw** method.

The **GrowMode** field determines how the view will be changed when the window is resized. **GrowMode** is assigned using the reserved **gf-** constants:

```
GrowMode  :=  gfGrowHiX  +  gfGrowHiY;
```

As a result the right and bottom side of the view will follow the right and bottom sides of the window. The **Options** field determines particular characteristics of the view. It is assigned using the **of-** constants:

```
Options  :=  Options  OR  ofFramed;
```

Option **ofFramed** sets the internal flag for drawing a frame around the view.   The **TInterior.Draw** method directly displays the view. The parent **TView.Draw** method is called in the new **Draw** method to display the view in the standard Turbo Vision way, using the new options. Besides this, we'll output two strings on the screen using the **TView.WriteStr** method.

WriteStr(X, Y: integer; St: string) outputs string **St** starting from the point X, Y of the color that is specified by the **Color** index from the **TView palette**. Turbo Vision provides special palettes (inner arrays) for setting colors.

Each byte of a palette contains a color attribute of the corresponding element of the screen. In order to set the view color you have to set the corresponding index (**Color** in our case) of the palette array. You can only activate the **WriteStr** method in the **Draw** method.

Now it's time to define the constructor for the **TAboutWindow** object:

```
CONSTRUCTOR TAboutWindow.Init(R:TRect; Wname:string;
                                        Wnumber:word);
VAR  Interior: PInterior;
BEGIN
  TWindow.Init(R, Wname, Wnumber); { initialize
                                     the window }
  GetClipRect(R);      { get minimum window size }
  R.Grow(-1,-1); { decrement current window size }
  Interior := New(PInterior, Init(R)); { define
                                 TInterior object }
  Insert(Interior); { bind the object
                                 with the window }
END;  { Init }
```

The new **Init** constructor calls the parent **TWindow.Init** to perform standard Turbo Vision initialization. The **R** parameter sets the window coordinates, the **Wname** string contains the name of the window, and **Wnumber** contains its number.

Now we'll specify the place where the **TInterior** view is allocated in the About window. The coordinates of the minimum rectangle needed for displaying the window are returned in the **R** parameter by the **GetClipRect(VAR R: TRect)** method of the **TView** object. The

TRect.Grow(-1,-1) method decrements the window coordinates. The coordinates for allocating the **TInterior** view in the **TAboutWindow** are now set.

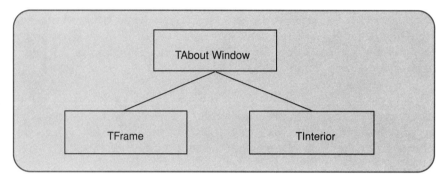

Figure 18-13
"About" Window Group of Views

When the view is initialized by the **New** procedure you have to include it in the window group using the standard **TGroup.Insert** method. You can also include other views in the same way which will then be displayed on the screen.

```
PROCEDURE TpAppl.AboutSystem;
{ make window for About command}
VAR
  P : PAboutWindow;
  R : TRect;
BEGIN
  R.Assign(20, 5, 60, 14);    { set window size }
  P := New(PAboutWindow, Init(R, 'About',
                                wnNoNumber));
  DeskTop^.Insert(P); { bind the window with
                                the desktop }
END;   { AboutSystem }
```

When you activate the **cmAbout** command it has the following effects: the **AboutSystem** method gets the window coordinates using the **TRect.Assign** method, the window (i.e. object of **TAboutWindow** type) is initialized using the **New** procedure and the **Init** constructor, and the window is inserted in the **DeskTop** group using **DeskTop^.Insert**. In the initialization statement, we have used the **wnNoNumber** constant which specifies that the window will not have a number. The **AboutSystem** method will produce the following window:

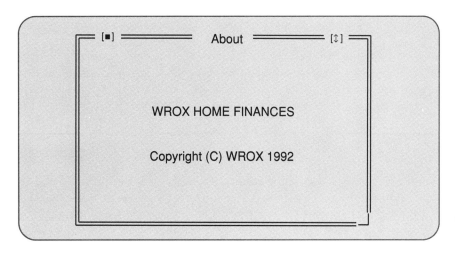

Figure 18-14
The "About"
Window

As with ordinary IDE windows, you can perform any actions with this window. You can open a great number of independent About windows using the **cmAbout** command, all of which will be displayed on the screen. To close a particular window you have to click the [■] field using the mouse. This is the only way we can close the window at the moment because we did not bind the internal **cmClose** command with any key combination. However, you can also close a window using the additional nested call of the **NewStatusKey** method in text **InitStatusLine** method:

```
PROCEDURE TpAppl.InitStatusLine;
VAR  R: TRect; { object for rectangular }
BEGIN
  GetExtent(R); { sets boundaries of the status line }
  R.A.Y := pred(R.B.Y);          { bottom line }
  StatusLine := New(PStatusLine, Init(R,
    NewStatusDef(0, $FFFF,
      NewStatusKey('~F5~ Month', kbF5, cmMonth,
      NewStatusKey('~F6~ Year', kbF6, cmYear,
      NewStatusKey('~Alt-F4~ Close', kbAltF4,
                                cmClose, { add call }
      NewStatusKey('~F10~ Menu', kbF10, cmMenu,
      NewStatusKey('~Alt-X~ Exit', kbAltX,
                                cmQuit, nil))))),
    nil)));
END;  { InitStatusLine }
```

You can now close the window using the **ALT-F4** hotkey. For complete information about methods and constants for window design you should refer to your Turbo Vision Guide or IDE Help. You can also find out how to organize vertical or horizontal bars and scrolling using standard **TScrollBar** and **TScroller** objects.

Dialog Boxes

When displaying About information, you only need to open a window once and output text strings in it. This means that you are not using the full potential of standard windows; for example, resizing. The nature of standard windows means that they are much more useful for editing text or displaying dynamic information.

For displaying static text Turbo Vision has **dialog boxes**. The **Dialogs** unit has standard objects for creating dialog boxes:

TDialog	- defines the main group of views for a dialog box.
TButton	- defines the button.
TRadioButtons	- defines radio buttons.
TInputLine	- inputs a string.
TCheckBoxes	- defines check boxes.

We'll use the familiar **TView** and **TGroup** objects for windows.

A **dialog box** is simply a special kind of window which is called a **modal**, because it sets the program operation mode. For making dialog windows we'll use the **TDialog** type, which is a descendant of the **TWindow** object. When the dialog box is active, you cannot open other windows and the dialog box waits for you to respond. Before we start making dialog boxes, we have to extend the **USES** line:

```
USES Objects, Drivers, Views, Menus, Dialogs, App;
```

Note that you don't need to derive a new object from the **TDialog** type. We will use objects of the base **TDialog** type because dialog boxes are modal and differ only in content.

Buttons

To pass from standard windows to dialog ones you have to delete the
definition of the **TInterior** and **TAboutWindow** types and rewrite the
AboutSystem method:

```
PROCEDURE TpAppl.AboutSystem;
{ make dialog box }
VAR
  C: Word;
  D: PDialog;
  R: TRect;
BEGIN
  R.Assign(20, 5, 60, 14);
  D := New(PDialog, Init(R, 'About'));
                          { make new dialog box }
  WITH D^ DO BEGIN
    R.Assign(0, 0, 40, 9);
    Options := Options OR ofCenterX;
    R.Grow(-1, -1);
    Dec(R.B.Y, 2);
    Insert(New(PStaticText, Init(R,
                        { make TStaticText and }
      #13 +^C+NamePro +#13 +
                    { insert it in  the dialog box }
      #13 +^C+CopyRight +#13)));
    R.Assign(16, 6, 22, 8);      { insert button in
                                    the dialog box }
    Insert(New(PButton, Init(R, 'O~K~', cmOK,
bfNormal)));
  END;
  C := DeskTop^.ExecView(D); { execute dialog box }
  Dispose(D, Done); { delete dialog box from Heap }
END;  { AboutSystem }
```

Figure 18-15 (over the page) shows The About dialog box.

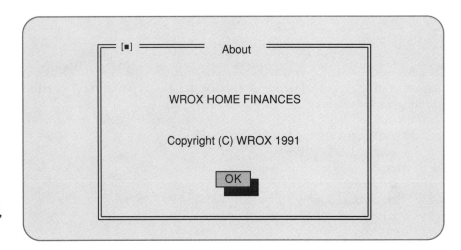

Figure 18-15
**The "About"
Dialog Box.**

To create a dialog box you have to initialize the object of the **TDialog**
type using the **Init** method. The first parameter of this method sets the
coordinates of the rectangle, the second specifies the name of the dialog
box. Then insert control objects and other views into the dialog box in
the same way as you did previously with view groups.

In our example, the **TStaticText** view is inserted. This is one of the
standard Turbo Vision views. It is used for making static text messages
on the screen. To initialize the **TStaticText** object you have to specify
the rectangle's coordinates and the message string. The **ofCenterX**
constant determines that the   **TStaticText** view will be displayed in
the owner window (dialog box in our case) and all lines will be centered
on the X-axis. The whole message string is divided into several screen
lines by the CR (#13) character. You can center any of them by beginning
each line with ^C control character.

Once you have formed all the views for the dialog window, you can start
on the control elements. In our example the dialog box contains only one
control element, the OK button. It is created by the standard method
TButton. **Button** is a rectangle with a text label. The **TDialog** object
handles events that are generated by the user, and pressing a button is
one of these events. When you press the button by clicking it with a
mouse or using the keyboard, the event handler **TDialog.HandleEvent**
generates the corresponding commands.

The **Dialogs** unit provides five standard dialog commands that deal
with the   **TButton** object: **cmOK, cmCancel, cmYes, cmNo, cmDefault**.

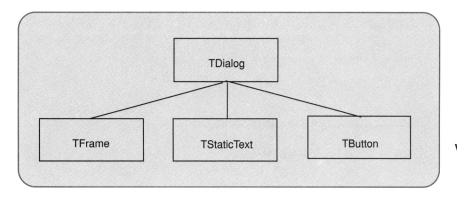

Figure 18-16
**Group of
Views for the
"About"
Dialog Box.**

The first four are displayed on the screen by specific buttons. When you push a particular button, the dialog box is closed and the corresponding command is returned as a result of the dialog box execution.

When **ESC** is pressed or the close icon [■] is clicked, the **TDialog.HandleEvent** generates the **cmCancel** command. In applications the Cancel button is often used for this command. It's sufficient to have the OK button to control the About dialog box. This button is bound with the **cmOK** command. Commands **cmOK**, **cmYes**, and **cmNo** are conventionally used for answering OK, Yes or No respectively. The **cmDefault** command indicates that the default button has been pressed. You can organize the processing of default buttons by overriding the **TButton.HandleEvent** handler (see Turbo Vision Guide).

Besides the command, each button is assigned with a standard **bf-** constant, that specifies the button type:

> **bfNormal**   - the button is normal and needs pressing.
> **bfDefault**   - the button will be selected by default when the **ENTER** key is pressed. There is only one of these buttons in each dialog box. As a rule, this is the button that is bound with the **cmDefau1**t command.

You can define a button using the following standard methods:

> **TRect.Assign**   - define rectangle for the object.
> **TButton.Init**   - initialize control element.
> **TDialog.Insert**   - add the object to dialog box.

To initialize the **TButton** object for the About box we specified:

1. Button's coordinates

2. Name string (OK)

3. Corresponding command (cmOK)

4. Button type (**bfNormal**)

The About dialog box is now ready. To execute it, use the following method:

```
TGroup.ExecView(P:  PView):  word;
```

This method stores the current desktop state, executes the dialog box, deletes it from the screen, returns the result command and restores the desktop. Note that the dialog box is executed instead of being inserted in the desktop as it is with standard windows.

The last step in the **AboutSystem** method is to delete the dialog box from the Heap using the **Dispose** procedure:

```
Dispose(D,  Done);
```

where **D** is the dialog box and **Done** is the destructor. All elements inserted in the dialog box (**TButton**, **TStaticText**) are deleted too. Using the dispose procedure means that executing the **AboutSystem** method does not reduce the available Heap memory.

Radio Buttons, Input Line and Label

The dialog box About is used for displaying a message. It does not perform any control operations for the program. As its name implies, the dialog box can also be used for making dialog in the program, in that it sets various modes of program execution. As an example we will show how to create the Set date command for our menu system (see Chapter 15, where it is implemented using the **Service** unit).

In our example the Set date menu option corresponds to the **cmSetDate** user command. The **NewDate** method that will process the **cmSetDate** command appears in the **TpAppl** type. **TpAppl.HandleEvent** binds `cmSetDate` with the **NewDate** method:

```
PROCEDURE TpAppl.HandleEvent(VAR Event: TEvent);
BEGIN
  TApplication.HandleEvent(Event);
                        { activate parent method }
  IF (Event.What = evCommand) THEN BEGIN
                        {if the command is entered}
    CASE (Event.Command) OF      { user command }
    cmAbout: AboutSystem; { help about the program }
  cmSetDate: NewDate;    { set new date in
                                  the program }
      ELSE    Exit;        { end of event handling }
    END;
    ClearEvent(Event); { event is successfully
                                    handled }
  END;
END;  { HandleEvent }
```

The **NewDate** method changes the current program date (month and year). This action can be performed using standard control objects:

TRadioButtons - specifies one of the 65536 radio buttons. We will use it for month specification.

TInputLine - inputs string using built-in string editor. We will use it to input year specification in the form of a string.

TLabel - defines the string labels of the objects (**TInputLine, TRadioButtons**) inside the dialog box for mouse clicking.

These objects and **TButton** will be used for creating the dialog box named 'Enter Date'. First we will add variables and constants to the definition section (see Chapter 15):

```
CONST
  Months: array[1..12] of string[9] =
      ('January','February','March','April','May',
              'June','July','August','September',
              'October','November','December');
VAR
  cMonth, cYear, R: word;
```

Now we can create the **TpAppl.NewDate** method:

```
PROCEDURE TpAppl.NewDate;
TYPE
  DialogData = RECORD { data definitions for dialog
                                              box }
    MonthDt: word;
    InputSt: string[4];
  END;
VAR
  D: PDialog;
  R: TRect;   B: PView;
  C, Y, M, I: Word;
  St: string[4];
  RealData: DialogData;
BEGIN
  R.Assign(20, 4, 60, 19);
  D := New(PDialog, Init(R, 'Enter Date'));
                              {create  new dialog box}
  WITH D^ DO BEGIN
    R.Assign(3, 2, 18, 14);
    B := New(PRadioButtons, Init(R, { make buttons
                                      TRadioButtons }
      NewSItem(Months[1],   NewSItem(Months[2],
                            NewSItem(Months[3],
      NewSItem(Months[4],   NewSItem(Months[5],
                            NewSItem(Months[6],
      NewSItem(Months[7],   NewSItem(Months[8],
                            NewSItem(Months[9],
      NewSItem(Months[10],  NewSItem(Months[11],
                            NewSItem(Months[12],
      nil)))))))))))));
    Insert(B);  { insert TRadioButtons in dialog box }
    R.Assign(6, 1, 12, 2);         { make a label for
                                      TRadioButtons }
    Insert(New(PLabel, Init(R, '~M~onth', B)));
    R.Assign(29, 1, 35, 2);       { create TInputLine
                                      for string input }
    B := New(PInputLine, Init(R, 4));
    Insert(B);     { insert TInputLine in dialog box }
    R.Assign(22, 1, 28, 2); { make a label for
                                      TInputLine }
```

```
   Insert(New(PLabel, Init(R, '~Y~ear', B)));
   R.Assign(22, 9, 28, 11);      { insert buttons in
                                       dialog box }
   Insert(New(PButton, Init(R, 'O~K~', cmOK,
                             bfDefault)));
   R.Assign(22, 12, 32, 14);
   Insert(New(PButton, Init(R, 'Cancel', cmCancel,
                                     bfNormal)));
END;
M := cMonth-1;
REPEAT
  I := 0; { flag normal execution of input }
  Y := cYear; Str(Y:4, St); { string for year value}
  RealData.MonthDt := M;    { form initial values
                                    for dialog box }
  RealData.InputSt := St;
  D^.SetData(RealData);       { set these values in
                                   the dialog box }
  C := DeskTop^.ExecView(D); { execute dialog box }
  IF C <> cmCancel THEN BEGIN   { if no ESC or [•] }
    D^.GetData(RealData);          { get new values }
    M := RealData.MonthDt;
    Val(RealData.InputSt, Y, I); { test year value }
    IF Y < 1900 THEN  I := 1      { execute dialog
                                     box once again }
    ELSE BEGIN
       cMonth := M+1;  cYear := Y;   { form year and
                                              month }
    END;
  END;
  UNTIL (I = 0);
  Dispose(D, Done);     { delete dialog box from Heap }
END; { NewDate }
```

The following is new main program block:

```
BEGIN
  GetDate(cYear, cMonth, R, R); { read system
                                            date }
  wApp.Init; { init application }
  wApp.Run;  { run application }
  wApp.Done; { close  application  }
END.
```

The **NewDate** method uses **cMonth** and **cYear** global variables that define the month and year. The standard **GetDate** procedure from the **Dos** unit initializes these variables with the current computer date values. (You have to include the **Dos** unit by the **USES** command). Figure 18-17 shows the result of executing the **NewDate** method:

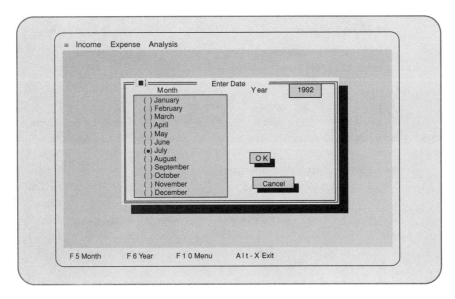

Figure 18-17
The "Enter Date" Dialog Box

With the About dialog box, first of all we create the **TRect.Assign** method and then the **TDialog.Init** constructor. We then add another object to the dialog box group.

We'll start with the **TRadioButtons** view, which makes a cluster of radio buttons with month names. This object is a descendant of the standard **TView** object and is defined by the **PView** pointer. Then, the rectangle coordinates for the object are calculated to place all the buttons on the screen. The **TRadioButtons.Init** constructor initializes the **TRadioButtons** object. Its second parameter is a pointer to the list of dynamic strings. The list is defined by the standard **TSItem** type:

```
TYPE
  PString = ^string;
  PSItem = ^TSItem;
  TSItem = RECORD
    Value: PString;
    Next: PSItem;
  END;
```

The list is formed by nested calls of the **NewSItem** procedure, and each list element is a string that corresponds to a particular button. Radio buttons are included in the dialog box by the **TGroup.Insert** method.

It is a good idea to follow each screen object with a **text label** that characterizes the object, and organizes immediate transfer of control to the object. To make a label you should use the standard **TLabel** object, which you create by calling the **TLabel.Init** method with the following parameters:

1. Position coordinates.

2. Label string (you can highlight any letter in the string using (~) character. Pressing the letter will immediately call the specified object).

3. The pointer to the object, that you specify by the label (set **Nil** if there is no object).

You define a label directly after the object which is specified by the label. An object that has a label can be activated in three different ways: using a mouse, cursor movement keys or the **ALT + <highlighted letter key>** combination.

The new **TInputLine** object reads the string from the input field which is a special screen area defined by the **TRect.Assign** method. If the string does not fit in, then horizontal scrolling is made. The maximum input field size is set by the second parameter of the constructor.

When the **TInputLine** object is added to the dialog box it is bound to the label Year. Besides the label, we can also make a **history list** for the **TInputLine** view. A history list contains the list of input before strings and is displayed on the screen with ▌↓▌ characters on the right of the input field. So, instead of retyping a view you can select it from the list. To make the history list you have to define an object of **THistory** type and bind it with the **TInputLine** object as we bound labels.

The next step is to add the OK and Cancel buttons to the dialog box. The OK button has **bfDefault** type which means that if you press **ENTER** the dialog box will be closed and the **cmOK** command will be returned.

So our box Enter Date consists of **TRadioButtons** object with Month label, **TInputLine** object with Year label and two buttons : OK and Cancel.

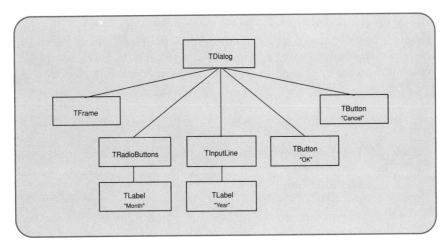

Figure 18-18
The Group of Views of the "Enter Date" Dialog Box.

You can activate any object by clicking the label with the mouse or using the **TAB** and **SHIFT-TAB** keys or pressing hotkeys of highlighted letters. The order in which you add the object to the dialog box determines the transfer order on the screen (Month —> Year —> OK —> Cancel).

Now we'll consider how to set initial values and get changed values, for the **TRadioButtons** and **TInputLine** views. This is done using a special record and the standard **SetData** and **GetData** methods. The record contains data fields for all dialog box objects. For example, the **DialogData** record contains the **MonthDt:** word field for the active radio button (0..65535) and the **InputSt:** string[4] field for the **TInputLine** view string. The sequence of the fields corresponds to the sequence in which the objects were added to the dialog box.

The **SetData** method uses **RealData** as a parameter for setting initial values in the dialog box. Figure 18-17 shows the dialog box with the following **RealData** setting:

```
RealData.MonthDt := 7;
RealData.InputSt := 1992;
```

If the dialog is successfully completed, then the **GetData** method returns new values in **RealData**. The **REPEAT..UNTIL** loop tests the conversion of an input string to a number. If the string cannot be converted the dialog is repeated. Every time an error string is input, the dialog box is closed and immediately opened again. This happens because the testing procedure is outside the dialog box. You can test inside the box using the new descendant of **TInputLine**.

The Enter Date dialog box is now ready. You can include any number of views in the dialog boxes. Any time you do this, change the record **DialogData**.

You can also use a cluster of check boxes in the dialog box (see Chapter 1) defined by the **TCheckBoxes** view. It can contain from 1 to 16 control elements. For example Figure 2-4 shows the check boxes Options with 4 controls in the Replace dialog box. Each check box can be set on the screen independently, turned either on or off. The data for check boxes is transferred as a number of the word type. Each of the 16 bits corresponds to one check box and defines its state: 1 - on, 0 - off. Check boxes are included in the same way as buttons, input lines and radio buttons. You can find all the necessary information about methods and constants for making dialog boxes in the Turbo Vision Guide or IDE help.

Graphics Output in Turbo Vision

In our HomeFinances program, the **cmMonth** and **cmYear** commands output the results in the graphics mode. Unfortunately, Turbo Vision can only work in the text mode. To avoid problems that might arise from this, follow our algorithm:

1. Deactivate the main Turbo Vision control objects and free the memory.

2. Initialize the graphics mode and perform graphics output.

3. Restore the memory and activate the main Turbo Vision control objects.

Graphics initialization remains unchangeable (see Chapter 16). We will complete the process using two methods which are included in the **TpAppl** type:

```
TYPE
  TpAppl = OBJECT(TApplication)
   PROCEDURE HandleEvent(VAR Event: TEvent); VIRTUAL;
   PROCEDURE InitMenuBar; VIRTUAL;
   PROCEDURE InitStatusLine; VIRTUAL;
   PROCEDURE AboutSystem;
   PROCEDURE NewDate;
   PROCEDURE ToGraph;    { switch to graphics mode }
   PROCEDURE ReturnText;{ return to the text mode }
  END;
```

The **ToGraph** method deactivates the main Turbo Vision control objects, frees the memory and sets the graphics mode:

```
PROCEDURE TpAppl.ToGraph;
BEGIN
   DoneSysError; { deactivate Turbo Vision
                                error processing }
   DoneEvents; { terminate event handling and
                                mouse control }
   DoneVideo;        { deactivate video processing }
   DoneMemory;                     { free memory }
   SetGraphMode(GetGraphMode);{ set graphics mode }
   END;                             { ToGraph }
```

The **DoneSysError** procedure deactivates Turbo Vision error processing. **DoneEvents** deactivates event handling and mouse control. **DoneError** deactivates video processing. **DoneMemory** frees memory. The **ReturnText** method performs the opposite of these actions:

```
PROCEDURE TpAppl.ReturnText;
BEGIN
  SetTextJustify(CenterText, TopText);
  SetColor(GetMaxColor);
  OutTextXY(GetMaxX div 2, GetMaxY-
  (TextHeight('N')+4),'Press any key to continue...');
  AnyKey;
  RestoreCrtmode;   { return to the text mode }
  InitMemory;       { initializes Turbo Vision
                                memory manager }
  InitVideo;        { activate video processing }
  InitEvents;       { initializes event manager and
                                mouse control }
  InitSysError;     { initialize Turbo Vision
                            error processing }
  Redraw;           { redraw old views on the screen }
END;                        { ReturnText }
```

The **InitMemory** procedure initializes the Turbo Vision memory manager. **InitVideo** initializes video manager. **InitEvents** initializes event manager and mouse control. **InitSysError** initializes the error manager. The **ReturnText** method calls these standard procedures in the same order as the **TApplication.Init** constructor. There is no need to initialize views again because we did not dispose of them in the **ToGraph** method. The **Redraw** method restores and displays the group of all existing views (in our case desktop, menu bar and status line).

The **ReturnText** method uses the **AnyKey** procedure from the **Service** unit (see Chapter 15). It waits until any key is pressed, then the **RestoreCrtMode** procedure returns the text mode and restores the standard Turbo Vision screen.

Since Turbo Vision does not work in the graphics mode, program control and data processing has to be performed by the programmer. As this unfortunate transfer from the rich Turbo Vision programming techniques affects the quality of the programs, we advise you, where possible, to only use text modes in Turbo Vision programs. You will find the complete text of the Turbo Vision version of the HomeFinances program in Appendix B.

Summary

Now that you have a Turbo Vision version of the HomeFinances program you can compare it with the previous program in Chapter 15. Although we haven't used Turbo Vision to its full capacity, the second version is undoubtedly more effective and better designed.

As far as designing programs in Turbo Vision goes, it's a good idea to divide every program into two sections: **interactive** and **internal**. The internal section contains all algorithms and calculations that are not visible to the user. For example, in our HomeFinances program we hid the operations with the **BASE.DTA** file and the income/expenditure calculations. The results of the work with the internal section must be presented in forms suitable for Turbo Vision views. The internal section can be designed both by traditional and OOP techniques. As Turbo Vision is based on OOP however, it is more natural to implement this section using the OOP approach. Moreover, using OOP you can operate with Turbo Vision tools: sorting procedures, file managing, etc. The interactive section contains views and the event handler can only be written using Turbo Vision techniques.

In conclusion we want to stress that Turbo Vision will help you create more effective programs and to become more familiar with OOP. Turbo Vision will demonstrate the main advantages of the new OOP approach, and it will make it easier for you to study modern object oriented software.

HOMEFINANCES PROGRAM

There are two versions of the HomeFinances program. One is for use with standard Turbo Pascal features (presented in Appendix A) and the other is intended for Turbo Vision (Appendix B). To compile the programs you need to copy the **EGAVGA.BGI** file from the main Turbo Pascal system subdirectory. Both versions contain the same procedures and functions. It is a good idea to assemble them in separate files employing the {$I} directive. We will look at these files in Appendix A only and will not repeat the explanations in Appendix B. For this reason, we have divided the HomeFinances program into 4 groups:

▲ Global definitions.

▲ Procedures and functions for processing data files and performing other   service actions.

▲ Procedures and functions for graphic output.

▲ Main program.

We'll continue by considering each group in turn.

Global Definitions

```
TYPE
  Base = RECORD              { file record }
         Month  : byte;      { month }
         Year   : word;      { year }
         Income : real;      { monthly income }
         Food,               { food expenses }
         Accommodation,      { living expenses }
         Clothing,           { clothes expenses }
         Education,          { education expenses }
         MedicalCare,        { expenses for medical care }
         Leisure,            { leisure expenses }
         Other  : real;      { other expenses }
       END;
```

```
CONST
  FileName = 'BASE.DTA';
  NamePro = 'WROX HOME FINANCES';
  CopyRight = 'Copyright (C) WROX 1992';
  Months: array[1..12] of MenuStr = ('January','February','March',
        'April','May','June','July','August','September',
        'October','November','December');
  sMain = 3;   sInc = 2;   sExp = 7;   sAn = 2;
  { command menu definition }
  aMain: array[1..sMain] of MenuStr = ('Income', 'Expense',
                                'Analysis');
  iMain: byte = 1;    { index of current menu bar item }
  aInc: array[1..sInc] of MenuStr = ('Income', 'Set date');
  iInc: byte = 1;     { index of current menu "Income" item }
  aExp: array[1..sExp] of MenuStr = ('Food','Accommodation',
      'Clothing','Education','Medical care','Leisure','Other');
  iExp: byte = 1;     { index of current menu "Expense" item }
  aAn: array[1..sAn] of MenuStr = ('Month', 'Year');
  iAn: byte = 1;      { index of current menu "Analysis" item}
  NameX = 'X month';   NameY = 'sum Y';
VAR
  wFile: file of Base;        { data file }
  ArrRec: array[1..12] of Base; { base records per year }
  wRec,                    { current file record }
  fRec: Base;              { first file record }
  cMonth, cYear,           { current month and year }
  cPos,         { position of the current file record }
  Fs: word;                { file size }
```

Definition data will be placed in the **TYPEDEF.PAS** file.

Procedures and Functions for Processing Data Files

```
FUNCTION ConvDate(Year, Month: word): word;
{ Calculates date value in month }
BEGIN
  ConvDate:= (Year-1900)*12 +pred(Month);
END; { ConvDate }

FUNCTION LoadRec(M, Y: word; VAR Rec: Base): boolean;
{ Reads data file record, returns read value as Rec parameter.
  The record contains M-month and Y-year values. Adds empty records if
      the file is empty or there is no record for current date }
VAR
  NewRec: Base;           { for empty file record }
  I, J: word;
BEGIN
  LoadRec:= False;
  FillChar(NewRec, SizeOf(Base), 0); { initializes fields }
```

```
  IF Fs = 0 THEN BEGIN                { empty file }
    NewRec.Month:= M;   NewRec.Year:= Y;
    Write(wFile, NewRec);             { creates first record }
    fRec:= NewRec;  Rec:= NewRec;
    Fs:= Fs+1;  Cpos:= 0;  END
  ELSE BEGIN                          { file is not empty }
    I:= ConvDate(Y, M);              { current date in month }
    { date value from the first record }
    J:= ConvDate(fRec.Year, fRec.Month);
    IF I < J THEN   Exit;  { exit: date is lower than first date }
    I:= I-J;              { month difference between dates }
    IF Fs < I+1 THEN BEGIN      { adds new records }
      Seek(wFile, Fs-1);        { points the last file record }
      Read(wFile, Rec);
      WITH NewRec DO BEGIN      { adds new records to the file }
        Month:= Rec.Month;      { from the last record }
        Year:= Rec.Year;
        { add new records to the end of the file }
        FOR J:=1 TO I+1-Fs DO BEGIN
          IF (Month<12) THEN inc(Month) { turns to the next month }
          ELSE BEGIN
            inc(Year);   Month:= 1; { turns to the next year }
          END;
          Write(wFile, NewRec); { writes new records in the file }
        END;
      END;
      Fs:= Fs+J;  Cpos:= Fs; { new number of records in the file }
      Rec:= NewRec;   END
    ELSE BEGIN              { the record for current date exists }
      Cpos:= I+1;              { current record pointer }
      Seek(wFile, Cpos-1);   { points the last file record }
      Read(wFile, Rec);
    END;
  END;
  LoadRec:= True;
END; { LoadRec }

PROCEDURE SaveWRec;
{ Save current file record, cPos variable contains record number,
  wRec contains current record value }
BEGIN
  Seek(wFile, cPos-1);
  Write(wFile, wRec);     { writes the current record to the file }
END; { SaveRec }

PROCEDURE ExitWork;
{ Closes data file and exits program }
BEGIN
  Close(wFile);    ExitProgram;
END; { ExitWork }
```

```
PROCEDURE Abort(S: string);
{ Exits program and outputs error message }
BEGIN
  ExitWork;
  Writeln('ERROR: ',S);   Halt(1);
END;  { Abort }

FUNCTION GetExpense(Rec: Base): real;
{ Calculates sum of all expenses according to Rec record }
BEGIN
  WITH Rec DO
    GetExpense:= Food+ Accommodation+ Clothing+ Education+
              MedicalCare+ Leisure+ Other;
END;  { GetExpense }

PROCEDURE InitWork;
{ Program initialization: reads system date, opens data file,
  initializes graphics, restores text mode, outputs program label }
VAR
  DriverVar, ModeVar, ErrCode: integer;  { for graphics driver }
  I: word;
BEGIN
  GetDate(cYear, cMonth, I, I);  { reads system date }
  Assign(wFile, FileName);
  {$I-} Reset(wFile); {$I+}      { opens old file }
  IF (IOResult <> 0) THEN   Rewrite(wFile); { opens new file }
  Fs:= FileSize(wFile);          { current size of file }
  IF Fs <> 0 THEN BEGIN          { reads first file record }
    Seek(wFile, 0);
    Read(wFile, fRec);
  END;
  IF NOT LoadRec(cMonth, cYear, wRec) THEN { reads file record }
    { exits program if there is no record for the date }
    Abort('Invalid date');
  DriverVar:= Detect;
  InitGraph(DriverVar, ModeVar,''); { initializes graphics }
  ErrCode:= GraphResult;
  IF ErrCode <> grOk THEN   Abort(GraphErrorMsg(ErrCode));
  RestoreCrtMode;                { restores text mode }
  WrtLabel(NamePro, CopyRight); { outputs program label }
END;  { InitWork }
```

These procedures and functions will be placed in the **F_PROC.PAS** file.

Procedures and Functions for Graphics Output

The following procedures and functions include the familiar **Coord, Chart** and **Pie** functions (see Chapter 16) as well as some other procedures and functions used for customizing graphics on real data from the **BASE.DTA** file:

```
PROCEDURE Coord(X0, Y0, Sx, Cx, Vx, Sy, Cy, Vy: integer;
             NameX, NameY: string; ColorC, ColorN: word);
{ Draws the two-dimensional coordinate system (see Chapter 16)
  X0, Y0 - start point coordinates;
  Sx - graduation step size in pixels on X;
  Cx - number of steps on X;
  Vx - integer value for first step on X;
  Sy - graduation step size in pixels on Y;
  Cy - number of steps on Y;
  Vy - integer value for first step on Y;
  NameX, NameY - X, Y axes names;
  ColorC, ColorN - axis colour and axis letter's colour }
VAR
  St: string[6];
  I, J: word;
BEGIN
  SetColor(ColorC);   { sets the colour of the X and Y axes }
  Line(X0, Y0, X0+Sx*Cx, Y0);            { outputs X axis }
  SetTextJustify(CenterText, TopText);
  FOR I:=1 TO Cx DO BEGIN          { graduates the X axis }
    J := X0+Sx*I;   Line(J, Y0-2, J, Y0+2);
    Str(Vx*I, St);      { converts the number into a string }
    OutTextXY(J, Y0+8, St);
  END;
  Line(X0, Y0, X0, Y0-Sy*Cy);           { outputs the Y axis }
  SetTextJustify(RightText, CenterText);
  FOR I:=1 TO Cy DO BEGIN          { graduates the Y axis }
    J := Y0-Sy*I;   Line(X0-2, J, X0+2, J);
    Str(Vy*I, St);      { converts the number into a string }
    OutTextXY(X0-4, J, St);
  END;
  SetColor(ColorN);          { sets the colour of the name }
  IF (TextWidth(NameY) DIV 2) >= X0 THEN BEGIN
    I := LeftText;
    J := 1;   END
  ELSE BEGIN
    I := CenterText;
    J := X0;
  END;
  SetTextJustify(I, CenterText);   { outputs the axes names }
  OutTextXY(J, Y0-Sy*Cy-20, NameY);
  SetTextJustify(LeftText, CenterText);
  OutTextXY(X0+Sx*Cx+10, Y0, NameX);
END;   { Coord }

PROCEDURE Chart(X0, Y0, Sx, Cx, Wx, Sy, Vy: integer;
             VAR Values; ColorBar, FillCode: word);
{ Draws the bar chart (see Chapter 16)
  X0,Y0 - bar chart start point;
  Sx - graduation size in pixels on X;
  Cx - number of graduations on X;
  Wx - column width in pixels on X;
```

```
  Sy - graduation size in pixels on Y;
  Values - array of column Y coordinates;
  ColorBar - column colour;
  FillCode - column fill style }
VAR
  ArrY: array[1..50] of integer ABSOLUTE Values;
  I, X2, Y2: integer;
BEGIN
  SetFillStyle(FillCode, ColorBar);
  SetColor(ColorBar);
  FOR I := 1 TO Cx DO BEGIN
    IF ArrY[I] > 0 THEN BEGIN
      X2 := X0+Wx;
      Y2 := Y0-Trunc((ArrY[I]/Vy)*Sy);
      Bar(X0, Y0, X2, Y2);
      Rectangle(X0, Y0, X2, Y2);
    END;
    X0 := X0+Sx;
  END;
END;  { Chart }

PROCEDURE Pie(X, Y, Radius, Count: integer; VAR Percents, Names);
{ Draws the pie chart (see Chapter 16)
  X, Y - start point coordinates;
  Radius - sector radius in pixels;
  Count - number of sector or components;
  Percents - array of percentage of each component;
  Names - array of component names }
TYPE  NameStr = MenuStr;
CONST  MaxValues = 30;
VAR
  ArrPer: array[1..MaxValues] of byte ABSOLUTE Percents;
  ArrNames: array[1..MaxValues] of MenuStr ABSOLUTE Names;
  MaxColor, FillPie, ColorPie, Xasp, Yasp,
  Angle, AngleMed, AngleCur: word;
  Xb, Yb, Wb, Hb, Xp, Yp, Psum, I: integer;
  Radians: real;
  St : string[5];
BEGIN
  Angle := 0;                  { first corner of the diagram }
  FillPie := SolidFill;   ColorPie := Blue; { first values }
  GetAspectRatio(Xasp, Yasp);  { relational X and Y coordinates }
  MaxColor := GetMaxColor;   Psum := 0;
  Xb := X+Radius+30;
  Yb := Y -Round(Radius*Xasp/Yasp) +30;
  Wb := 50;   Hb := TextHeight('N')*2;
  FOR I := 1 TO Count DO BEGIN
    IF I = Count THEN BEGIN                { final sector }
      ArrPer[I] := 100 -Psum;
      AngleCur := 360 -Angle;  END
    ELSE
      AngleCur := Round(ArrPer[I]*3.6);  { reorganizes }
    { Calculates the mid-point of the sector. Header to be output
      at this position }
```

```
   AngleMed := AngleCur DIV 2 +Angle;
   Radians := AngleMed*Pi/180;
   SetFillStyle(FillPie, ColorPie);
   PieSlice(X, Y, Angle, Angle+AngleCur, Radius);
   Angle := Angle +AngleCur;
   Psum := Psum +ArrPer[I];
   { calculates the boundary coordinates of the sector and outputs
     the percentage }
   Xp := X +Round(Cos(Radians) *Radius);
   Yp := Y -Round((Xasp/Yasp)*Round(Sin(Radians) *Radius));
   IF AngleMed < 90 THEN
     SetTextJustify(LeftText, BottomText)
   ELSE IF AngleMed < 180 THEN
     SetTextJustify(RightText, BottomText)
   ELSE IF AngleMed < 270 THEN
     SetTextJustify(RightText, TopText)
   ELSE  SetTextJustify(LeftText, TopText);
   Str(ArrPer[I], St);    OutTextXY(Xp, Yp, St+' %');
   IF FillPie < CloseDotFill THEN   Inc(FillPie);
   IF ColorPie < MaxColor THEN   Inc(ColorPie);
   { outputs the sector name }
   Bar(Xb, Yb, Xb+Wb, Yb+Hb);   Rectangle(Xb, Yb, Xb+Wb, Yb+Hb);
   SetTextJustify(LeftText, CenterText);
   { output the name }
   OutTextXY(Xb+Wb+4, Yb+ Hb DIV 2, ArrNames[I]);
   Yb := Yb+Hb*2;
  END;
END;  { Pie }


FUNCTION RealToStr(R: real; W, D: byte): string;
{ Converts real number R in a string }
VAR  St : string[20];
BEGIN
  Str(R:W:D, St);
  RealToStr := St;
END;  { RealToStr }


PROCEDURE DrawChart(Y: word);
{ Draws bar chart using current year data from data file }
CONST   Cx = 12;                { 12 months }
VAR
  ArrIn, ArrExp: array[1..Cx] of real;
  InData, ExpData: array[1..Cx] of integer;
  X0, Y0, Sx, Wx, Sy, Cy, Vy, I, J: integer;
  Imin, Imax, Isum, Emin, Emax, Esum, Max: real;
  Count1, Count2: byte;
  Rec: Base;
  St: string;
BEGIN
  FillChar(ArrIn, SizeOf(ArrIn), 0);  { zeroes array elements }
  FillChar(ArrExp, SizeOf(ArrExp), 0);
  I:= ConvDate(fRec.Year, fRec.Month);   J:= 0;
  IF (Y = fRec.Year) THEN   J:= I
  ELSE IF (Y > fRec.Year) THEN   J:= ConvDate(Y, 1);
```

```
IF J > 0 THEN              { forms ArrIn and ArrOut arrays }
  IF Succ(J-I) <= Fs THEN BEGIN
    { sets file pointer to first record for current year }
    Seek(wFile,J-I);
    REPEAT
      Read(wFile, Rec); { reads file record }
      IF (Rec.Month = cMonth) AND (Rec.Year = cYear) THEN
        Rec:= wRec;
      WITH Rec DO BEGIN
        ArrIn[Month]:= Income;
        ArrExp[Month]:= GetExpense(Rec);
      END;
    UNTIL (Eof(wFile) OR (Rec.Month = 12));
  END;
Imax:= 0;   Emax:= 0;   Isum:= 0;   Esum:= 0;
Imin:= 0;   Emin:= 0;   Count1:= 0;   Count2:= 0;
FOR I:=1 TO Cx DO BEGIN    { prepares data arrays for Chart }
  InData[I]:= Round(ArrIn[I]);
  ExpData[I]:= Round(ArrExp[I]);
  IF ArrIn[I] > 0 THEN BEGIN
    IF (Imin > ArrIn[I]) OR (Imin = 0) THEN  Imin:= ArrIn[I];
    IF Imax < ArrIn[I] THEN   Imax:= ArrIn[I];
    Isum:= Isum +ArrIn[I];   Inc(Count1);
  END;
  IF ArrExp[I] > 0 THEN BEGIN
    IF (Emin > ArrExp[I]) OR (Emin = 0) THEN  Emin:= ArrExp[I];
    IF Emax < ArrExp[I] THEN   Emax:= ArrExp[I];
    Esum:= Esum +ArrExp[I];   Inc(Count2);
  END;
END;
{ outputs bar chart name }
Str(Y:4, St);
SetTextJustify(CenterText, TopText);
OutTextXY(GetMaxX DIV 2, 0, 'Analysis for '+St+' year');
I:= GetMaxX DIV 4;   J:= TextHeight('N');
SetColor(LightCyan);
OuttextXY(I, J*3, 'INCOME:');  { outputs income values }
OutTextXY(I, J*6, 'In all = ' +RealToStr(Isum,8,2));
IF Count1 > 0 THEN   BEGIN
  OutTextXY(I,J*7,'Max    = ' +RealToStr(Imax,8,2));
  OutTextXY(I,J*8,'Min    = ' +RealToStr(Imin,8,2));
  OutTextXY(I,J*9,'Middle = ' +RealToStr(Isum/Count1,8,2));
END;
I:= I*3;
SetColor(LightGreen);
OuttextXY(I, J*3, 'EXPENSE:'); { outputs expense values }
OutTextXY(I, J*6, 'In all = ' +RealToStr(Esum,8,2));
IF Count2 > 0 THEN   BEGIN
  OutTextXY(I,J*7,'Max    = ' +RealToStr(Emax,8,2));
  OutTextXY(I,J*8,'Min    = ' +RealToStr(Emin,8,2));
  OutTextXY(I,J*9,'Middle = ' +RealToStr(Esum/Count2,8,2));
END;
IF Count1+Count2 = 0 THEN  Exit; { if not values - exit }
```

```
  { prepares data for Coord and Chart procedures }
  IF Imax > Emax THEN   Max:= Imax
  ELSE   Max:= Emax;
  Cy:= 10;                      { 10 graduation steps on Y }
  Vy:= Succ(Round(Max) DIV Cy);
  Inc(Vy, (100 -Vy MOD 100)); { graduation step size for Y axis }
  Y0:= GetMaxY -J*6;   X0 := GetMaxX DIV 12;
  Sx:= (GetMaxX -X0*5) DIV Cx;
  Sy:= (GetMaxY -J*(6+12+4)) DIV Cy;
  Coord(X0,Y0,Sx,Cx,1,Sy,Cy,Vy,NameX,NameY,Cyan, LightRed);
  Wx:= (Sx -12) DIV 2;          { column width }
  Chart(X0+4,Y0,Sx,Cx,Wx,Sy,Vy,InData,LightCyan,LtSlashFill);
  Chart(X0+8+Wx,Y0,Sx,Cx,Wx,Sy,Vy,ExpData,LightGreen,SolidFill);
  IF Isum > Esum THEN           { prepares summary string }
    St:= 'Summary: GOOD! INCOME is greater than EXPENSE!'
  ELSE
    St:= 'Summary: BAD! You have to reduce your EXPENSE!';
  SetColor(Yellow);  SetTextJustify(CenterText, TopText);
  OutTextXY(GetMaxX DIV 2, J*12, St); { outputs summary string }
END;  { DrawChart }
```

```
PROCEDURE DrawPie(Rec: Base);
{ Draws pie chart according to Base record fields}
TYPE
  { this record will access the Base field using ABSOLUTE keyword }
  FreeRec = RECORD
          Month  : byte;
          Year   : word;
      Income : real;
       ValR   : array[1..sExp] of real;
    END;
VAR
  Names: array[1..sExp] of MenuStr;
  Percents: array[1..sExp] of byte;
  X, Y, Count, Radius, I: integer;
  St: string[20];
  R: real;
  AltRec: FreeRec ABSOLUTE Rec;
  { after this you can access any field of Base record as
    the element of ValR array of FreeRec record }
BEGIN
  FillChar(Percents,SizeOf(Percents),0); { zeroes arrays elements }
  Y:= GetMaxY DIV 2;
  X:= GetMaxX DIV 2 - GetMaxX DIV 6;
  Radius:= GetMaxX DIV 4;
  R:= GetExpense(Rec);
  WITH Rec DO BEGIN
    Str(Year:4, St);
    SetTextJustify(CenterText, TopText);
    OutTextXY(GetMaxX DIV 2, 0,
            'Analysis for '+Months[Month]+' '+St);
```

```
   Str(Income:8:2, St);
   SetColor(LightCyan);
   { outputs month incomes }
   OuttextXY(GetMaxX DIV 4, 3*TextHeight('N'),'INCOME: '+St);
   Str(R:8:2, St);   SetColor(LightGreen);
   { outputs monthly expenses }
   OuttextXY((GetMaxX DIV 4)*3,3*TextHeight('N'),'EXPENSE: '+St);
 END;
 SetColor(GetMaxColor);
 Count:= 0;            { prepares data about percentage }
 FOR I:= 1 TO sExp DO
   { if the present expense item exists }
   IF AltRec.ValR[I] > 0 THEN BEGIN
     Inc(Count);
     Percents[Count]:= Round(100 *AltRec.ValR[I]/R);
     Names[Count]:= aExp[I];  { name of expense item }
   END;
 Pie(X, Y, Radius, Count, Percents, Names);  { draws pie chart }
END;  { DrawPie }
```

These procedures and functions will be placed in the **G_PROC.PAS** file.

The Main Program

```
PROGRAM HomeFinances;
{ The program analysis family year income and expenditure }
USES Crt, Dos, Graph, Service;

{$I TYPEDEF.PAS}
{$I F_PROC.PAS}
{$I G_PROC.PAS}

PROCEDURE OutBase(X,Y: byte; Name: string; Rec: Base);
{ Draws income and expense for the file record in the screen window:
  X, Y - window coordinates;
  Name - window name;
  Rec - file record }
VAR
  St: string[4];
  R: real;
BEGIN
  WITH Rec DO BEGIN
    Str(Year:4, St);
    Frame(X, Y, X+35, Y+3, Name+': '+Months[Month]+' '+St);
    WriteXYc('Income:  ',X+2,Y+1,NormColor); { outputs the name }
    SetCol(HighColor);
    Write(Income:10:2);               { outputs the income value }
    WriteXYc('Expense: ',X+2,Y+2,NormColor); { outputs the name }
```

```
    R:= GetExpense(Rec);                    { total expense value }
    SetCol(HighColor);
    Write(R:10:2);                    { outputs the expense value }
  END;
END; { OutBase }


PROCEDURE OutTwoBases;
{ Draws income and expense for the first and the current file
  records }
BEGIN
  IF (fRec.Year = wRec.Year) AND (fRec.Month = wRec.Month) THEN
    OutBase(1,20,'First date',wRec)  { for the first file record }
  ELSE  OutBase(1, 20, 'First date', fRec);
  OutBase(45,20,'Current date',wRec); {for the current file record}
END; { OutTwoBases }


FUNCTION GetReal(R:real; X,Y:byte; NameField, St:string): real;
{ Draws input real number in the window:
  R - current number;
  X, Y - window coordinates;
  NameField - logical name of the number;
  St - the string describes read operation: 'New' or 'Add' }
VAR
  S: string;
  CopyR: Real;
  I: word;
BEGIN
  WrtHelp('ENTER exit');                    { help string }
  REPEAT
    CopyR := R;
    Frame(X, Y, X+35, Y+3, 'Enter '+NameField); { window frame }
    WriteXYc('Old value: ', X+2, Y+1, NormColor);
    SetCol(HighColor);  Write(R:10:2); { outputs previous value }
    WriteXYc(St+' value: ', X+2, Y+2, NormColor);
    SetCol(HighColor);  Readln(S);     { inputs number string }
    Val(S, CopyR, I);
    IF S = '' THEN BEGIN
      I := 0;   CopyR := 0;             { if the string is empty }
    END;
    Window(X,Y,X+35,Y+3);  SetCol(NormColor);  ClrScr;
    Window(1,1,80,25); { return to the normal size of the window }
  UNTIL (I = 0);        { loop until current number will be input }
  GetReal := CopyR;
END; { GetReal }
PROCEDURE InputData(Cm: word);
{ Inputs income and expense values for the current wRec record.
  Cm specifies ordinal number of the field of Base record
  starting from the Income field }


FUNCTION GetField(X, Y: byte; Value: real; Name: string): real;
{ Changes Value parameter in the window. New value is the sum of
  current and input ones. Checks for positive values only }
```

```
VAR
  D: real;
BEGIN
  D:= GetReal(Value,X,Y,Name,'Add') +Value; { changes Value }
  IF D < 0 THEN D := Value;                { check new value }
  GetField := D;
END;    { GetField }

BEGIN   { InputData }
  WITH wRec DO          { changes real fields of wRec record }
    CASE Cm OF
      0: Income:= GetField(3, 4, Income, aMain[1]);
      1: Food:= GetField(25, 2+Cm, Food, aExp[Cm]);
      2: Accommodation:= GetField(25,2+Cm,Accommodation,aExp[Cm]);
      3: Clothing:= GetField(25, 2+Cm, Clothing, aExp[Cm]);
      4: Education:= GetField(25, 2+Cm, Education, aExp[Cm]);
      5: MedicalCare:= GetField(25,2+Cm,MedicalCare,aExp[Cm]);
      6: Leisure:= GetField(25, 2+Cm, Leisure, aExp[Cm]);
      7: Other:= GetField(25, 2+Cm, Other, aExp[Cm]);
    END;
  OutTwoBases;        { outputs new income and expense values }
END; { InputData }

PROCEDURE NewDate;
{ Enter new date }
VAR
  Rec: Base;
  M: byte;
  Y: word;
  St: string[4];
BEGIN
  Y:= Round(GetReal(cYear, 15, 4, aAn[2], 'New')); { inputs year }
  IF ((Y = 0) OR (Y < 1990)) THEN  Y:= cYear; { check year value }
  Str(Y:4, St);
  Frame(15, 4, 40, 19, 'Enter Month '+St);    { window frame }
  M := cMonth;
  IF VMenu(Months, M, 21, 5, 12) THEN BEGIN   { month menu }
    SaveWRec;                 { saves current record in the file }
    { reads new record for the new date }
    IF LoadRec(M,Y,Rec) THEN BEGIN
      wRec := Rec;
      cMonth := M;   cYear := Y;
    END;
  END;
  Window(15, 4, 40, 19);  SetCol(NormColor);  ClrScr;
  Window(1, 1, 80, 25);     { restores normal window size }
  OutTwoBases;              { outputs income and expense values }
END; { NewDate }
PROCEDURE ReturnText;
{ Restores text mode }
BEGIN
  { outputs message and makes delay }
  SetTextJustify(CenterText, TopText);  SetColor(GetMaxColor);
  OutTextXY(GetMaxX div 2, GetMaxY-(TextHeight('N')+4),
```

```
        'Press any key to continue...');   AnyKey;
  RestoreCrtmode;                { restores text mode }
  SetCol(NormColor); ClrScr; { clears screen }
  OutTwoBases;                { outputs income and expense values }
END; { ReturnText; }


PROCEDURE MonthBal;
{ Draws the month results of the analysis in the form of
  pie chart }
BEGIN
  SetGraphMode(GetGraphMode); { sets previous graphics mode }
  DrawPie(wRec);  { draws pie chart for the current wRec record }
  ReturnText;                { restores text mode }
END; { MonthBal }


PROCEDURE YearBal;
{ Draws the year results in the form of bar chart }
BEGIN
  SetGraphMode(GetGraphMode); { sets previous graphics mode }
  DrawChart(cYear); { draws bar chart for the current cYear year }
  ReturnText;                { restores text mode }
END; { YearBal }
BEGIN   { HomeFinances }
  InitWork;                { program initialization }
  OutTwoBases;                { outputs income and expense values }
  WHILE HMenu(aMain, iMain, 1, sMain) DO
    CASE iMain OF
      1: WHILE VMenu(aInc, iInc, 3, 2, sInc) DO
           IF iInc = 1 THEN  InputData(0) { enters income value }
           ELSE  NewDate;                { enters date }
      2: WHILE VMenu(aExp, iExp, 12, 2, sExp) DO
           InputData(iExp);                { enters expense values }
      3: IF VMenu(aAn, iAn, 22, 2, sAn) THEN
           CASE iAn OF
             1: MonthBal;              { month analysis }
             2: YearBal;              { year analysis }
           END;
    END;
  SaveWRec;              { saves the current record }
  ExitWork;              { exits the program }
END.   { HomeFinances }
```

Instructions for Use

The HomeFinances program allows you to enter and analyze income and
expenditure data. The data is organized by month and is stored in separate
records in the **BASE.DTA** file. The program keeps account of the data already
stored in the system and automatically adjusts the data you enter for each
new month. Furthermore, the program allows you to access the values for

any month or year which means that you can alter the figures entered for the previous month for example. The results of the analysis of data are presented in the graphics mode.

A pie chart is used to show how the expenditure is allocated for the current month (Food, Accommodation, Clothing, Medical care, Leisure, Other). A two-dimensional bar chart is used to show the changes in the income and expenditure for the current year (see chapter 16). When you start HomeFinances, the first screen picture you get shows the system name and the copyright. To get into the main menu, press any key. The main menu contains three main regimes: Income, Expense, Analysis. To select an option, position the cursor on the one you want, then press **ENTER** (see Chapter 15).

The Income menu contains two commands: Income and Set date. When you select the Income command, a window appears on the screen showing the income value for the current month. You can increase this value by adding a positive number, or decrease it by entering a negative one which means that you can easily alter the income value for the current month.

The Set date command allows you to change the value of the current date in the program. When you select this command, a vertical menu appears on the screen listing all the months. When you select a month, a separate window appears on the screen into which you can enter the new values for the year, then press **ENTER**. If the value of the date has been changed, then the data for the old date is stored in the **BASE.DTA** file and the values for the new date are calculated.

The Expense menu contains seven commands that correspond to the various outgoing expenses: Food, Accommodation, Clothing, Education, Medical care, Leisure, Other. By selecting any of these commands you can change the value of the current type of expense. The same applies to changing these values as for the Income command.

Finally, the Analysis menu contains two commands which give you access to the figures for: Month and Year. When you select the Month command, a pie chart appears on the screen giving a percentage representation of the expenses for the current month. Selecting the Year gives you a two-dimensional bar chart of the income and expenditure for the current year. If you have changed the value of the current data using the Set date command, you can easily analyse the results for any previous month or year. To exit the HomeFinances program, return to the main menu and press **ESC**.

HOMEFINANCES PROGRAM IN TURBO VISION

The Turbo Vision HomeFinances program text is made up of the same functions and procedures that were described in Appendix A. These will be initialized in the basic program by the {$I} directive. To distinguish between the two programs, we have called this one TvHomeFinances. To compile the program you need to copy the **EGAVGA.BGI** file from the main Turbo Pascal system subdirectory.

```
PROGRAM TvHomeFinances;
USES Crt, Dos, Graph, Objects, Drivers, Memory, Views,
     Menus, Dialogs, App, Service;
CONST
  cmAbout= 100;            { about command }
  cmIncome= 101;           { changes income value }
  cmFood= 102;             { changes expenses value for food }
  cmAccommodation=103;     { changes expenses value for accommodation}
  cmClothing= 104;         { changes expenses value for clothing }
  cmEducation= 105;        { changes expenses value for education }
  cmMedicalCare= 106;      { changes expenses value for medical care }
  cmLeisure= 107;          { changes expenses value for leisure }
  cmOther= 108;            { changes expenses value for other }
  cmSetDate= 109;          { sets date }
  cmMonth= 110;            { month analysis }
  cmYear= 111;             { year analysis }
TYPE
  TpAppl = OBJECT(TApplication)
      PROCEDURE HandleEvent(VAR Event: TEvent); VIRTUAL;
      PROCEDURE InitMenuBar; VIRTUAL;
      PROCEDURE InitStatusLine; VIRTUAL;
      PROCEDURE AboutSystem; { method for the cmAbout command }
      { for the commands cmIncome..cmOther }
      PROCEDURE InputData(Cm: word);
      PROCEDURE NewDate;       { method for the cmSetDate command }
      PROCEDURE MonthBal;    { method for the 0cmMont hcommand }
      PROCEDURE YearBal;     { method for the cmYear command }
      PROCEDURE ToGraph;
      PROCEDURE ReturnText;
```

```
   END;
VAR
  wApp: TpAppl;              { instance of the TpAppl object type }

{$I TYPEDEF.PAS}
{$I F_PROC.PAS}
{$I G_PROC.PAS}

PROCEDURE TpAppl.HandleEvent(VAR Event: TEvent);
{ Event handler }
BEGIN
 TApplication.HandleEvent(Event); { activates parent method }
 IF (Event.What=evCommand) THEN BEGIN {if the command is entered}
   CASE (Event.Command) OF   { user command }
    cmAbout: AboutSystem;         { program help information }
                               { input income and expense values }
 cmIncome..cmOther: InputData(Event.Command);
  cmSetDate: NewDate;            { sets date }
   cmMonth: MonthBal;            { month analysis }
    cmYear: YearBal;             { year analysis }
      ELSE   Exit;               { end of event handling }
    END;
    ClearEvent(Event);           { event is successfully handled }
  END;
END; { HandleEvent }

PROCEDURE TpAppl.InitMenuBar;
{ Sets program menu bar }
VAR  R: TRect;               { object for rectangle }
BEGIN
  GetExtent(R);              { sets boundaries for the menu bar }
  R.B.Y:= succ(R.A.Y);      { top screen line }
 MenuBar:= New(PMenuBar, Init(R, NewMenu(
   NewSubMenu('~_~', hcNoContext, NewMenu(   { "_" }
    NewItem('~A~bout...', '', 0, cmAbout, hcNoContext,
      nil)),
   NewSubMenu('~I~ncome',hcNoContext,NewMenu( { "Income" }
     NewItem('~I~ncome', '', 0, cmIncome, hcNoContext,
     NewItem('~S~et date', '', 0, cmSetDate, hcNoContext,
      NewLine(
     NewItem('~E~xit', 'Alt-X', kbAltX, cmQuit, hcNoContext,
      nil))))),
   NewSubMenu('~E~xpense', hcNoContext, NewMenu( { "Expense" }
     NewItem('~F~ood', '', 0, cmFood, hcNoContext,
    NewItem('~A~ccommodation','',0,cmAccommodation,hcNoContext,
     NewItem('~C~lothing', '', 0, cmClothing, hcNoContext,
     NewItem('~E~ducation', '', 0, cmEducation, hcNoContext,
     NewItem('~M~edical care','',0,cmMedicalCare,hcNoContext,
     NewItem('~L~eisure', '', 0, cmLeisure, hcNoContext,
     NewItem('~O~ther', '', 0, cmOther, hcNoContext,
      nil)))))))),
   NewSubMenu('~A~nalysis', hcNoContext, NewMenu( { "Analysis" }
     NewItem('~M~onth', 'F5', kbF5, cmMonth, hcNoContext,
```

```
    NewItem('~Y~ear', 'F6', kbF6, cmYear, hcNoContext,
      nil))),
 nil)))))));
END; { InitMenuBar }


PROCEDURE TpAppl.InitStatusLine;
{ Sets status line }
VAR  R: TRect;              { object for rectangle }
BEGIN
 GetExtent(R);             { sets boundaries for the status line }
 R.A.Y:= pred(R.B.Y);     { bottom line }
 StatusLine:= New(PStatusLine, Init(R,
  NewStatusDef(0, $FFFF,
    NewStatusKey('~F5~ Month', kbF5, cmMonth,
    NewStatusKey('~F6~ Year', kbF6, cmYear,
    NewStatusKey('~F10~ Menu', kbF10, cmMenu,
    NewStatusKey('~Alt-X~ Exit', kbAltX, cmQuit, nil)))),
   nil)
 ));
END; { InitStatusLine }


PROCEDURE TpAppl.AboutSystem;
{ Makes dialog box "About" }
VAR
 C: Word;
 D: PDialog;              { object for the dialog box }
 R: TRect;                { object for the rectangle }
BEGIN
 R.Assign(20, 5, 60, 14); { sets boundaries of the dialog box }
 D:= New(PDialog, Init(R, 'About'));   { makes new dialog box }
 WITH D^ DO BEGIN
   R.Assign(0, 0, 40, 9);           { sets view size }
  Options:= Options OR ofCenterX;{ sets options of view output }
   R.Grow(-1, -1);                 { decrements current view size }
   Dec(R.B.Y, 2);
  Insert(New(PStaticText, Init(R, { makes TStaticText and }
    #13 +^C+NamePro +#13 +    { inserts it in the dialog box }
    #13 +^C+CopyRight +#13)));
   R.Assign(16, 6, 22, 8); { inserts button in the dialog box }
  Insert(New(PButton, Init(R, 'O~K~', cmOK, bfNormal)));
 END;
 C:= DeskTop^.ExecView(D); { executes dialog box }
 Dispose(D, Done);          { deletes dialog box from the Heap }
END; { AboutSystem }


FUNCTION GetReal(R:real; NameField:string; St:string): real;
{ Forms dialog box to input income and expense values }
TYPE
 DialogData = RECORD    { data type description for dialog box }
  InputSt: string[30];
  END;
```

```
VAR
  D: PDialog;                { object for the dialog box }
  Tr: TRect;                 { object for the rectangular }
  B: PView;                  { object for the view }
  C, I: Word;
  S: string;
  RealData: DialogData;      { dialog box data }
BEGIN
  Tr.Assign(20, 5, 60, 14); { sets boundaries of the dialog box }
  { makes new dialog box }
  D:= New(PDialog, Init(Tr, 'Enter '+NameField));
  WITH D^ DO BEGIN
    Tr.Assign(3, 2, 38, 3); { sets view size }
    Str(R:10:2, S);          { converts number to string }
    { inserts view }
    Insert(New(PStaticText, Init(Tr, 'Old value: '+S)));
    Tr.Assign(13, 4, 27, 5);  { sets TInputLine size }
    B:= New(PInputLine, Init(Tr,12)); { defines TInputLine object }
    Insert(B);                { inserts TInputLine }
    Tr.Assign(2, 4, 12, 5);   { sets TLabel size }
    { inserts TLabel }
    Insert(New(PLabel, Init(Tr, St+' ~V~alue', B)));
    Tr.Assign(18,6,24,8);     { makes and inserts the buttons }
    Insert(New(PButton, Init(Tr, 'O~K~', cmOK, bfDefault)));
    Tr.Assign(26, 6, 36, 8);
    Insert(New(PButton, Init(Tr, 'Cancel', cmCancel, bfNormal)));
  END;
  REPEAT
    { forms initial values for the dialog box }
    RealData.InputSt:= ''; I:= 0;
    D^.SetData(RealData); { sets these values in the dialog box }
    C:= DeskTop^.ExecView(D);     { executes the dialog box }
    IF C <> cmCancel THEN BEGIN   { if no ESC or [•] }
      D^.GetData(RealData);       { gets new values }
      IF RealData.InputSt = '' THEN BEGIN { is string empty? }
        R:= 0;  I:= 0;  END       { exit }
      ELSE                        { tests string value }
      Val(RealData.InputSt,R,I); END {convert string into number}
    ELSE BEGIN                    { if ESC or [•] }
      R:= 0;   I:= 0;             { exit }
    END;
  UNTIL (I = 0);         { loop until number value will be valid }
  GetReal:= R;
  Dispose(D, Done);               { deletes dialog box from Heap }
END; { GetReal }

PROCEDURE TpAppl.InputData(Cm: word);
{ Inputs income and expense sums when Cm: cmIncome..cmOther command
  is activated }


FUNCTION GetField(Value: real; Name: string): real;
{ Changes Value parameter in the dialog box. New value is the sum
```

```
  of current and input ones. Checks for positive values only }
VAR  D: real;
BEGIN
  D:= GetReal(Value, Name, 'Add') +Value; { changes Value }
  IF D < 0 THEN D := Value;                { checks new value }
  GetField := D;
END; { GetField }


BEGIN   { InputData }
  WITH wRec DO   { changes real fields of wRec record }
    CASE Cm OF
      cmIncome: Income:= GetField(Income, 'Income');
        cmFood: Food:= GetField(Food, 'Food');
 cmAccommodation: Accommodation:= GetField(Accommodation,
                                          'Accommodation');
    cmClothing: Clothing:= GetField(Clothing, 'Clothing');
   cmEducation: Education:= GetField(Education, 'Education');
  cmMedicalCare: MedicalCare:= GetField(MedicalCare,
                                     'Medical care');
     cmLeisure: Leisure:= GetField(Leisure, 'Leisure');
       cmOther: Other:= GetField(Other, 'Other');
    END;
END; { InputData }


PROCEDURE TpAppl.NewDate;
{ Enteres new date }
TYPE
  DialogData = RECORD      { dialog box data }
    MonthDt: word;
    InputSt: string[4];
  END;
VAR
  D: PDialog;                { object for the dialog box }
  R: TRect;                  { object for the rectangle }
  B: PView;                  { object for the view }
  C, I, Y, M: Word;
  St: string[4];
 RealData: DialogData;
 Rec: Base;
BEGIN
 R.Assign(20, 4, 60, 19); { sets boundaries of the dialog box }
 D:= New(PDialog,Init(R,'Enter Date')); { creates new dialog box }
 WITH D^ DO BEGIN
   R.Assign(3, 2, 18, 14);
   B:= New(PRadioButtons, Init(R, { makes buttons TRadioButtons }
   NewSItem(Months[1], NewSItem(Months[2], NewSItem(Months[3],
   NewSItem(Months[4], NewSItem(Months[5], NewSItem(Months[6],
   NewSItem(Months[7], NewSItem(Months[8], NewSItem(Months[9],
   NewSItem(Months[10], NewSItem(Months[11], NewSItem(Months[12],
    nil))))))))))))
   ));
   Insert(B);        { inserts TRadioButtons in the dialog box }
   R.Assign(6, 1, 12, 2);   { makes the label for TRadioButtons }
```

```
   Insert(New(PLabel, Init(R, '~M~onth', B)));
    R.Assign(29, 1, 35, 2); { makes TInputLine for input string }
    B:= New(PInputLine, Init(R, 4));
     Insert(B);          { inserts TInputLine in the dialog box }
    R.Assign(22, 1, 28, 2); { makes the label for TInputLine }
   Insert(New(PLabel, Init(R, '~Y~ear', B)));
    R.Assign(22, 9, 28, 11); { inserts buttons in the dialog box }
   Insert(New(PButton, Init(R, 'O~K~', cmOK, bfDefault)));
    R.Assign(22, 12, 32, 14);
   Insert(New(PButton, Init(R, 'Cancel', cmCancel, bfNormal)));
  END;
 M:= cMonth-1;
 REPEAT
   I:= 0;                   { flag of normal execution of input }
   Y:= cYear;  Str(Y:4, St); { string for year value }
   RealData.MonthDt:= M;   { forms initial values for the dialog }
   RealData.InputSt:= St;
   D^.SetData(RealData);   { sets these values in the dialog box }
   C:= DeskTop^.ExecView(D);   { executes dialog box }
    IF C <> cmCancel THEN BEGIN  { if no ESC or [•] }
     D^.GetData(RealData);       { gets new values }
    M:= RealData.MonthDt;
    Val(RealData.InputSt, Y, I); { tests year value }
     IF Y < 1900 THEN I:=1; END { executes dialog box once again }
    ELSE BEGIN                   { if ESC or [•] }
     Y:= cYear;  M:= cMonth-1;  { return to the previous values }
    END;
  UNTIL (I = 0); { loop until current year value will be input }
  Dispose(D, Done);            { deletes dialog box from Heap }
  IF ((Y <> cYear) OR (M+1 <> cMonth)) THEN BEGIN
    SaveWRec;                { saves current record in the file }
    { loads new record from the file }
   IF LoadRec(M+1,Y,Rec) THEN BEGIN
     wRec:= Rec;                { new current record }
     cMonth:= M+1;  cYear:= Y;  { forms year and month }
    END;
  END;
END; { NewDate }


PROCEDURE TpAppl.ToGraph;
{ Sets graphics mode }
BEGIN
 DoneSysError;   { deactivates Turbo Vision error processing }
 DoneEvents;     { terminates event handling and mouse control }
```

```
  DoneVideo;      { deactivates video processing }
  DoneMemory;      { free memory }
  SetGraphMode(GetGraphMode); { sets graphics mode }
END;  { ToGraph }


PROCEDURE TpAppl.ReturnText;
{ Restores text mode }
BEGIN
  { outputs message and makes a delay }
  SetTextJustify(CenterText, TopText);  SetColor(GetMaxColor);
  OutTextXY(GetMaxX div 2, GetMaxY-(TextHeight('N')+4),
    'Press any key to continue...');  AnyKey;
  RestoreCrtmode;  { returns to the text mode }
  InitMemory;      { initializes Turbo Vision memory manager }
  InitVideo;       { activates video processing }
  InitEvents;      { initializes event manager and mouse control }
  InitSysError;    { initializes Turbo Vision error processing }
  Redraw;          { redraws old views on the screen }
END;  { ReturnText; }


PROCEDURE TpAppl.MonthBal;
{ Draws result of the month analysis in the form of pie chart }
BEGIN
  ToGraph;          { sets graphics mode }
  DrawPie(wRec);   { draws pie chart for the current wRec record }
  ReturnText;       { restores text mode }
END;  { MonthBal }


PROCEDURE TpAppl.YearBal;
{ Draws result of the year analysis in the form of bar chart }
BEGIN
  ToGraph;           { sets graphics mode }
  DrawChart(cYear); { draws bar chart for the current cYear year }
  ReturnText;        { restores text mode }
END;  { YearBal }


BEGIN   { TvHomeFinances }
  InitWork;         { program initialization }
  wApp.Init;        { initializes application }
  wApp.Run;         { runs application }
  wApp.Done;        { closes application }
  ExitWork;         { closes file and exits the program }
END.    { TvHomeFinances }
```

Instructions for Use

As the design and application of the TvHomeFinances program are virtually the same as the HomeFinances program, we will only describe the aspects that are different.

As with all Turbo Vision programs, TvHomeFinances can be operated using both the keyboard and a mouse (see Chapter 18).

The main menu of the TvHomeFinances program is expanded with the regime "≡", which has only one command, About. When you select this command a window containing descriptive information about the program and the copyright appears on the screen (see Chapter 18).

The Income menu has an additional command Exit. Selecting this command exits the program. A short cut for exiting this program is to press **ALT-X**.

Another short cut, which lets you call the commands Month and Year, is to use the hotkeys **F5** and **F6** respectively.

APPENDIX C

ASCII TABLE

	0	1	2	3	4	5	6	7	8	9	A	B	C	D	E	F
00	NUL	☺	☻	♥	♦	♣	♠	•	◘	○	◎	♂	♀	♪	♫	☼
	0	1	2	3	4	5	6	7	8	9	10	11	12	13	14	15
10	►	◄	↕	‼	¶	§	▬	↨	↑	↓	→	←	∟	↔	▲	▼
	16	17	18	19	20	21	22	23	24	25	26	27	28	29	30	31
20		!	"	#	$	%	&	'	(	)	*	+	,	–	.	/
	32	33	34	35	36	37	38	39	40	41	42	43	44	45	46	47
30	0	1	2	3	4	5	6	7	8	9	:	;	<	=	>	?
	48	49	50	51	52	53	54	55	56	57	58	59	60	61	62	63
40	@	A	B	C	D	E	F	G	H	I	J	K	L	M	N	O
	64	65	66	67	68	69	70	71	72	73	74	75	76	77	78	79
50	P	Q	R	S	T	U	V	W	X	Y	Z	[	\	]	^	_
	80	81	82	83	84	85	86	87	88	89	90	91	92	93	94	95
60	`	a	b	c	d	e	f	g	h	i	j	k	l	m	n	o
	96	97	98	99	100	101	102	103	104	105	106	107	108	109	110	111
70	p	q	r	s	t	u	v	w	x	y	z	{	|	}	~	⌂
	112	113	114	115	116	117	118	119	120	121	122	123	124	125	126	127

Continued overleaf

	0	1	2	3	4	5	6	7	8	9	A	B	C	D	E	F
80	Ç 128	ü 129	é 130	â 131	ä 132	à 133	å 134	ç 135	ê 136	ë 137	è 138	ï 139	î 140	ì 141	Ä 142	Å 143
90	É 144	æ 145	Æ 146	ô 147	ö 148	ò 149	û 150	ù 151	ÿ 152	Ö 153	Ü 154	¢ 155	£ 156	¥ 157	Pₜ 158	ƒ 159
A0	á 160	í 161	ó 162	ú 163	ñ 164	Ñ 165	ª 166	º 167	¿ 168	⌐ 169	¬ 170	½ 171	¼ 172	¡ 173	« 174	» 175
B0	░ 176	▒ 177	▓ 178	│ 179	┤ 180	╡ 181	╢ 182	╖ 183	╕ 184	╣ 185	║ 186	╗ 187	╝ 188	╜ 189	╛ 190	┐ 191
C0	└ 192	┴ 193	┬ 194	├ 195	─ 196	┼ 197	╞ 198	╟ 199	╚ 200	╔ 201	╩ 202	╦ 203	╠ 204	═ 205	╬ 206	╧ 207
D0	╨ 208	╤ 209	╥ 210	╙ 211	╘ 212	╒ 213	╓ 214	╫ 215	╪ 216	┘ 217	┌ 218	█ 219	▄ 220	▌ 221	▐ 222	▀ 223
E0	α 224	ß 225	Γ 226	π 227	 228	σ 229	µ 230	τ 231	Φ 232	θ 233	Ω 234	δ 235	 236	ø 237	∈ 238	∩ 239
F0	≡ 240	± 241	≥ 242	≤ 243	⌠ 244	⌡ 245	÷ 246	 247	° 248	∙ 249	· 250	√ 251	ⁿ 252	² 253	■ 254	255

APPENDIX

D

APPENDIX D

Key Codes

Key	Normal	Shifted	Ctrl	Alt
F1	27 59	27 84	27 94	27 104
F2	27 60	27 85	27 95	27 105
F3	27 61	27 86	27 96	27 106
F4	27 62	27 87	27 97	27 107
F5	27 63	27 88	27 98	27 108
F6	27 64	27 89	27 99	27 109
F7	27 65	27 90	27 100	27 110
F8	27 66	27 91	27 101	27 111
F9	27 67	27 92	27 102	27 112
F10	27 68	27 93	27 103	27 113
←	27 75	52	27 115	none
→	27 77	54	27 116	none
↑	27 72	56	none	none
↓	27 80	50	none	none
PGUP	27 73	57	27 132	none
PGDN	27 81	51	27 118	none
HOME	27 71	55	27 119	none
END	27 79	49	27 117	none
INS	27 82	48	27 165	none
DEL	27 83	46	27 166	none
BACKSPACE	8	8	127	none
TAB	9	27 15	none	none
RETURN	13	13	10	none
ESC	27	27	27	none
0	48	41	none	27 129
1	49	33	none	27 120
2	50	64	27 3	27 121
3	51	35	none	27 122
4	52	36	none	27 123
5	53	37	none	27 124
6	54	94	30	27 125

7	55	38	none	27 126
8	56	42	none	27 127
9	57	40	none	27 128
A	97	65	1	27 30
B	98	66	2	27 48
C	99	67	3	27 46
D	100	68	4	27 32
E	101	69	5	27 18
F	102	70	6	27 33
G	103	71	7	27 34
H	104	72	8	27 35
I	105	73	9	27 23
J	106	74	10	27 36
K	107	75	11	27 37
L	108	76	12	27 38
M	109	77	13	27 50
N	110	78	14	27 49
O	111	79	15	27 24
P	112	80	16	27 25
Q	113	81	17	27 16
R	114	82	18	27 19
S	115	83	19	27 31
T	116	84	20	27 20
U	117	85	21	27 22
V	118	86	22	27 47
W	119	87	23	27 17
X	120	88	24	27 45
Y	121	89	25	27 21
Z	122	90	26	27 44
*	42	none	27 114	none
+	43	43	none	none
-	45	95	31	27 130
=	61	43	none	27 131
@	44	60	none	none
/	47	63	none	none
;	59	58	none	none
~	96	126	none	none
[	91	123	27	none
]	93	125	29	none
\	92	124	28	none
'	96	126	none	none

TABLE OF PROGRAMS

Chapter	File Name on Disk	Item Name
2	IDEALWEI.PAS	PROGRAM IdealWeight;
2	FIRSTEXP.PAS	PROGRAM Firstexp;
4	DEMOREP.PAS	PROGRAM DemoRepeat;
4	DEMOWHIL.PAS	PROGRAM DemoWhile;
4	SIMPLES.PAS	PROGRAM SimplesSum;
6	DEMWRITE.PAS	PROGRAM DemoWrite;
6	DEMOPRIN.PAS	PROGRAM DemoPrinting;
6	DEMOUSER.PAS	PROGRAM DemoUserTypeOutput;
6	DEMODIAL.PAS	PROGRAM DemoDialogue;
7	DEMOASC.PAS	PROGRAM DemoASCII;
7	DEMOPRO.PAS	PROGRAM DemoProcedure;
7	DEMPOWER.PAS	PROGRAM DemoPower;
7	DEMOPAR.PAS	PROGRAM DemoParameters;
7	RECURS.PAS	PROGRAM Recursion;
8	USE_MATH.PAS	PROGRAM SimpleMath;
8	MATH.PAS	UNIT Math;
9	DEMORECO.PAS	PROGRAM DemoRec;
10	DSTRING.PAS	PROGRAM DemoStringGo;
11	BLOCK.PAS	PROGRAM DemoIOBlock;
12	TESTNEW.PAS	PROGRAM TestNew;
12	TESTMARK.PAS	PROGRAM TestMark;
12	SLIST.PAS	PROGRAM SimpleList;
13	DWIND.PAS	PROGRAM DemoWindow;
13	DSCREEN.PAS	PROGRAM DemoScreenLine;
14	PRTIP.PAS	PROGRAM TestFunc;
14	SCANCODE.PAS	PROGRAM DemoScanCode;
14	IORES.PAS	PROGRAM DemoIOResult;
14	SCALE.PAS	PROGRAM DemoScale;
14	ACCOMPL.PAS	PROGRAM DemoAccomplish;
14	RINGING.PAS	PROGRAM DemoRinging;
14	MUSIC.PAS	PROGRAM MakeMusic;

14	INSTRUM.PAS	PROGRAM DemoInstrument;
14	ASM.PAS	PROGRAM DemoAsm;
14	DEMOFCH.PAS	PROGRAM DemoFCH;
14	DEMOMOVE.PAS	PROGRAM DemoMove;
15	SERVICE.PAS	UNIT Service;
15	EX_SERV.PAS	PROGRAM HomeFinances;
16	DEMOSVP.PAS	PROGRAM DemoSetViewPort;
16	COORD.PAS	PROCEDURE Coord;
16	CHART.PAS	PROCEDURE Chart;
16	DEMCHART.PAS	PROGRAM DemoChart;
16	PIE.PAS	PROCEDURE Pie;
16	DEMPIE.PAS	PROGRAM DemoPie;
17	PHONES.PAS	PROGRAM Phones;
17	OBJPHON2.PAS	UNIT ObjPhon2;
17	OBJPHON1.PAS	UNIT ObjPhon1;
17	OBJPHONE.PAS	UNIT ObjPhone;
17	PHONES2.PAS	PROGRAM Phones2;
18	APPL1.PAS	USES Objects, Drivers, Views, Menus, Dialogs, App;
18	APPL2.PAS	USES Dos, Objects, Drivers, Views, Menus, Dialogs, App;

APPENDIX A   HomeFinances Program
APP_A in **HOMEFNCS** on Disk
APPENDIX B   TVHomeFinances Program
APP_B in **HOMEFNCS** on Disk

Index

Instant C++ Programming

If you want a swift route to proficiency in C++, this no-nonsense, fast-paced tutorial

teaches you all you need to know in an instant and gets you writing programs

from day one. The book is ideal for the programmer moving to a new language.

Lots of example code and self-check exercises enable you to quickly become proficient

in C++ and then move to object-oriented programming.

Ian Wilks ISBN 1-874416-29-X
$19.95 / C$27.95 / £18.49

The Beginner's Guide to OOP using C++

This Beginner's Guide teaches OOP to programmers from the procedural world,

assuming a small amount of programming knowledge. You will learn all you

need to know about the C++ language - not only the tools, but also the

methodology to use them.

L. Romanovskaya et al ISBN 1-874416-27-3
$29.95 / C$41.95 / £27.99

The Beginner's Guide to C

This is a well-structured tutorial on application programming, not merely

a language reference. The author builds a complete application with the

reader, step by step, leaving them with a useful tool and a sense of

achievement. The ANSI C language is given comprehensive coverage in a

friendly environment.

Ivor Horton ISBN 1-874416-15-X
$24.95 / C$34.95 / £22.99

WIN FREE BOOKS

TELL US WHAT YOU THINK!

Complete and return the bounce back card and you will:

- Help us create the books you want.
- Receive an update on all Wrox titles.
- Enter the draw for 5 Wrox titles of your choice.

FILL THIS OUT to enter the draw for free Wrox titles

Name _____

Address _____

_____

_____

_____ Postcode/Zip _____

Occupation _____

How did you hear about this book ?

☐ Book review (name) _____

☐ Advertisement (name) _____

☐ Recommendation

☐ Catalog

☐ Other _____

Where did you buy this book ?

☐ Bookstore (name) _____

☐ Computer Store (name) _____

☐ Mail Order

☐ Other _____

What influenced you in the purchase of this book ?

☐ Cover Design

☐ Contents

☐ Use of Color

☐ Other (please specify)

How did you rate the overa contents of this book ?

☐ Excellent

☐ Good

☐ Average

☐ Poor

What did you find most useful about this book ?

What did you find least useful about this book ?

Please add any additional comments. _____

What other subjects will you buy a computer book on soon ?

What is the best computer book you have used this year ? _____

WROX PRESS INC.

Wrox writes books for you. Any suggestions, or ideas about how you want information given in your ideal book will be studied by our team. Your comments are always valued at WROX.

Free phone from USA 1 800 814 3461
Fax (312) 465 4063

Compuserve 100063,2152.
UK Tel. (4421) 706 6826   Fax   (4421) 706 2967

Computer Book Publishers

NB. If you post the bounce back card below in the UK, please send it to:
Wrox Press Ltd. Unit 16 Sapcote Industrial Estate, 20 James Road,
Tyseley, Birmingham B11 2BA

NO POSTAGE
NECESSARY
IF MAILED
IN THE
UNITED STATES

BUSINESS REPLY MAIL
FIRST CLASS MAIL   PERMIT#64   CHICAGO,IL.

POSTAGE WILL BE PAID BY ADDRESSEE

WROX PRESS
2710 WEST TOUHY AVE
CHICAGO IL 60645-3008
USA